TRADE ISSUES, POLICIES AND LAWS

TRADE LIBERALIZATION AND PROTECTIONISM

TRADE ISSUES, POLICIES AND LAWS

Additional books in this series can be found on Nova's website at:

https://www.novapublishers.com/catalog/index.php?cPath=23_29&seriesp=Trade+Issues%2C+Policies+and+Laws

Additional e-books in this series can be found on Nova's website at:

https://www.novapublishers.com/catalog/index.php?cPath=23_29&seriespe=Trade+Issues%2C+Policies+and+Laws

TRADE ISSUES, POLICIES AND LAWS

TRADE LIBERALIZATION AND PROTECTIONISM

BALTHASAR HAHN
AND
CARL JAEGER
EDITORS

Nova Science Publishers, Inc.
New York

For permission to use material from this book please contact us:
Telephone 631-231-7269; Fax 631-231-8175
Web Site: http://www.novapublishers.com

LIBRARY OF CONGRESS CATALOGING-IN-PUBLICATION DATA

Trade liberalization and protectionism / editors, Balthasar Hahn and Carl Jaeger.
p. cm.
Includes index.
ISBN 978-1-60876-837-0 (hardcover)
1. Free trade. 2. Protectionism. I. Hahn, Balthasar. II. Jaeger, Carl.
HF1713.T69475 2009
382'.7--dc22

2009045941

Published by Nova Science Publishers, Inc. ✢ New York

CONTENTS

PREFACE

This book makes an intensive review of the literature on trade liberalization and its impacts on growth and distribution in developing countries. Moreover, the authors scrutinize some controversial national initiatives that are gradually fragmenting the international economic field. The urgent need that multilateral institutions have to push trade higher up in the list of the political priorities is emphasized. In addition, the biggest producers and exporters of agricultural products have been adopting the genetic engineering in order to improve the factors productivity and the firms' profits. The authors examine the potential motivations behind the different policies on GM products adopted by US and EU. Additionally, the welfare effect of bilateral free trade agreement (FTA) in a vertical trade structure is investigated in this book. A three-country model is considered with one country exporting intermediate good and two countries exporting final good. Other chapters explore the major theories of international trade from antiquity up to the neoclassical economics in the latter part of the nineteenth century. Effective trade policies for developed countries today are also discussed, as well as international trade, both exports and imports, in countries such as India and China. It is the authors' contention that these two countries pose particular challenges and offer particular opportunities in the evolving trade-development nexuses.

Chapter 1 explores the major theories of international trade from antiquity up to the neoclassical economics in the latter part of the nineteenth century. This intellectual odyssey begins with the analysis of the long-distance trade among the territories of the ancient world. Greek historians and philosophers laid the foundation upon which other thinkers developed the theories of trade culminating in the influential writings of the classical economists; in particular, David Hume, Adam Smith, and David Ricardo. The authors end their survey with the contributions of John Stuart Mill, the final major figure of the classical economics.

Prior to the dawn of the Mercantilist era in the sixteenth century, any insight concerning long-distance trade had been an integral and inseparable part of the general theory of the market, which remained largely undeveloped until the seventeenth century. Mercantilist theories of foreign trade were followed by relatively advanced theories in the eighteenth century, preparing the path towards the discovery and articulation of trade theories; above all, the theory of comparative advantage.

Chapter 2 makes an intensive review of the literature on trade liberalization and its impacts on growth and distribution in developing countries. A growing surge of literature on internal and external trade reforms for the last two decades comprises both transition and developing economies. Most of the theoretical studies are, in fact, the extensions of Stolper-Samuelson theorem. Empirical studies, however, differ based on their methodological approaches; but they can be broadly grouped into cross-country regression analysis, country-specific partial analysis, and general equilibrium analysis. This paper concludes that trade reforms are growth enhancing but they require complementary policies to make the growth pro-poor. So long as the macroeconomic parameters improve or do not deteriorate, at least, the potential impacts are sustainable.

Chapter 3 discusses the MERCOSUR (Mercado Común del Sur, Southern Common Market)[1] agreement, which is a Regional Integration Agreement (RIA) among two of the largest states of Latin America, Argentina and Brazil, and two of the smallest, Paraguay and Uruguay. Besides its four original members, six other Latin-American countries are associate members of the agreement: Bolivia, Chile, Peru, Colombia, Ecuador and Venezuela.[2]

The core agreement (Argentina, Brazil, Paraguay and Uruguay) comprises a population of approximately 200 million people, encompasses an area of 12 million square kilometers, had a gross domestic product (GDP) of about US$ 670 billion in 1996 and accounted for about 50 percent of Latin American industrial output and total exports.[3] Despite the fact that MERCOSUR is the second largest RIA in the Western Hemisphere (after NAFTA) and that Argentina and Brazil are sufficiently large trading countries to influence world prices in some markets, the Common Market of the South is a relative small international trader accounting for only 1 percent of world markets.[4]

---

[1] The MERCOSUR agreement is also known as MERCOSUL (Mercado Comum do Sul).
[2] Cf. MERCOSUR (2009).
[3] Cf. Diao & Somwaru (1999), p. 27.
[4] Cf. Olarreaga, Soloaga & Winters (1999), pp. 2 ff.

Chapter 4 makes an attempt to assess the impact of trade liberalization on services sector employment. Based on the time series macro data, the elasticity of organised services sector employment with respect to value added and exports and imports have been estimated. After controlling for growth it is difficult to identify a positive and significant impact of international trade on employment in the organized service sector. The authors have also tried to work out the direct and indirect effects of exports and imports on employment after deciphering their effects included in overall growth. However, the positive effects are mostly negligible. For the informal or unorganized services sector employment the impact does not seem to be greatly different from what is observed in the case of the organized services sector employment. Also as per the company level data international trade does not seem to be an important determinant of employment in the services sector.

As explained in Chapter 5, the traumatism associated with the closing trade of the 1930s led to ask for (in a more or less conscious) protecting the free trade debate in terms of binary choice. In the West, while tightening of trade policy is to resurface the idea of a drop-sufficient and is the subject of a condemnation in principle. The terms associated with the word protectionism are often charged with a negative connotation: temptation, spectrum, poison, trap, danger....

In these debates, it was largely forgotten in reality protectionism is a gradual concept. Free trade is an extreme case, that of a zero degree of protection. At the other extreme is the autarky absolute if the authorities avoid smuggling. Historically own in recent years, protection is the rule and free trade the exception. However in economic theory, the reverse is true. Debate protection versus free trade should replace questions about the determination of trade policy relevant. Good policy depends heavily on the structures of the national economy, its specialties, its forward or its relative backwardness in terms of development.

International trade, both exports and imports, can contribute to development and poverty alleviation by expanding markets, promoting competition, and raising productivity, each of which has the *potential* for increasing the real incomes of poor people. The potential of international trade to alleviate poverty comes from its ability to expand markets and thereby create new production and consumption opportunities for people. Such market expansion can help to generate employment and incomes for poor people. That said, long-term development and poverty alleviation requires *both* technological upgrading *and* the education and skills acquisition necessary to support it. In Chapter 6, the authors consider these issues in some detail and then turn to the emerging and important cases of India and China. It is their contention that these two countries pose particular challenges and offer particular opportunities in the evolving trade-development nexuses.

A protectionist policy on the part of the government is a recurrent behavior especially evident under severe crisis. Behind this attitude is the assumption that short-run benefits for nationals overcome the costs associated with protectionism. As a matter of fact, from a long-run perspective, the costs must include the expected reactions from the other trade partners. This, in turn, challenges even the responsibility hypothesis that supports the short-run behavior of the government as national citizens may indeed be characterized by a sufficiently large time-horizon allowing for an electoral punishment of the incumbent. The current global crisis is already contracting global trade at a rate of knots, spreading negative effects among countries, which is magnifying the impact of the fall-off in domestic demand. Nationals' crisis-fighting plans have spawned new obscure ways of protectionism, by discriminating against foreign firms, workers and investors. In Chapter 7 the authors scrutinize some controversial national initiatives that are gradually fragmenting the international economic field. The authors will emphasize the urgent need that multilateral institutions have to push trade higher up in the list of the political priorities, putting the recent Doha agenda on the right track.

The biggest producers and exporters of agricultural products have been adopting genetic engineering in order to improve the factors productivity and the firms profits. In the last decade, the United States of America (U.S.) and the European Union (EU) have established a high divergent regulation on production, distribution and consumption of genetically modified organisms (GMOs). Apparently, the EU′s complex legislative framework related to GMOs was intended to satisfy the European consumers which are concerned about food safety and wish to make a more informed choice about the food they eat. The aim of Chapter 8 is to understand the potential motivations behind the different policies on GM products adopted by the U.S. and EU.

Chapter 9 investigates the welfare effect of the bilateral free trade agreement (FTA) in a vertical trade structure. The authors consider a three-country model with one country exporting intermediate goods (upstream country) and two countries exporting final goods (downstream countries). The authors focus on the situation where both the upstream and downstream countries impose positive import tariffs before forming the FTA. The authors then consider an FTA between the upstream country and one of the downstream countries. The other downstream country is regarded as a nonmember country. After forming the FTA, all of the tariffs between the member countries are eliminated, whereas the tariffs between the FTA member and nonmember are maintained. The authors have two scenarios in relation to the FTA; the first one is the case where external tariff reform by the FTA member country is not allowed, and the second one is the case where external tariff reform is allowed. Then, in the first scenario, the FTA unambiguously decreases the nonmember's welfare, while it may or may not increase the FTA members' welfare. The latter result depends on the number of firms producing the intermediate and the final goods and on the levels of the initial tariffs. Irrespective of an increase of the FTA members' welfare, Pareto-improving FTA is not possible. In contrast, in the second scenario, if an external tariff reform, *i.e.* a reduction of tariff by the FTA member, is available, there exist some possibilities that the FTA increases both of the FTA members' welfare without changing the nonmember's welfare. Therefore, Pareto-improving welfare is possible.

In: Trade Liberalization and Protectionism
Editors: B. Hahn et al, pp. 1-30
ISBN: 978-1-60876-837-0

Chapter 1

THE DEVELOPMENT OF INTERNATIONAL TRADE THEORY: FROM XENOPHON TO JOHN STUART MILL

Farhad Rassekh*
Economics, University of Hartford

Abstract

The presents essay explores the major theories of international trade from antiquity up to the neoclassical economics in the latter part of the nineteenth century. This intellectual odyssey begins with the analysis of the long-distance trade among the territories of the ancient world. Greek historians and philosophers laid the foundation upon which other thinkers developed the theories of trade culminating in the influential writings of the classical economists; in particular, David Hume, Adam Smith, and David Ricardo. We end our survey with the contributions of John Stuart Mill, the final major figure of the classical economics.

Prior to the dawn of the Mercantilist era in the sixteenth century, any insight concerning long-distance trade had been an integral and inseparable part of the general theory of the market, which remained largely undeveloped until the seventeenth century. Mercantilist theories of foreign trade were followed by relatively advanced theories in the eighteenth century, preparing the path towards the discovery and articulation of trade theories; above all, the theory of comparative advantage.

*E-mail address: rassekh@hartford.edu. (Corresponding author)

1. From Antiquity to the Sixteenth Century

A visitor to the major cities of the Classical world – cities such as Athens, Rome, Alexandria, and Constantinople – would have found not only local goods but also imported olive, wine, grain, silk, spices, and handcrafted items. A large repertoire of historical accounts by the Greeks and Romans in antiquity records the commercial activities of merchants transporting goods across the known world in pursuit of profits. Commerce had connected various regions of the Classical world and had caused interdependence among them so deeply that Neville Morley in *Trade in Classical Antiquity* (2007) notes, "If Egypt had suddenly been conquered by the Persians, one might suggest, the effects on the city of Rome would have been catastrophic…" (p. 96). Just as the Chinese in the twenty-first century manufacture goods for American markets, "Attic potters and pot-painters" in the first century "produced shapes and designs especially for the Etruscan market…" The commercial network in antiquity was so strong and the movement of "people, goods, and information" was so free and frequent that "the Greek and Roman worlds would have looked very different without wine, or imported fine-ware pottery, or incense" (Morley, p. 96). Greek orator Aelius Aristides (117 – 181 C.E.) in reference to the city of Rome noted, "so many merchant ships arrive here, conveying every kind of goods from every people every hour, every day, so that the city is like a marketplace common to the whole earth" (quoted in Morley, p. 33).[1]

While long-distance trade remained a fact of life in antiquity, certain influential Greek philosophers advocated self-sufficiency in order to minimize contact with foreigners, whom they called barbarians and regarded as inferior. Consistent with his advocacy of state's control of the economy, Plato (427 – 347 B.C.E.) recommended that "foreign imported materials for a use that is not necessary" be banned, and that the exports of "any of the stuff which should of necessity remain in the country" be prohibited (quoted in Douglas Irwin, 1996, pp. 14 -15). Nevertheless, Plato realized that foreign trade cannot be completely eliminated, for it "is practically impossible to establish the city in a region where

[1] Ancient empires such as the Persian, Greek, and Roman as well as relatively more recent empires of Islam and Mongol generally instituted a market economy and protected free movements of people, goods, and ideas within their own territories. Ronald Findlay and Kevin O'Rourke (2007) note that within the Islamic territories during the few centuries following the advent of Islam in the seventh century, dubbed "The Golden Age of Islam," there existed "apparently no restrictions at all on the free flow of people, ideas, techniques, fashions, goods, and capital…in spite of the frequent political conflicts and warfare between individual Muslim states" (p. 61).

it will not need imports" (Ibid., p. 13). Aristotle (384 – 322 B.C.E.) assumed a similar position and argued that cities be developed where they could be self-sufficient while not objecting to the "importation of commodities that they do not happen to have in their own country and the export of their surplus products" (quoted in Irwin, p. 14). The Greek historian Xenophon (430 – 354) offered a much more sympathetic view of foreign trade and directed attention to the advantage of merchants transporting goods in pursuit of profits:

> Because of their great passion for grain, merchants sail wherever they hear there is an abundance of it, across the Aegean, the Euxine and the Sicilian Sea, so that they can seize it. And when they have taken as much of it as they can onto their ships, they carry it across the sea, even storing it in the same ship in which they are sailing. And when they need money, they do unload this grain anywhere they happen to be, but rather they take it and sell it wherever they hear that grain is selling for the highest price, where men place the highest value on it. (Quoted in Morley, pp. 30-31)

Xenophon's observation – that merchants in the pursuit of profits transport grains from where it is abundant (cheap) to where it is scarce (dear) – has continued to be the basis for long-distance trade to the present time. Cicero (106 – 46 B.C.E.) made the same observation, but as a moralist he focused on the proper conduct of trade rather than the economic consequences of trade. Thus he approved of imports "from all parts of the world and distributing to many" as long as it is done "without misrepresentation" (quoted in Irwin, p. 13). Apparently, Cicero believed that merchants of long-distance trade faced a moral dilemma because they had an opportunity to profit at the expense of distributors and consumers. To illustrate the dilemma, he depicted the following scenario:

> Suppose that there is a time of dearth and famine at Rhodes, with provisions being sold at fabulous prices; and suppose that an honest man has imported a large cargo of grain from Alexandria and that to his certain knowledge several other importers have set sail from Alexandria, and that in the course of the voyage he has sighted their vessels laden with grain and headed for Rhodes; is he bound to report this fact to the people of Rhodes, or is he to keep his own counsel and sell his goods at the highest market prices? (Quoted in Morley, p. 17)

Cicero's question further testifies to the fact that long-distance trade in the first century had reached a significant level to merit such scrutiny. More importantly, it illustrates the fact that foreign trade has always been a contentious issue on both economic and moral grounds.

A few generations after Cicero, the Greek historian Plutarch (46 – 120 C.E.) observed that foreign trade makes possible the consumption of goods that are superior to local goods or not produced at home. Plutarch's observation has remained as applicable today in making a case for free trade as it was in antiquity. Any insight or observation in antiquity including Plutarch's, however, was eclipsed and displaced by a doctrine that influenced economic thinking for centuries to come. Jacob Viner, in his classic book, *Studies in the Theory of International Trade* (1937/1975), notes:

> In the ancient Greek and Roman classics is to be found the doctrine that differences in natural conditions in different countries made trade between these countries mutually profitable. The early Christian philosophers took over this doctrine and gave it a theological flavor. God had endowed different regions with limited but varied products to give mankind an incentive to trade, so that through a world economy they would become united in a world society. This was apparently common doctrine among the English theological writers of the sixteenth century and later. (P. 100)

In his first lecture at Wabash College in 1959, Viner called this idea "Universal Economy" and referred to it as "the oldest and longest-lived economic doctrine" (1959/1991, p. 42). Viner quoted the historian Florus, a contemporary of Roman Emperor Augustus (63 B.C.E. – 14 C.E.), who wrote, "Suppress commerce and you tear apart the bonds of human race" (Ibid, p. 41). Similarly, Plutarch expressed the universal economy doctrine in support of long-distance commerce, and noted that commerce through "[The sea] has rendered sociable and tolerable our existence" and that "the exchange of goods" has brought "community and friendship" (Ibid, p. 41). Viner points out that this idea, after the rise of Christianity, assumed a theological garb. John Chrysostom, a fourth century preacher and a student of Libanius, summed up this doctrine as follows: "God filled the earth with goods but gave each region its own particular products, so that, moved by need, we would communicate and share among ourselves, giving others that of which we have abundance and receiving that which we lack" (quoted in Morley, p. 20).[2]

However, since foreign commerce took place largely over the sea and sailors faced the risk of piracy, conflict, and storms, some observers objected to the doctrine of universal economy. Morley quotes Ambrose a Classical writer who argued:

> God did not make the sea for sailing on, but for the sake of the beauty of the element. The sea is tossed by storms; you ought to fear it, not to use it. The

[2] Libanius, a pagan teacher, strongly believed in the doctrine of universal economy. On this point see Viner, 1959 / 1991, p. 42.

> innocent element is not to blame; it is man's own rashness that puts him in peril. Someone who never goes to the sea has no need to fear shipwreck. The sea is given to supply you with fish to eat, not to endanger your self upon it; use it for food, not for commerce. (P. 29)

Nonetheless, the doctrine of universal economy carried the day because commerce proved to be beneficial and, more importantly, the doctrine entered the theological discourse and received the endorsement of influential religious thinkers. Given the dominance of Christianity in all spheres of Western culture that began in the fourth century, it is not surprising that universal economy assumed a religious dimension. Stripped of its theological garb, however, two aspects of this doctrine have survived since its introduction over two millennia ago. The first one attributes trade to resource endowments, a theory that has dominated the field of international trade theory since Eli Heckscher (1919/1991) and Bertil Ohlin (1933) identified factor endowments as the primary source of comparative advantage in international trade.

The second aspect of the doctrine of universal economy – the idea that commerce promotes amity and unity among nations – became quite popular in the eighteenth and nineteenth centuries. In an important contribution to this idea's history, Albert Hirschman (1982) quotes many sympathetic scholars including Thomas Paine (1737 – 1809) who wrote in 1792:

> [Commerce] is a pacific system, operating to cordialise mankind, by rendering Nations, as well as individuals, useful to each other...The invention of commerce...is the greatest approach towards universal civilization that has yet been made by any means not immediately flowing from moral principles. (Quoted in Hirschman, p. 1465)

Hirschman calls this idea the "*doux-commerce*" thesis. The historian Jacques Barzun (1981, p. 703) notes that the eighteenth century thinkers regarded international commerce as a means of establishing world peace. The French philosopher Montesquieu (1689 – 1755) argued that "the spirit of commerce unites nations" and Benjamin Rush, a signer of the U.S. Declaration of Independence, viewed commerce as "the means of uniting the different nations of the world" (both quotations are in Ralph Lerner, 1979, p. 15). Similarly, John Stuart Mill (1848/2006) wrote of the benefits of international trade:

> But the economical advantages of commerce are surpassed in importance by those of its effects which are intellectual and moral. It is hardly possible to overrate the value, in the present low state of human improvement, of placing human being in contact with persons dissimilar to themselves, and with modes of

> thought and action unlike those with which they are familiar. Commerce is now what war once was, the principal source of this contact... There is no nation which does not need to borrow from others, not merely particular arts or practices, but essential points of character in which its own type is inferior. Finally, commerce first taught nations to see with good will the wealth and prosperity of one another...It is commerce which is rapidly rendering war obsolete, by strengthening and multiplying the personal interests which are in natural opposition to it. And it may be said without exaggeration that the great extent and rapid increase of international trade, in being the principal guarantee of the peace of the world, is the great permanent security for the uninterrupted progress of the ideas, the institutions, and the character of the human race. (Pp. 581-2)

Such views testify to the triumph of the doctrine of universal economy. However, along with the rise of modern natural science in the sixteenth century, there emerged new economic theories, most conspicuously and prominently theories of foreign trade, to which we now turn.

2. Mercantilism

Thomas Mun (1571 – 1641) summed up the essence of mercantilism as follows, "to increase our wealth and treasure is by foreign trade, wherein we must ever observe this rule: to sell more to strangers yearly than we consume of theirs in value" (1664, p. 11). Although Mun is generally regarded as the most influential expositor of mercantilism, mercantilist tracts appeared long before Mun wrote his book *England's Treasure by Forraign Trade* in 1630 (published posthumously by his son in 1664). Sir Thomas Smith in 1549 had argued that foreign trade deficit impoverishes the national economy and benefits the trading partners. He wrote, "we must always take heed that we buy no more of strangers than we do sell them; for so we should impoverish ourselves and enrich them" (quoted in Irwin, 1996, p. 27). Indeed, mercantilist policies aimed at generating a trade surplus by limiting imports and promoting exports, which would cause an inflow of precious metals. To varying degrees, mercantilists regarded precious metals as the wealth of nations, and many of them went as far as declaring foreign trade as "the only source of wealth" (quoted in Viner, 1937, p. 3). Mercantilism viewed international trade as a zero-sum game, similar to international wars in which one nation wins only at the expense of the other nation's loss. The mercantilist literature justified and fueled the desire of newly established European nations for international domination and contributed to the colonial aspirations that finally ended in the twentieth century.[1]

Many thinkers in the mercantilist era turned their attention to international relations and foreign trade as a source of national power and wealth because in this period international conflicts were a constant on the continent of Europe. Leonard Gomes (2003) notes:

> Warfare was almost a normal relationship among European superpowers – England, Spain, France, and the Dutch Republic – as they engaged in geopolitical and dynastic struggles throughout most of the period. There was complete peace in only a single year during the period 1600 – 1667. Commercial rivalry – 'jealously of trade' as it was called – was a frequent cause of open conflict in sixteenth- and seventeenth-century Europe. (P. 6)

Although mercantilism as a body of theoretical knowledge and policy prescriptions dominated the European economic thought in the sixteenth and seventeenth centuries, the intellectual origin of mercantilism, can be traced to the Greek poet and merchant Solon who lived in the early sixth century B.C.E. Barry Gordon in *Economic Analysis before Adam Smith, Hesiod to Lessius* (1975) notes that Solon considered

> foreign trade ... as the leading edge of an expansionary movement. In a list of six worthy occupations, sea commerce is given first place ahead of agriculture, manufactures, teaching, prophecy and medicine. This emphasis on trade, monetization of the economy, and the alliance of political with economic power suggest that it is appropriate to apply the term 'mercantilist' to Solon's programne. The future of Athens was being shaped in accordance with policies akin to those adopted by nation-states of Europe in the late sixteenth and early seventeenth centuries A.D. (Pp. 7 – 8).

Gordon further notes that the Greek sophist philosophers, who "were a potent force in the intellectual life of Athens between about 450 and 350 B.C.", advanced economic views that "had a strong mercantilist bias" (p. 17). Socrates, Plato, and Aristotle argued against the sophist philosophy, but made no attempt to refute mercantilism. The refutation had to wait until the eighteenth century when two leading figures of classical economics David Hume and Adam Smith effectively crushed mercantilism. But Hume and Smith wrote, *not* against the ancient sophists, rather against the mercantilism of their own age, although Smith did use

[1] For a concise summary of Mercantilist thought, see Laura Lahaye (2008).

the word "sophistry" in relation to mercantilism in at least four places in *The Wealth of Nations*.[2]

Gordon cites a surviving treatise, entitled, *Ways and Means to Increase the Revenues of Athens*, "written about the middle of the fourth century B.C. by a contemporary of Plato…[which] remained the only essay to be devoted exclusively to this particular topic [mercantilism] for well over 1500 years" (p. 17). The treatise argues that the prosperity of a city depends on the amount of silver it can acquire. Similarly, the mercantilist literature of the sixteenth and seventeenth centuries argue that the prosperity of a nation depends on the amount of precious metals it can acquire from the outside. Both arguments reflect the political reality of their own times: The treatise had a focus on the advancement of city-state in Ancient Greece while the later mercantilist literature aimed at enriching the recently established nations in Europe. As William Allen (1987) notes, "The precept and proposals of mercantilism were the economic component of state-building, providing much of the rationale and suggesting some of the procedures of national unification, seen especially in England, France and Spain" (p. 446).

What explains the nearly two millennia gap between the appearance of the essay *Ways and Means* and the emergence of the mercantilist literature of the later period? A plausible explanation is that the period from 500 B.C.E. to 1500 C.E. roughly corresponds to the time when empires ruled vast areas. These empires including Greek, Persian, Roman, Carolingian, Sung, Islam, and Mongol were more interested in expanding and / or preserving the lands they had acquired than enriching them through foreign trade. Indeed the way these empires ruled their territories, especially the operation of free markets, simply did not lend itself to mercantilist ideologies and policies. Hence no substantive literature on mercantilism appeared for nearly 2000 years. However, during this period numerous thinkers analyzed economic activities and offered views that finally led to the development of modern economics beginning with the writings of David Hume and Adam Smith that we will present in the next section.

As noted before, mercantilists based their theories on the conviction that an economy benefits from trade surplus and suffers from trade deficit. This conviction, however, rests on two fallacies. The first one regards precious metals as wealth, which would increase with trade surplus. This fallacy was so effectively debunked in the eighteenth century that hardly anyone believes in it any more. The second fallacy maintains that a trade surplus positively contributes

---

[2] For example, he wrote of "the sophistry of the mercantile system" (1776/1981, p. 927). It appears, however, Smith used the word "sophistry" not as a reference to the ancient sophists, rather as a pejorative term against mercantilism.

to labor employment in the country. This is called "the balance-of-labor doctrine" that was regarded as *the end* to be achieved by *the means* of trade surplus.[3] Unlike the first fallacy, the second one has survived to the present time among the politicians and intellectuals. Consider that as recently as the 1980s it was quite common to blame the U.S. trade deficit with Japan as the cause of declining employment in manufacturing, and since the 1990s the blame has shifted to the U.S. trade deficit with China. The conviction that imports are responsible for economic vows such as unemployment, especially if the country is running a trade deficit, remains an enduring fallacy that has refused to die despite much analytical works and historical evidence against it in the last three hundred years. This issue is explored below.

3. Debunking Mercantilism

Although mercantilist ideology has always been appealing to merchants, statesmen, and many writers throughout history, keen observers have noticed that mercantilist policies do not withstand empirical scrutiny. In fact trade policies that are exactly opposite to those of mercantilism have often coincided with the prosperity of nations. In 1670 Roger Coke noted that "The Dutch we see import all, yet thrive upon trade, and the Irish export eight times more than they import, yet grow poorer" (quoted in Irwin, 1996, p. 48).

Over three hundred years later in our time, economists have resorted to the same logic to debunk the mercantilist myth that trade surplus signifies economic strength. For example, George Hatsopoulos, *et al*, (1988) note, "from 1980 through 1986 Bolivia consistently ran a trade surplus. Exports exceeded imports by more than 60% in most years...yet from 1980 to 1986 the per capita output in the already desperately poor Bolivian economy fell by 26%" (p. 299). More generally, Peter Lindert and Jeffrey Williamson (2003) point out that there is not even one country

> that chose to be less open to trade and factor flows in the 1990s than in the 1960s and rose in the global living-standard ranks at the same time. As far as we can tell, there are no anti-global victories to report for the postwar Third World. We infer that this is because freer trade stimulates growth in Third World economies...

---

[3] See Viner, 1937, p. 55.

Although empirical observations that contradict the predictions of a proposition sufficiently reject the general validity of the proposition, theoretical analysis is necessary to expose the fallacy of an entrenched idea such as mercantilism.

An intellectual development in the last decade of the seventeenth century and the early decades of the eighteenth century significantly contributed to debunking mercantilism and making the case for free trade. This intellectual development centered on the harmony between the pursuit of private interests and of public interests. Pierre de Boisguilbert (1646 – 1714) around the years 1690-1710 argued that people contribute to "the general good" while they "are occupied night and day with their own particular interests" and care the least about the general good (quote in Irwin, 1996, p. 65). The influential Bishop Joseph Butler in a sermon in 1726 said, "by acting merely from regard (suppose) to reputation, without any consideration of the good of others, men often contribute to public good. In both these instances…[men] carry on ends, the preservation of the individual and good of society, which they themselves have not in their view or intention" (quoted in Milton Myers, 1983, p. 60).

Once the idea of the harmony between the private and public interests was developed and accepted, a group of thinkers extended the idea to international trade. The most prominent figures of this group include Dudley North (1641 – 1691), Charles Davenant (1656 – 1714), and Henry Martyn (d.1712) who proposed that the pursuit of free trade promotes the general welfare. Of these, North, unambiguously and consistently, advanced the clearest argument on the identity between the individual and public interests when international trade is freely practiced. In 1691, he wrote: "there can be no trade unprofitable to the public; for if any prove so, men leave it off; and wherever the traders thrive, the public; of which they are a part, thrives also" (quoted in Gomes, p. 21). Davenant in an essay in 1696 argued against the laws that would restrict trade: "Trade is in its Nature Free, finds its own Channel, and best directeth its own Course: and all Laws to give it Rules and Directions, and to Limit and Circumscribe it, may serve the Particular Ends of Private Men, but seldom Advantageous to the Publick…such laws are needless, unnatural, and can have no Effect conducive to the Public Good" (quoted in Istvan Hont, pp. 216-217).

Martyn in his book, *Considerations upon the East India Trade* (1701) greatly advanced the arguments against mercantilism by showing why protectionism cannot be beneficial to the economy. Trade restrictions, he argued, necessarily lead to the production of goods that require more resources at home than abroad: "a law to restrain us to use only English manufactures, is to oblige us to make them first, is to oblige us to provide for our consumption by the labor of many, what might as well be done by that of few, is to oblige us to consume the labor of many when that of few might be sufficient" (quote in Irwin, p. 57). If more workers than necessary produce a good, then the economy will operate below its potential even at full employment. In modern jargon, trade restrictions will necessarily place the economy on a lower production possibilities curve because in a protected economy some resources have zero marginal productivity or their opportunity cots are so high that by working in the protected industries they make a negative contribution to the economy's output. The case for free trade that Adam Smith and other scholars in the eighteenth century advanced, as we shall see, rest on a different kind of argument and did not exhibit the same degree of sophistication that we find in Martyn's.[4]

David Hume (1711– 1776), who wrote on numerous subjects including economics, ranks among the most influential thinkers of the eighteenth century.[5] In a series of essays, Hume consistently and persuasively argued for the expansion of foreign trade by emphasizing on the benefits of exports as well as imports. In an essay titled, "Of Commerce" he noted, "a kingdom, that has a large import and export, must abound more with industry, and that employed upon delicacies and luxuries, than a kingdom which rests contended with its native commodities" (Rotwein, p. 13). The inclusion of "large imports" marked a radical departure from mercantilism that had stressed import restrictions. In particular, Hume exposed the fallacy of mercantilism with two arguments. The first one centered on the specie-flow mechanism that clearly shows the impossibility of maintaining a trade surplus. In the second argument, Hume reversed a tenet of mercantilism by showing that through international commerce an economy prospers from the prosperity of its trading partners.

The first argument concerning the specie-flow mechanism rests on the quantity theory of money, which Hume presented in an essay titled, "Of the Balance of Trade." Here Hume argues that prices change proportionately with a change in money supply with no long-run impact on the economy. Whether "four-fifths of all the money in GREAT BRITAIN to be annihilated in one night" or "all the money of GREAT BRITAIN were multiplied fivefold in a night…the price of all labour and commodities" change "in proportion" to the change in money supply (Ibid,, pp. 60-61). Thus the mercantilist policy of increasing exports, which brings in more gold and silver is unsustainable and self-defeating; for, prices

[4] Despite his brilliant mind, Martyn was not immune from national prejudice. He vehemently opposed free trade with France (Gomes, 2003, p. 23).

[5] Eugene Rotwein (1955) has collected all of Hume's writings on economics in one volume, which the present essay uses as the source for exploring Hume's views on mercantilism.

> rise to such an exorbitant height, that no neighbouring nations could afford to buy from us; while their commodities, on the other hand, became comparatively so cheap, that, in spite of all the laws which could be formed, they would be run in upon us, and our money flow out; till we fall to a level with foreigners, and lose that great superiority of riches... (Ibid, p. 63)

Hume exhibited a deep understanding of self-regulating system of international payments through the endogenous changes in the exchange rate. He wrote, "When we import more goods than we export, the exchange turns against us, and this becomes a new encouragement to export..." (Rotwein, p. 64). This analysis deals one more blow to mercantilism because it implies that reducing imports will reduce exports by strengthening the exchange rate and making exports more expensive.

Hume's second argument, exposing the fallacy of mercantilism, concerns certain ignorance regarding foreign trade relations. A dominant view in the seventeenth and eighteenth centuries held that international trade would lead to fear, suspicion, and prejudice that Hume and other thinkers at the time called "Jealously of Trade." Istvan Hont (2005) notes that "jealously of trade" had mutated from "Jealousy of State," extracted from Thomas Hobbes's *Leviathan* (1650) in which he had written of "Jealously of Kings and Persons of Sovereign Authority" (Hont, p. 2). Hont points out that in the seventeenth and eighteenth centuries the term jealously connoted "a competitive stance motivated by ambition, envy, and resentment" (Ibid, p. 3) and it "was a disparaging phrase, referring to a pathological conjunction between politics and the economy that turned the globe into a theater of perpetual commercial war" (Ibid, p. 6). Many Enlightenment thinkers, above all David Hume and Adam Smith, labored hard to show that jealousy of trade is driven by national hatred and prejudice, resting on ignorance concerning the benefits of international commerce. The sentiments that jealousy of trade evokes have survived to the present time.

In the essay "Of the Balance of Trade" Hume, notes "Our jealousy and our hatred of France are without bounds; and...have occasioned innumerable barriers and obstructions upon commerce...But what have we gained by the bargain? We lost the FRENCH market for our woollen manufactures, and transferred the commerce of wine to SPAIN and PORTUGAL, where we buy worse liquor at a higher price" (Rotwein, pp. 66-67). Hume presents his most comprehensive analysis of this argument against mercantilism in an essay titled, "Of the Jealously of Trade." In the opening paragraph of the essay he writes:

> Nothing is more usual, among states which have made some advances in commerce, than to look on the progress of their neighbours with a suspicious eye,

> to consider all trading states as their rivals, and to suppose that it is impossible for any of them to flourish, but at their expense. In opposition to this narrow and malignant opinion, I will venture to assert, that the encrease of riches and commerce in any one nation, instead of hurting, commonly promotes the riches and commerce of all its neighbours; and that a state can scarcely carry its trade and industry very far, where all the surrounding states are buried in ignorance, sloth, and barbarism. (Ibid., p. 78)

Hume argues quite persuasively that the more prosperous and more advanced a country's trading partners are the more benefits accrues to the country. He writes that richer neighbors can afford to buy more of our goods, which in return contributes to our riches, thereby motivating us to consume more of their goods. He invokes a sort of divine economy doctrine to argue that "a diversity of geniuses, climates, and soils" among different nations secures "mutual intercourse and commerce" (Ibid., p. 79). He concludes the essay with these words,

> I shall therefore venture to acknowledge, that, not only as a man, but as a BRITISH subject, I pray for the flourishing commerce of GERMANY, SPAIN, ITALY, and even FRANCE itself. I am at least certain, that GREAT BRITAIN, and all those nations, would flourish more, did their sovereigns and ministers adopt such enlarged and benevolent sentiments towards each other. (Ibid., p. 82)

One year after the appearance of "Of the Jealously of Trade", Adam Smith published his first book *The Theory of Moral Sentiments* (1759/1984), which he regarded "superior to the *Wealth of Nations* and took the trouble to revise and expand it for a sixth edition…in 1790, the year of his death" (T. D. Campbell, p. 16). In a section of the book on "Character of Virtues" he writes, "The love of our own nation often disposes us to view, with the most malignant jealously and envy, the prosperity and aggrandizement of any other neighbouring nation" (TMS, p. 228). He then uses the example of jealously between France and Great Britain to expose the fallacy of mercantilism:

> France and England may each of them have some reason to dread the increase of the naval and military power of the other; but for either of them to envy the internal happiness and prosperity of the other, the cultivation of its lands, the advancement of its manufactures, the increase of its commerce, the security and number of its ports and harbours, its proficiency in all the liberal arts and sciences, is surely beneath the dignity of two such great nations. These are all real improvements of the world we live in. *Mankind are benefited, human nature is ennobled by them.* In such improvements each nation ought, not only to endeavour itself to excel, but from the love of mankind, to promote, instead of obstructing the excellence of its neighbours. These are all proper objects of

> national emulation, not of national prejudice or envy. (TMS, p. 229, emphasis added)

Thus, by invoking the nobility of human nature and the love of mankind, Smith's argument against jealously of trade has a moral dimension that resonates well with Hume's view on (both internal and international) commerce. In fact in a passage in *The Wealth of Nations* where Smith focuses on the contributions of commerce to "the improvements of the country," he gives credit to Hume:

> commerce and manufactures gradually introduced order and good government, and with them, the liberty and security of individuals, among the inhabitants of the country, who had before lived almost in a continual state of war with their neighbors, and of servile dependency upon their superiors. This, though it has been the least observed, is by far the most important of all their effects. Mr. Hume is the only writer who, so far as I know, has hitherto taken notice of it. (WN, 412)

Smith views mercantilism as a system that confers benefits on merchants and manufacturers at the expense of everyone else whom he calls "the great body of the people." In *The Wealth of Nations*, he argues this "great body of the people" should have the freedom "to buy whatever they want of those who sell it cheapest" (pp. 493-494). This freedom extends to purchasing imported goods, as presented in the following passage, which overlaps with Martyn's argument for free trade. Smith argues,

> If a foreign country can supply us with a commodity cheaper than we ourselves can make it, better buy it of them with some part of the produce of our own industry employed in a way in which we have some advantage. The general industry of the country, being always in proportion to the capital which employs it, will not thereby be diminished, no more than that of the above-mentioned artificers; but only left to find out the way in which it can be employed with the greatest advantage. It is certainly not employed to the greatest advantage when it is thus directed towards an object which it can buy cheaper than it can make. The value of its annual produce is certainly more or less diminished when it is thus turned away from producing commodities evidently of more value than the commodity which it is directed to produce. According to the supposition, that commodity could be purchased from foreign countries cheaper than it can be made at home. It could, therefore, have been purchased with a part only of the commodities, or, what is the same thing, with a part only of the price of the commodities, which the industry employed by an equal capital would have produced at home, had it been left to follow its natural course. The industry of the country, therefore, is thus turned away from a more to a less advantageous employment, and the exchangeable value of its annual produce, instead of being

> increased, according to the intention of the lawgiver, must necessarily be diminished by every such regulation. (WN, p. 457)

Smith further argues that import duty and export bounty are unjust because they enrich merchants and manufacturers at the expense of consumers. In his words,

> In the restraints upon of all foreign commodities which can come into competition with those of our own growth or manufacture, the interest of the home-consumer is evidently sacrificed to that of the producer. It is altogether for the benefit of the latter that the former is obliged to pay that enhancement of price which this monopoly almost always occasions.
> It is altogether for the benefit of the producer that bounties are granted upon the exportation of some of his productions. The home-consumer is obliged to pay, first, the tax which is necessary for paying the bounty, and secondly, the still greater tax which necessarily arises from the enhancement of the price of the commodity in the home market. (WN, pp. 660 – 661)

In addition to the foregoing arguments, Smith proposes that free trade enhances economic growth and reduces poverty. He explains how division of labor increases productivity and living standards but, he points out, division of labor "is limited by the extent of the market." International commerce, by widening the market, results in a more extensive division of labor and higher productivity. He notes that the "discovery of America" opened "a new and inexhaustible market to all the commodities of Europe, it gave occasion to new divisions of labour and improvements of art" (WN, p. 448).

Smith provided empirical support for his theory that division of labor improves living standards. In a lecture in 1763 he observed that the living standards of a "day-labourer in England or Holland" exceed those of an "Indian prince" or an "African king" (1982, pp. 339 – 340). He attributed the higher living standards in such societies to division of labor that results from commercial activities. Thus free trade by expanding the size of the market further advances the well-being of "day-labourers." For Smith, such policy assumes a moral dimension as gleaned from the following passage:

> No society can surely be flourishing and happy, of which the far greater part of the members are poor and miserable. It is but equity, besides, that they who feed, cloath and lodge the whole body of people, should have such a share of the produce of their own labour as to be themselves tolerably well fed, cloathed and lodged. (WN, p. 96)

Smith, however, allowed a few exceptions to free trade. Given the international hostility of his time, he argued that every country must be strong enough to defend itself, for "defence…is of much more importance than opulence." He argued, "There seem, however, two cases in which it will generally be advantageous to lay some burden upon foreign, for the encouragement of domestick industry. The first is when some particular sort of industry is necessary for the defence of the country" (WN, p. 463). Thus Smith endorsed the Navigation Acts which were enforced in his time and provided Great Britain with a strong naval power for national defense. "The second case, in which it will generally be advantageous to lay some burden upon foreign for the encouragement of domestick industry, is, when some tax is imposed at home upon the produce of the latter. In this case, it seems reasonable that an equal tax should be imposed upon the like produce of the former" (WN, p. 465). Further, Smith endorsed retaliatory measures "when there is a probability that they will procure the repeal of the high duties or prohibitions" but he disapproved of retaliation when "there is no probability that any such repeal can be procured, it seems a bad method of compensating the injury done to certain classes of our people, to do another injury ourselves, not only to those classes, but to almost all the other classes of them" (WN, p. 468).

Despite the few exceptions noted above, Smith remains the patron- saint of free trade in the annals of economic history. His writings have never ceased to influence economic thought and policies. In 1793, three years after Smith's death, the Scottish philosopher Dugald Stewart (1752 – 1828) gave an "Account of the Life and Writings of Adam Smith" before the Royal Society. In the "Account" Stewart referred to Smith as "a genius, which was destined not only to extend the boundaries of science, but to enlighten and reform the commercial policy of Europe" (1793/1982, p. 270).

4. David Ricardo and the Theory of Comparative Advantage

David Ricardo (1772 – 1823) ranks as one of the greatest economic minds of all times. He made several seminal contributions to economics including the theory of comparative advantage that Ronald Findlay (2008) has called "the deepest and most beautiful result in all of economics" (p. 28).

The theory of comparative advantage constitutes the cornerstone of the theory of international trade. Having an absolute advantage means being able to produce a good with fewer resources or more efficiently than others. Having a comparative advantage means being able to produce a good at a lower cost. This theory maintains that although an economy, say E_1, may have an absolute advantage over another economy, say E_2, in producing all goods, it is impossible for E_1 to produce everything at a lower cost. Accordingly, there is always a range of goods that E_1 can produce at lower costs than E_2 as well as a range of goods that it can produce only at higher costs. This is true regardless of the educational, technological, and institutional attainment of the economies engaged in international trade.

Moreover, under free trade all economies would export goods in which they have a comparative advantage and import goods in which they have a comparative disadvantage. Such an exchange would maximize the gains from trade. (We will explain the distribution of gains from trade later). This theory is fundamental to the market since it implies that all economies, including those that have an absolute disadvantage relative to others, can engage in mutually beneficial exchange. As Roy Ruffin (2002) put it "Every country has a place at the table of world markets, no matter how high the country's competitively determined wages or how poor its circumstances of production…" (p. 734)

The logic of comparative advantage is not limited to international trade and applies equally to the exchange of goods and services among individuals and business firms. This theory implies that unequal levels of productivities between two economies are a source of mutual benefits to market participants even if one of the economies is more productive than the other in all goods.

Although much has been written on whether Robert Torrens (1780 – 1764), David Ricardo, or (to a lesser extent) James Mill (1773 – 1836) discovered the theory of comparative advantage, the fact remains that it was Ricardo who presented the theory as we know it today.[6] In chapter VII of his major work *The Principles of Political Economy and Taxation* in 1817, Ricardo explains the core of the theory. Following a general argument in favor of free trade, Ricardo introduces a hypothetical model in which Portugal is more efficient than England in the production of both wine and cloth. "England …to produce the cloth may require the labor of 100 men… to make the wine, it might require the labor of 120 men…To produce the wine in Portugal might require only the labor of 80 men…to produce the cloth…might require the labor of 90 men..." (Ricardo, 1817/1996, p. 94). Ricardo then argues that it would be advantageous to both

[6] For a history of this argument, see Douglas Irwin (1996) and Andrea Maneschi (1998). Ruffin (2002) by delving into the theory itself (for example, articulating the assumptions needed for the veracity of the theory) as well as the writings and correspondences of Torrens, Ricardo, and Mill has persuasively argued that indeed Ricardo should receive credit for having discovered the theory.

countries if English cloth is exchanged for Portuguese wine “notwithstanding that the commodity imported by Portugal could be produced there with less labor than in England” (Ibid., p. 94). In modern jargon, Portugal has an absolute advantage over England and a comparative advantage in wine while England has an absolute disadvantage relative to Portugal and a comparative advantage in cloth.

In the paragraph following his analysis of comparative advantage, Ricardo argues that capital and labor are mobile within a country but not between countries. He speaks of “the difficulty with which capital moves from one country to another” and argues that if capital and labor were mobile internationally, in his example, they would move from England to Portugal, and as a result, "there could be no difference in the rate of profit, and no other difference in the real or labor required to convey them to the various market where they were to be sold." Capital and labor would move from England to Portugal where labor is more productive in both cloth and wine production, and this “would be undoubtedly advantageous to the capitalists of England, and to the consumers in both countries” (Ricardo, 1817/1994, p. 95). Ricardo’s comparative advantage model rests on the assumption of factor mobility within an economy but on factor immobility between economies.

Another significant aspect of Ricardo’s analysis is that he applied comparative advantage to production and exchange among individuals. He wrote:

> Two men can both make shoes and hats, and one is superior to the other in both employments; but in making hats he can only exceed his competitor by one-fifth or 20 percent, and in making shoes he can excel him by only one-third or 33 percent;-will it not be for the interest of both that the superior man should employ himself exclusively in making shoes, and the inferior man in making hats? (P. 95n)

This paragraph, which Ricardo included in a footnote, illustrates how free markets through comparative advantage benefit the society.

The concept of comparative advantage is so counter-intuitive that even some prominent economists in the nineteenth century either did not understand it or failed to appreciate its significance. Arthur Bloomfield (1989/1994) notes, “Even as eminent an economist as Jules Dupuit argued that a country could have nothing to gain from foreign trade if it could produce everything more cheaply than elsewhere” (p. 236). This statement by Dupuit in 1861, long after Ricardo, James Mill, John Stuart Mill and others had explicated the theory, is shocking and testifies to the counterintuitive nature of comparative advantage.

John Stuart Mill (1806 – 1873) in an essay he wrote in 1829 but published in 1844, credits Ricardo for having elucidated the theory of comparative advantage and then gave a precise description of the theory of comparative advantage. Mill wrote:

> It is not a difference in the *absolute* cost of production, which determines the interchange, but a difference in the *comparative* cost. It may be to our advantage to procure iron from Sweden in exchange for cottons, even though the mines of England as well as her manufactories should be more productive than those of Sweden; for if we have an advantage of one-half in cottons, and only an advantage of a quarter in iron, and could sell our cottons to Sweden at the price which Sweden must pay for them if she produced them herself, we should obtain our iron with an advantage of one-half, as well as our cottons. (1844/2006, p. 233)

Ricardo originated the term "comparative advantage" but not in chapter seven on foreign trade where he introduced the concept; rather, in chapter nineteen, which is also on foreign trade. He wrote, "A new tax...may destroy the comparative advantage which a country before possessed in the manufacture of a particular commodity" (p. 183). It remains a puzzle that he did not introduce the term where he explained his model of comparative advantage. But this puzzle, if it qualifies as one, fades quickly compared to the perplexing fact that in the heated debate over repeal of Corn Laws in England from roughly 1815 to 1846, the leading economists of the time including Ricardo, William Nassau Senior, John Ramsey McCulloch, and John Stuart Mill who all favored the repeal did not invoke comparative advantage to support their position.

Cheryl Schonhardt-Bailey (2006) has written a comprehensive book on the repeal of the Corn Laws that ushered in the period of free trade in the Great Britain in 1846. She argues

> that interests drove repeal to the doors of Parliament, ideas inspired constituents and legislators alike to endorse free trade .... and institutions shaped *and* shaped by the interests and ideas that drove repeal. In short, repeal must be understood as the product of interests, ideas, *and* institutions. (p. 28, italics original)

Schonhardt-Bailey argues that interests and ideas succeeded in repeal of the Corn Laws because the "institutions of parliamentary of democracy in the 1840s had become far more conciliatory to liberal reform than they had been just a few decades before." More importantly, "economic interests led Britain to repeal, but ideas and institutions delivered the final outcome." The perplexing fact remains that comparative advantage, the most important idea in trade theory, did not enter into the debate on repealing the Corn Laws. The term "comparative advantage" is not even mentioned in Schonhardt-Bailey's 426-page long book on the subject.

One possible reason is that it took a long time for the leading economists to appreciate the decisive role of comparative advantage in favor of free trade. Leonard Gomes (1990) points out that although the "economists were on the side of free trade...arguments based on comparative-cost reasoning featured only marginally, if at all, in their attacks on agricultural protection" (pp. 44-5).

A more plausible reason is that Ricardo, John Stuart Mill, and other economists of that era regarded comparative advantage primarily as an *explanation* for the fact that trade takes place among nations, rather than as an argument to be invoked in favor of international trade. Whenever these authors put forth an argument in favor of free trade, they usually resorted to the same rationale we find in *the Wealth of Nations*. For example, a few short paragraphs before introducing the theory of comparative advantage, Ricardo reiterated a theme that Smith and Hume had made a center piece of their arguments in favor of free trade. Ricardo wrote:

> Under a system of perfectly free commerce, each country naturally devotes its capital and labour to such employments as are most beneficial to each. *This pursuit of individual advantage is admirably connected with the universal good of the whole.* By stimulating industry, by rewarding ingenuity, and by using most efficaciously the peculiar powers bestowed by nature, it distributes labour most effectively and most economically. while, by increasing the general mass of productions, it diffuses general benefit, and binds together by one common tie of interest and intercourse, the universal society of nations throughout the civilized world. It is this principle which determines that wine shall be made in France and Portugal, that corn shall be grown in America and Poland, and that hardware and other goods shall be manufactured in England. (P. 93, emphasis added)

Thus free trade not only binds people "throughout the civilized world" but also constitutes the most efficient and productive mechanism for the allocation of resources. The italicized sentence "*This pursuit of individual advantage is admirably connected with the universal good of the whole*" conveys the same sentiment as many passages in *The Wealth of Nations* including where Smith discusses foreign trade and invokes his famous metaphor of the invisible hand.[7] Similarly, John Stuart Mill in two essays, one titled, "The Corn Laws" (1825/2006) and the other, "Petition on Free Trade" (1841/2006) argues that protective tariffs benefit one group at the expense of another one, which is fundamentally the same as Adam Smith's argument that protectionism benefits

[7] Consider that Smith says an individual by "pursuing his own interest he frequently promotes that of the society more effectually than when he really intends to promote it" (WN, p. 456).

"merchants and manufacturers" at the expense of the "great body of people." To the economists of the nineteenth century, the theory of comparative advantage had a descriptive, rather than a prescriptive, utility.

5. Adam Smith and the Theory of Comparative Advantage

Given the centrality of comparative advantage to international trade and its significance to economic thinking in general as well as the stature of Adam Smith in shaping classical economics, some scholars have criticized Smith for having failed to discover this theory. For example, Arthur Bloomfield (1975/1994) while praising Smith for his "over-all performance in the analysis of international trade" and saying that Smith "deserves respectful attention" notes, "Admittedly, Smith did not come up with comparative costs, reciprocal demand, or others of the concepts and tools that were to be developed by later classical writers" (p. 138). Bloomfield is not alone in this criticism.[8]

This is a startling criticism. Faulting Smith for not having discovered the theory of comparative advantage is like criticizing Galileo for not having formulated the theory of Gravity, and chastising Isaac Newton for not having discovered the theory of Relatively. Science is a cumulative and collaborative enterprise that advances over time. Adam Smith drew on the contributions of many thinkers from Greek philosophers in antiquity to numerous writers in his own time, and in turn inspired David Ricardo to study economics.[9] Every generation of thinkers provides the analytical tools for the later generations in all sciences including economics. As Mark Blaug (2001) has observed:

> Economic knowledge is path-dependent. What we now know about economic system is not something we have just discovered, but it is the sum of all discoveries, insights and false starts in the past. Without Hayek and Robbins and Pigou, no Keynes; without Keynes, non Friedman; without Friedman, no Lucas; without Lucas, no…(p. 156)

And we might add, without Smith, no David Ricardo and, as a result, no formulation of comparative advantage in 1817, at least not the way Ricardo presented. But there is more to the story here. Upon a careful examination of *The*

---

[8] See also Hla. Myint (1977).

[9] The influence of Smith on Ricardo is noted in the opening page of the 1996 print of Ricardo's *Principles of Political Economy* (1817/1996).

Wealth of Nations, it turns out that Smith did understand the basic idea of comparative advantage. In fact Lars Magnusson (2004) refers to Smith as "a founding father of the comparative cost theory" (p. 31). As noted before, the theory of comparative advantage rests on the proposition that it is impossible for an economy (E_1) to produce everything at a lower cost than another economy (E_2) even if E_1 is more efficient (requires fewer resources) than E_2 in producing everything. The proposition implies that trade between the two economies will benefit both of them; for, each will import the good that would cost more to make at home. In the early part of *The Wealth of Nations*, Smith exhibited an awareness of this proposition:

> The most opulent nations, indeed, generally excel all their neighbours in agriculture as well as in manufactures; but they are commonly more distinguished by their superiority in the latter than in the former. Their lands are in general better cultivated, and having more labour and expence bestowed upon them, produce more in proportion to the extent and natural fertility of the ground. But this superiority of produce is seldom much more than in proportion to the superiority of labour and expence. In agriculture, the labour of the rich country is not always much more productive than that of the poor; or, at least, it is never so much more productive, as it commonly is in manufactures. The corn of the rich country, therefore, will *not always*, in the same degree of goodness, come cheaper to market than that of the poor. (WN, p. 16, emphasis added)

In the last sentence, if instead of "*not always*" (my italics) Smith had used the word "never," or simply had not used the word "*always*," this paragraph would have qualified as a clear statement of comparative advantage; for, it says that even though labor productivity in corn production is higher in a rich country than in a poor country, the rich country does not produce the corn more cheaply. That is, the rich country has an absolute advantage, but not a comparative advantage, in corn production. In fact Smith's model with two countries (rich and poor), two sectors (manufacture and agriculture), and one factor (labor) resembles the textbook version of the Ricardian model. Smith's further analysis of the model can (and should) be read in terms of comparative advantage

> ...though the poor country, notwithstanding the inferiority of its cultivation, can, in some measure, rival the rich in the cheapness and goodness of its corn, it can pretend to no such competition in its manufactures; at least if those manufactures suit the soil, climate, and situation of the rich country. The silks of France are better and cheaper than those of England, because the silk manufacture, at least under the present high duties upon the importation of raw silk, does not so well suit the climate of England as that of France. But the hard-ware and the coarse woollens of England are beyond all comparison superior to those of France, and

> much cheaper too in the same degree of goodness. In Poland there are said to be scarce any manufactures of any kind, a few of those coarser household manufactures excepted, without which no country can well subsist. (WN, pp. 16-17)[10]

Nevertheless, Smith should not be credited with the discovery of comparative advantage, but nor should he be criticized for not having articulated it as Ricardo did. Comparative advantage simply played no role in Smith's analysis of foreign trade. There is no hint of comparative advantage in the literature following Smith while after Ricardo the concept quickly became a staple of international trade theory.

6. The Contributions of John Stuart Mill

For both intellectual and commercial reasons, trade theory in the nineteenth-century assumed a prominent place in economics. Intellectually, the theory of comparative advantage raised the status of economic logic well beyond "the 18th century rule" that says trade is beneficial when commodities can be imported at a smaller cost than produced at home.[11] This rule does not excite one's intellect; for, it is an obvious and even a tautological proposition while comparative advantage is counterintuitive and produces unexpected results.

Commercially, the nineteenth century witnessed a dramatic increase in international trade. In fact many scholars have identified the early decades of the century as the dawn of modern globalization era. Kevin O'Rourke and Jeffrey Williamson (2002) note, "There was no big global bang in the 1490s, but there was a very big global bang in the 1820s" (p. 456).[12] Among the major factors contributing to the rapid rise in international trade were inventions such as steamships, train, refrigeration, and telegraph. Concurrently with the availability of these technologies, Western Europe, led by England began to realize the fruits of the Industrial Revolution including higher labor productivity and mass production of manufactured goods. Although in the eighteenth century, thinkers such as Hume and Smith had paid a great deal of attention to trade theory, the soaring international commerce in the nineteenth century garnered considerably

---

[10] For further elaboration, see Bruce Elmslie and Antoinette James (1993) and Elmslie (1994).

[11] Jacob Viner (937) coined the phrase "the 18th century rule." See Bloomfield (1989/1994) for elaboration.

[12] Angus Maddison (1995) also identifies 1820 as the beginning of modern globalization era. On the history of globalization, see also Gary Gereffi (2005).

more intellectual energy in order to explain the forces that shape international trade and determine the terms of trade.

O'Rourke and Williamson (1999) in their book, *Globalization and History*, have described the impact of technological innovation on the nineteenth-century trade. They refer to steamships as "the most important nineteenth-century contribution to shipping technology" (p. 33). Steamers began to navigate the waterways of the continental Europe and the United States in the first decade of the nineteenth-century as, for example, the steamer "Claremont made its debut on the Hudson in 1807" (ibid, p. 33). But it took a few decades for the steamers to be employed fully in international commerce. The construction of railways that had started in the early decades of the century took off around the year 1850 in Europe as well as in the United States. A few decades later India, Japan, Mexico, and China began the construction and expansion of railroads (Ibid, p. 34).[13] Another boost to transoceanic trade in the nineteenth-century came from the development of mechanical refrigeration that made the exportation of many food items to distant places possible.

O'Rourke and Williamson (1999) estimate that these inventions and innovations dramatically reduced the transportation costs both within and between countries. For example, from approximately mid-century to 1913 transport costs in real terms fell by 45 percent, leading to an unprecedented rise in international commerce (p. 36). Ronald Findlay and Kevin O'Rourke (2007) in chapters six and seven of their book *Power and Plenty* analyze in details the evolution of world trade from late eighteenth-century to the early twentieth-century. In particular, they document that international trade in primary products as well as in manufactured goods tripled between 1880 and 1913 (p. 412).

Ricardo's theory of comparative advantage convinced almost all professional economists that free trade is the optimal policy and, regardless of the economic idiosyncrasies of the trading partners, trade is mutually beneficial.[14] But what determines the distribution of the benefits? This question, apparently, never crossed Ricardo's mind. In reference to the question of the distribution of gains from trade, John Stuart Mill in his 1829 essay to which we referred earlier (1844/2006) writes:

---

[13] The railway in the U.S. expanded from 9,000 miles in 1850 to 250,000 miles in 1910. O'Rourke and Williamson (1999) argue that "the railroad was in many ways to the United States what the 1992 Single Market program was to the European Union" (p. 34).

[14] Prominent dissenters include, but not limited to, Friedrich List (1789 – 1846), John Rae (1796 – 1882), and Augustin Cournot (1801 – 1877).

> This, which was not an error, but a mere oversight of Mr. Ricardo, arising from his having left the question of the division of the advantage entirely unnoticed, was first corrected in the third edition of Mr. Mill's *Elements of Political Economy*...It can hardly, however, be said that Mr. Mill has prosecuted the inquiry any further; which, indeed, would have been quite as inconsistent with the nature of his plan as of Mr. Ricardo's. (P. 236)

Here John Stuart Mill develops the theory of reciprocal demand, which ranks as one of the most important contributions to the theory of international trade. In his *Principles of Political Economy* (1848/2006), citing the 1829 essay as the origin of the theory, Mill argues that the theory rests on the following observation: "The value of a thing in any place, depends on the cost of its acquisition in that place; which in the case of an imported article, means the cost of production of the thing which is exported to pay for it" (p. 595). Mill begins his analysis with a clear explication of the laws of demand and supply and the emergence of equilibrium from interactions between demand and supply. He then extends the analysis to international markets in which imports are paid for by exports. Mill argues that the terms of trade between two countries results from the demand function that each one has for the other country's exports.[15] The demand function represents the various units of imports a country is willing to purchase and pay for it with exports. The farther the terms of trade is from a country's production cost of imports (measured in terms of foregone exports), the larger the gains from trade.

The theory of reciprocal demand implies that if a country is large enough to influence the terms of trade by imposing a tariff, it can capture a bigger share of the gains from trade. This would require either the country's export price to rise or its import price to fall. But if the foreign demand for the country's export is highly elastic, a trade tax would fail to secure a larger portion of gains from trade. Moreover, retaliation can nullify the impact of tariff on the terms of trade and reduce the gains from trade in both countries by shrinking the volume of trade.[16]

The foregoing analysis implies that under free trade a small (poor) country (that is, a price-taker in world markets) benefits much more than a large (rich) trade partner. The reason for this paradoxical result is that the terms of trade

---

[15] Alfred Marshall (1842 - 1924) presents this analysis by a geometrical device, known as the offer curves, which has become the staple of every textbook in international trade.

[16] Robert Torrens had understood the possibility that a tariff could be beneficial to an importing country at the expense of the exporting country, but he failed to articulate the intricacies of how it might happen. John Stuart Mill gave a clear analysis of the issue that later became the seeds for the optimum tariff argument. On this point, see Irwin, 1996, chapter 7.

would be much closer to the cost (price) ratio of the large country and thus (relatively) farther from that of the small country. In Mill's own words:

> The richest countries, ceteris paribus, gain the least by a given amount of foreign commerce: since, having a greater demand for commodities generally, they are likely to have a greater demand for foreign commodities, and thus modify the terms of interchange to their own disadvantage. (Quoted in Gomes, 1990, p. 30)

This counter-intuitive result would be reversed if the rich country imposed a tariff on its imports from the small country, against which the small country cannot retaliate because it purchases too small a quantity of the traded good to be able to influence its price.

Another Mill's seminal contribution is the finding that the benefits of trade exceed any cost that may be imposed on some people such as those working in import-competing industries. Mill argues that the losers can be compensated so that everyone can actually benefit from trade. The neoclassical economists who followed Mill demonstrated mathematically what Mill had realized intuitively, namely the proposition that trade generates a net benefit. Wolfang Stolper and Paul Samuelson (1941/1994) who identified the beneficiary and the loser of free trade in their influential and cntroveial Stolper-Samuelsson theorem concluded their paper as follows:

> it has been shown that the harm which free trade inflicts upon one factor of production is necessarily less than the gain to the other. Hence, it is always possible to bribe the suffering factor by subsidy or other redistributive devices so as to leave all factors better off as a result of trade. (p. 61)

John Stuart Mill, the last major figure of classical economics, played the pivotal role in the evolution of classical economics into the neoclassical paradigm in 1870s.

7. Summary and Conclusions

Trade theory, the oldest branch of economics, has attracted the greatest minds in the profession from Adam Smith to John Stuart Mill to Paul Samuelsson. The intellectual history of trade theory originated two and one-half millennia ago in the hands of Greek historians and philosophers. Their attempt at explaining the reason for long-distance commerce marks the birth of trade theory, which remained a component of the general theory of the market until the seventeenth century when mercantilism emerged as a major school of thought in economics. Mercantilism rests on the erroneous view that the wealth of nations consists in precious metals to be acquired through export expansion and import restriction. Although mercantilism was effectively refuted by David Hume and Adam Smith in the eighteenth century, its remnants still guide the trade policy of many countries. Hume discovered the specie-flow mechanism, showing how this mechanism prevents a country from sustaining a trade surplus over the long-term. Smith debunked the idea that precious metals constitute the wealth of nations and argued that the expansion of markets through international trade raises labor productivity and thus living standards. Hume and Smith advanced a strong case for increasing international trade not only on economic ground but also on social and moral grounds.

David Ricardo raised the status of economics by demonstrating the utility of abstract models in economic analysis. No where has this been more apparent and path-breaking than in the demonstration of the theory of comparative advantage, the jewel of all trade theories. Ricardo quite effectively showed why mutually beneficial exchange rests on comparative and not absolute advantage. John Stuart Mill further advanced the trade theory by explicating the determination of the terms of trade through reciprocal demand of each country for its trade partner's exports. Ricardo and Mill revolutionized the field of international trade and crafted a scientific framework that has since served as the basis of the neoclassical trade theory.[17]

Reference

Allen, William R. (1987), *"Mercantilism," in The New Palgrave Dictionary of Economics,* Vol. 3, in John Eatwell, et al, (eds.), 1987, pp. 445 – 449, London: The Macmillan Press Limited.

Blaug, Mark (2001), "No History of Ideas, Please, We're Economists," *Journal of Economic Perspectives* 15, 1, pp. 145 – 164.

Bloomfield, Arthur I. (1975/1994), *"Adam Smith and the Theory of International Trade,"* in Essays in the History of International Trade Theory, in Arthur Bloomfield (ed.), Cheltenham, UK and Northampton, USA: Edward Elgar, pp. 109 - 144.

Bloomfield, Arthur I. (1989/1994), *"Aspects of the Theory of International Trade in France: 1800 – 1914,"* in Essays in the History of International Trade

[17] For the development of neoclassical international economics, see Leonard Gomes (1990).

Theory, in Arthur Bloomfield (ed.), Cheltenham, UK and Northampton, USA: Edward Elgar, pp. 233 – 262.

Campbell, T. D. (1971), *Adam Smith's Science of Morals*, London: George Allen & Unwin LTD.

Elmslie, Bruce and Antoinette James (1993), *"The Renaissance of Adam Smith in Modern Theories of International Trade,"* in Perspectives on the History of Economic Thought, Volume IX, in Robert F. Hebert (ed.), Published for the History of Economic Society by Edward Elgar.

Elmslie, Bruce (1994), Positive Feedback Mechanism in Adam Smith's Theories of International Trade," *The European Journal of the History of Economic Thought* 1, 2, Spring, pp. 253 – 271.

Findlay, Ronald (2008), *"Comparative Advantage," in Steven Durlauf and Lawrence Blume (eds),* in The New Palgrave: Dictionary of Economics, Second Edition, pp. 28 - 33.

Findlay, Ronald and Kevin O'Rourke (2007), *Power and Plenty: Trade, War, and the World Economy in the Second Millennium,* Princeton and Oxford: Princeton University Press.

Gereffi, Gary (2005), *"The Global Economy: Organization, Governance, and Development,"* in Neil J. Smeler and Richard Swenberg (eds.), in The Handbook of Sociology, 2nd edition, Princeton: Princeton University Press, pp. 160 – 182.

Gomes, Leonard (1990), *Neoclassical International Economics: An Historical Survey*, New York: St. Martin Press.

Gomes, Leonard (2003), *The Economics and Ideology of Free Trade: A Historical Review,* Cheltenham, UK and Northampton, USA: Edward Elgar.

Gordon, Barry (1975), *Economic Analysis before Adam Smith: Hesiod to Lessius*, Barnes and Noble Books.

Hatsopoulos, George, Paul Krugman, and Lawrence Summers (1988), "*U.S. Competitiveness: Beyond the Trade Deficit*," Science 241, July 15, pp. 299 – 307.

Heckscher, Eli (1919), *"The Effects of Foreign Trade on the Distribution of Income,"* in Heckscher-Ohlin Trade Theory in Harry Flam and M. June Flanders (1991), Cambridge: The MIT press.

Hirschman, Albert (1982), "Rival Interpretations of Market Society: Civilizing, Destructive, or Feeble?" *Journal of Economic Literature* 20, December, pp. 1463-1484.

Hont, Istavan (2005) *Jealousy of Trade: International Competition and the nation-State in Historical Perspective*, Cambridge, Mass: The Belknap of the Harvard University Press.

Hume, David (1758/1955) *"Of the Jealously of Trade,"* in David Hume: Writings on Economics, in Eugene Rotwein (ed.), Madison: University of Wisconsin Press, pp. 78 – 82.

Irwin, Douglas A. (1996), Against the Tided: An Intellectual History of Free Trade, Princeton: Princeton University Press.

Lahaye, Laura (2008), *"Mercantilism," in Steven Durlauf and Lawrence Blume (eds),* in The New Palgrave: Dictionary of Economics, Second Edition, pp. 568-569.

Lerner, Ralph (1979), *"Commerce and Character: The Anglo-American as New-Model Man,"* The William and Mary Quarterly 35. January, pp. 3-26.

Lindert, Peter and Jeffrey Williamson (2003), *"Does Globalization Make the World More Unequal?"* in Globalization in Historical Perspective, in M. Bordo, Allan M. Taylor and Jeffrey G. Williamson (eds.), Chicago: The University of Chicago Press, pp. 227 – 271.

Maddison, Angus (1995), *Monitoring the World Economy,* Paris: OECD Development Center.

Magnusson, Lars (2004), *The Tradition of Free Trade*, Abingdon, Oxfordshire: Rutledge.

Maneschi, Andrea (1998), *Comparative Advantage in International Trade: A Historical Perspective*, Cheltenham, UK and Northampton, USA: Edward Elgar.

Martyn, Henry (1701), *Considerations upon the East India Trade*, London: A. and J. Churchill.

Mill, John Stuart (1825/2006), *"The Corn Laws,"* in Essays on Economics and Society, 1824-1845, Collected Works of John Stuart Mill, Indianapolis: Liberty Fund, pp. 45 – 70..

Mill, John Stuart (1844/2006), "*Essays on Some Unsettled Questions of Political Economy,"* in Essays on Economics and Society, 1824-1845, Collected Works of John Stuart Mill, Indianapolis: Liberty Fund.

Mill, John Stuart (1841/2006), *"Petition on Free Trade,"* in Essays on Economics and Society, 1824-1845, Collected Works of John Stuart Mill, Indianapolis: Liberty Fund, pp. 761 -763.

Mill, John Stuart (1848/2006), *Principles of Political Economy,* Collected Works of John Stuart Mill, Indianapolis: Liberty Fund.

Morley, Neville (2007), *Trade in Classical Antiquity*, Cambridge: Cambridge University Press.

Mun, Thomas (1664), *England's Treasure by Forraign Trade*, London: T. Clark.

Myers, Milton (1983), *The Soul of Modern Economic Man*, Chicago: Chicago University Press.

Myint, Hla. (1977), "Adam Smith Thory of International Trade in the Perspective of Economic Development," *Economica*, 44, pp. 231 – 248.

Ohlin, Bertil (1933), *Interregional and International Trade,* Cambridge: Harvard University Press.

O'Rourke, Kevin H. and Jeffrey G. Williamson (1999), *Globalization and History-Evolution of a Nineteenth-Century Atlantic Economy,* Cambridge, Mass: The MIT Press.

O'Rourke, Kevin H. and Jeffrey G. Williamson (2002), "The Heckscher-Ohlin Model between 1400 and 2000: When It Explained Factor Price Convergence, and When It Did not, and Why," in Bertil Ohlin; *a Centennial Celebration,* 1899 – 1999, ed. by Ronald Findlay, Lars Jonung, and Mats Lundahl, Cambridge MA: The MIT Press, pp. 431 – 453.

Ricardo, David (1817/1996), *Principles of Political Economy and Taxation*, Great Mind Series, Amherst, New York: Prometheus Books.

Rotwein, Eugene (1955), David Hume: *Writings on Economics*, edited, Madison: University of Wisconsin Press.

Schonhardt-Bailey, Cheryl (2006), *From Corn Laws to Free Trade: Interests, Ideas, and Institutions in Historical Perspective,* Cambridge, Mass: The MIT Press

Smith, Adam (1759/1984), *The Theory of Moral Sentiments,* Indianapolis: Liberty Fund.

Smith, Adam (1776/1981), *An Inquiry into the Nature and Causes of the Wealth of Nations*, Indianapolis: Liberty Fund.

Smith, Adam (1982), *Lectures on Jurisprudence*, Indianapolis: Liberty Fund.

Stewart, Dugald (1793), *"Account of the Life and Writings of Adam Smith,"* in Adam Smith Essays on Philosophical Subjects, 1982, Indianapolis: Liberty Fund, pp. 269 – 351.

Viner, Jacob (1937/1975), *Studies in the Theory of International Trade*, New York: Augustus M. Kelly Publishers.

Viner, Jacob (1959/1991), *"Early Attitudes towards Trade and the Merchant",* in Essays on the Intellectual History of Economics, in Douglas A. Irwin (ed.), Princeton: Princeton University Press.

In: Trade Liberalization and Protectionism
Editors: B. Hahn et al, pp. 31-60
ISBN: 978-1-60876-837-0

Chapter 2

TRADE LIBERALIZATION, GROWTH AND DISTRIBUTION IN DEVELOPING COUNTRIES: LEADING EXPERIENCES

Sanjaya Acharya*
Tribhuvan University, Kathmandu, Nepal

Abstract

This paper makes an intensive review of the literature on trade liberalization and its impacts on growth and distribution in developing countries. A growing surge of literature on internal and external trade reforms for the last two decades comprises both transition and developing economies. Most of the theoretical studies are, in fact, the extensions of Stolper-Samuelson theorem. Empirical studies, however, differ based on their methodological approaches; but they can be broadly grouped into cross-country regression analysis, country-specific partial analysis, and general equilibrium analysis. This paper concludes that trade reforms are growth enhancing but they require complementary policies to make the growth pro-poor. So long as the

---

* E-mail address: sanjaya@newera.wlink.com.np and sanjaya_acharya@hotmail.com. Phone: 977-1-4423176, Fax: 977-1-4419562. Corresponding author: Dr. Acharya conducted this review paper while pursuing his doctoral research at Erasmus University Rotterdam, The Netherlands. He is grateful to Socio-Economic Research (SEOR) funding to this work. Currently, he is working as an Associate Professor of Economics at Tribhuvan University, Kathmandu. Moreover, he is also available at New ERA, PO Box 722, Kalopul, Rudramati Marga, Kathmandu, Nepal.

macroeconomic parameters improve or do not deteriorate, at least, the potential impacts are sustainable.

JEL Classification: O11, I3, O24, E65, F15, P46

Key Words: Economic liberalization, developing countries, growth, poverty, distribution

1. Introduction

In this paper, we review three important questions pertaining to economic liberalization and its distributional impacts. These three questions are: (a) What do theoretical studies tell on the relationship between liberalization and pro-poor growth? (b) What is the empirical evidence on this relationship between liberalization and distribution? (c) How did international assistance agencies, such as the World Bank and International Monetary Fund (IMF), and recipient governments in developing countries formulate their development policy in the context of knowledge on the relationship between liberalization and distribution? The orientation of this paper is to determine a good deal by the answers to these questions.

The rest of the sections in this paper are organized as follows: Section 2 reviews the theoretical studies on liberalization and distribution starting from the pioneer work of Stolper and Samuelson (1941). Likewise, review of the empirical works relating liberalization and distribution is the subject matter of Section 3. Section 4 gives a brief account of policy reforms initiated by the World Bank and IMF for integrating developing economies to the global economy. It covers the period after the mid 1980s disaggregated into 1986-89, 1989-92 and later extended till 1999, and 1999 onwards. This section sheds light on the relative shift of policy prescriptions of these two biggest global financial institutions in addressing the growth and stabilization problems of the developing world. We draw the conclusions of the paper in Section 5.

2. Theoretical Studies on Liberalization and Distribution

The theorem of Stolper-Samuelson (1941) is the first basic theoretical tool to deal with the distributional impacts of trade liberalization. Many theoretical and empirical studies on trade reform and its distributional impacts have their theoretical foundation on this theorem, which itself is based on Heckscher-Ohlin-Samuelson (HOS) Model. In this section we review relevant theoretical literature on the relationship between trade liberalization and income distribution.

The Stolper-Samuelson theorem states that under the assumptions of the Heckscher-Ohlin-Samuelson (HOS) model, an increase in the relative price of a good raises the return to the factor used intensively in the production of that good relative to all other prices and lowers the return to the other factors. The 2-good × 2-factor general equilibrium model provides the minimally complex micro-foundations for a well-specified macroeconomic model with international trade that can generate income distribution effects. The Stolper-Samuelson theorem takes over various assumptions of the HOS model. They are: rational behavior by households and firms, complete and perfectly competitive markets, and the trading countries possessing the identical tastes that can be represented by identical systems of (homothetic) community indifference curves. Moreover, each country is endowed with fixed quantities of two factors of production: (L) for labor and (H) for human capital, or simply skills and capital. Further assumptions include the homogeneity in the quality of factors, perfect mobility of them among sectors but not between the trading countries. Other assumptions of the model are that countries share the same technological opportunities, each good requires strictly positive inputs of both L and H to be produced in positive quantities, and production functions are linear homogeneous, twice differentiable, and strictly concave.

Regarding the factor intensity, the model assumes that, at all relevant factor prices, one of the goods in trade is always human capital intensive relative to the other. One of the two countries is taken to be relatively more richly endowed with human capital than the other. The last but very strong assumption is that international trade in goods is costless.

Applied to a poor and a rich trading countries, with more relative endowments in labor and capital, respectively, the theorem predicts that more trade will benefit labor in the poor country and, hence, progressive in its distribution effect. The opposite would apply for the rich country.

Many theoretical works related to trade liberalization and its distributional impacts stem from the foundation of Stolper-Samuelson theorem. We give a brief account of some relevant ones. Bourguignon and Morrison (1989) have dropped the assumption of flexible factor prices and their full employment to obtain the Keynesian approach of trade. In this model, demand plays a key role and has an interdependent relation with income distribution. According to this approach, trade affects income distribution via exogenously determined foreign demand. Though not directly related to the Stolper-Samuelson theorem, Alsenia and

Rodrik (1994) studied the relationship between politics and economic growth in a simple model of endogenous growth with distributive conflict among agents endowed with varying capital/labor shares. This study is not particularly devoted to trade and distribution issues; however, the politics of tax has well captured the direction of international trade in the model. They established several results regarding the factor ownership of the median individual and the level of taxation, redistribution, and growth. The wider the inequality of wealth and income, the higher is the rate of taxation and the lower growth.

Wood (1994) and Cline (1997) have made a comprehensive extension of the Stolper-Samuelson theorem from the viewpoint of making it practical to deal with concrete trade policy. Francois and Nelson (1998) introduced the inter-industry linkages and considered the mechanism that transmits the effect of goods' prices to factors' prices. According to this version, the change in goods' prices are transmitted first to value added prices and then to relative factor prices. In this case, the theorem will hold so long as the goods are homogenous; however, in case of the intermediate product differentiation, the theorem no longer holds. Some argue that an appropriate test of the Stolper-Samuelson theorem must take account of the fact that the theorem refers to a long-run relationship between relative commodity-prices and relative factor-prices. They used a unit root co-integration method developed by Johansen (1988) to evaluate the Stolper-Samuelson relationship.

According to Aghion, Caroli and Garcia-Penalosa (1999), in developing countries, trade liberalization is likely to have had conflicting effects on the distribution of earnings. On the one hand, standard trade theory implies that trade liberalization should result in a reduction of skill premium. On the other hand, trade flows bring in new technologies and ideas that enhance the productivity of all workers, but especially that of skilled workers. However, the notion of "skilled" and "unskilled" workers differs across countries. In less developed economies, those on the top of the earnings distribution often have no more than a secondary degree. Yet, they have skills that will be enhanced by the arrival of new technologies, thus, increase their wage relative to that of uneducated workers.

The impact of economic liberalization on poverty is mostly analyzed through its adjustment in the labor market. On the other side, the financial liberalization enhances financial intermediation and subsequent investment. In the wake of trade liberalization whether this increasing investment induces labor-intensive or capital-intensive modes of production along with the price movements makes all the difference regarding the distributional changes. Since the relative price shifts in favor of traded over non-traded goods in free trade, the distributional impact of it does depend on the factor intensity in both sectors. The changes in demand of the final products in domestic and international markets make all the factor reallocations and change in their relative returns. The wage earners will benefit more than profit earners from the trade liberalization if labor-intensive goods are traded more than capital-intensive goods.

3. Empirical Studies on the Relationship between Liberalization and Distribution

On the empirical front, the global economy has undergone increasing factor and product market liberalization during the last couple of decades. Developing economies are becoming more open, while factor shares and the patterns of income distribution and income inequalities are also changing over time.

The liberalization drive in the developing world was basically led by the IMF/World Bank's Structural Adjustment Program since the mid-1980s. The external sector liberalization was considered to integrate the domestic economy to the rest of the world; therefore, it was sometimes synonymously understood as the globalization process. To be more specific, many empirical papers have regarded trade liberalization as globalization; whereas some others such as Milanovic (2005a) have regarded capital account liberalization as globalization. However, in this paper, globalization refers to both of these concepts.

Three groups of empirical studies are available on trade liberalization and its distributional impacts mainly in developing countries. These are (a) cross-sectional regression analysis for groups of countries (b) partial analysis of trade and its distributional impact for specific countries, and (c) general equilibrium analysis for specific countries.

3.1. Cross-Country Analysis

Deininger and Squire (1996) prepared a first consistent database to make this type of studies. This opened the way for a series of influential econometric studies. Edwards (1997) analysis of trade policy and income distribution, using new income comparative data sets, showed no relationship between the two ends. The regression of the change in the Gini index between the 1970s and 1980s on a dummy indicating whether or not a country had engaged in trade liberalization as measured by the average black-market premium or the average collected tariff ratio helped Edwards reach this conclusion.

Spilimbergo, Londono, and Szekely (1999) studied the empirical links among factor endowments, trade, and personal income distribution. By using panel data, they showed that land and capital intensive countries have a less equal income distribution while skill intensive countries have a more equal income distribution. They showed that the effects of trade openness on inequality depend on factor endowments in a way consistent with several recent case studies but not with the Hecksher–Ohlin framework. The results are robust to the division of the sample according to the level of income, the inclusion of different regressors, the use of different measures of trade openness and relative factor abundance, and the tests for possible problems of endogeneity.

Atkinson (2003) was able to represent a decrease in inequality in the wake of globalization -- more specifically after the Second World War -- and a turning point around the 1980s when inequality began increasing again, which confirmed the "U-turn" hypothesis. Other studies that also derived similar results using different specifications, time periods, and data include Londono (2002), Green and Dickerson (2001), and Dollar and Kraay (2002). Berman, Birdsall, and Szekely (2003) concluded that more liberal trade regimes did not have an impact on wage differentials among different education categories in Latin American countries. But, financial liberalization and high-technology exports in the context of a liberal trade regime contributed to the rising inequality. Rajas-Romagosa (2005), analyzing cross-country regressions, showed that trade openness does not influence income inequality negatively in low-income countries although the effects are marginal and for most indicators of trade openness the effect was not significant.

Mainstream economists and international financial organizations claim that trade liberalization and factor mobility have increased economic growth in those countries which have successively integrated into the world economy and that these improved economic conditions have allowed these developing countries to reduce poverty (World Bank, 2002). Another representative study that reached to this conclusion was by Dollar and Kraay (2002). They found that inequality between the population-weighted mean incomes of the globalizing countries declined substantially between 1975 and 1995. In the global context, Milanovic (2005b) found a sharp increase in the global inequality between 1988 and 1993 and then moderate decline during the next five years. Sala-i-Martin (2002) and Bhalla (2002) also argued that the global inequality had gone down. On the other side, Lundberg and Squire (2003); and Barro (2000) found that their preferred measure of openness has measured increasing inequality in low-income countries. Milanovic and Squire (2005) also concluded that trade openness is associated with higher inter-occupational and inter-industry inequality in poorer countries -- those below the world medium income -- and the reverse in richer countries. But these studies are suffering from the lots of criticisms. First, their approach that combines household survey and national accounts (GDP data) is questionable. Second, the results drawn have been based on many heroic assumptions. Third, neither of these studies explored the causality between increased globalization and global inequality (Ibid, p. 8).

The general impression from a review of cross-country regressions is that the results of distributional effects of more trade are very mixed. The pooling of observations of developed and developing countries in one equation regression analysis is also not helpful tool in shedding the light on the mechanisms that couple trade to distribution.

3.2. Country Studies with Partial Analysis

These studies address the phenomenon of selected aspects of growth and distribution following the trade reform. Hansen and Harrison (1999) concluded that trade reform along with foreign direct investment, export orientation, and technological change had increased wage-inequality in Mexico. Robertson (2000) has also reached to similar conclusion. Bayer, Rajas and Vergara (1999) also found a similar effect of trade reform on wage inequality in Chile because skill-intensive and resource-based industries expanded following the liberalization. In this connection, Robbins and Gindling (1999) put a prominent argument regarding the effects of trade liberalization on the dispersion of wages in least developed countries (LDCs) that trade liberalization must lower the relative demand for more-skilled workers by inducing them to shift towards unskilled labor-intensive sectors. Based on a nonparametric approach, this paper presented the evidence that trade liberalization in Costa Rica led to an increase in relative demand of skilled workers. Other findings are consistent with the "skill-enhancing-trade hypothesis," whereby trade liberalization induces an acceleration of physical capital imports, which raises relative demand through capital–skill complimentarity.

Vos and Jong (2000) applied a methodology of "micro-simulations" to Ecuador and analyzed in detail which labor market factors are associated with most of the changes in income distribution -- and poverty, for that matter. The "counterfactual" scenario created in the micro-simulations was one of what poverty and income distribution would have looked like if the observed labor market shifts would not have taken place. The results suggested that the observed rise in income inequality seemed to be closely associated with the effects of trade liberalization, which led to greater demand for skilled workers and pushed unskilled workers into unemployment or informal/self-employed activities. This appears to have been counteracted somewhat by rising participation rates, falling unemployment and real wage increases during the period of stabilization and growth (1990-95), facilitated by greater capital inflows. The macroeconomic downturn intensified the inequalities and the steep rise in poverty.

Wei and Wu (2001) provide a case study of the impact of globalization on income inequality using data across Chinese regions. They criticized literature on cross-country studies because differences in legal systems and other institutions across countries were difficult to control for; and the data on inequality across them were not compatible. Authors claim that an in-depth case study of a particular country's experience can provide a more useful alternative to cross-country regressions. This study constructed an income ratio for about 100 Chinese cities -- urban areas and adjacent rural counties -- over the period 1988-1993. The major finding was that cities which experienced a greater degree of openness in trade also tended to demonstrate a greater decline in urban-rural income inequality. Thus, globalization has been helping to reduce, rather than increase, the urban-rural income inequality. However, this pattern in the data suggested that inferences based solely on China's national aggregate figures (overall openness and overall inequality) can be misleading. The negative association between openness and inequality holds true when authors apply a geography-based instrumental variable approach to correct for possible endogeneity of a region's trade openness.

Harrison, Rutherford and Tarr (2002) illustrated two approaches to design trade liberalization in Turkey which could ensure that the poor will not lose. This approach was followed with the assumption that trade liberalization results in aggregate welfare gain over all households but with the high possibility that the poorest households would lose. The first of the two approaches proposed was the direct compensation to losers. The second approach used limited policy reform, where exceptions to the across-the-board reform were chosen to meet the equity goal. In each case, the authors mapped out some of the efficiency costs of attaining these equity goals so as to inform policy makers about the least-cost way of attaining them.

The impact of opening trade is found to vary across regions of the came country. Hanson (2004) finds that labor income in low-exposure states in Mexico fell relative to high-exposure states by 10%; therefore, the wage poverty[1] in low

[1] The fraction of wage earners whose labor income would not sustain a family of four above the poverty consumption levels.

exposure states increased relative to high exposure states by 7% after the trade liberalization. Ravallion and Loskin (2004) have also reached a similar conclusion. They find both gainers and losers (contrary to the past claims) and the rural poor are worse off in average after trade reforms. More specifically, Bruno, Hanshom and Ashipala (2004) considered factors such as poor human development, lack of competitiveness and the less efficient traditional technology in domestic production as unfavorable conditions that allow the external forces to ruin the domestic village economy of the developing world in the course of trade liberalization.

Studies mentioned above illustrate the conditions -- much among that exist in specific countries and in specific regions within a country -- that can lead to positive or negative redistribution effects of trade. An in-depth country specific approach is more relevant than a cross-country regression analysis in gauging the relationship between trade and distribution.

3.3. Country Studies with General System Analysis

These analyses mostly base on computable general equilibrium (CGE) models. Decaluwe, Patry and Savard (1998) studied the impact of a trade shock and a tariff reform on household poverty for an archetype developing country. Following a change in the mean income, the income distribution shifted proportionally by the same variation. The poverty line changed following a variation in relative prices. With the new distributions and poverty line, the poverty levels of the base year were compared with the ex-post values. Basic poverty index measures were used to quantify the households' poverty levels. The decline in the world terms of trade indicated a drop in all household incomes and also a decrease in the poverty line. Unilateral trade liberalization also had negative impacts on all household incomes.

The dynamically recursive general equilibrium model of Morocco by Löfgren, El-Said and Robinson (1999) examined alternative trade and domestic policy scenarios with reference to its agreement with the European Union (EU) for 1998-2012. The model has a detailed treatment of the agricultural and rural economy in Morocco. The results for the trade liberalization scenarios indicated that tariff unification had small aggregate effects whereas the removal of non-tariff barriers had strong positive aggregate effects. However, trade liberalization appeared to disfavor the rural poor, especially in rain-fed areas. The simulation of the introduction of complementary domestic policies with a non-distorting transfer program, which fully compensates the owners of rain-fed resources and skill upgrading for the rural labor force, indicated that if combined with at least one of these complementary domestic policies, trade liberalization could increase the welfare of all household groups significantly and rapidly than if status-quo policies were followed.

Devarajan and Mensbrugghe (2000); Hertel, Preckel and Cranfield (2000); Ianchovichina, Nicita and Soloaga (2001) used a two-step computationally simple procedure to analyze the effects of Mexico's potential unilateral tariff liberalization. Simulation with price changes was applied to the household data in order to assess the effects of the policy simulation on poverty and income distribution. Mexico had already widely liberalized most of its imports by the mid 1990s -- a salient feature of its membership in the North American Free Trade Agreement (NAFTA) with Canada and the United States. Using the Global Trade Analysis Project (GTAP) as the price generator, the authors were able to model the differential tariff structure quite appropriately (almost zero for NAFTA members and higher tariffs for non-members). Starting with a low level of tariff protection, simulation results showed that the impact of tariff reform on welfare would be positive in general for all expenditure deciles. Moreover, when non-homothetic individual preferences were modeled, trade liberalization had a good prospect of benefiting people in the poorer deciles more than those in the richer ones.

In a general equilibrium analysis of Jordan's trade liberalization, Hosoe (2001) simulated the effects of Uruguay Round (UR) negotiations and Free Trade Agreement (FTA) with the European Union on Jordan's economic growth. The conclusion showed that UR would bring about trade expansion effects whereas FTA would make trade diversion effects favorably for imports from the EU. Under these circumstances, the chemical and the agricultural sectors would expand while the non-metal mineral sector would contract. In total, the overall effect of the trade liberalization was confirmed expansionary.

Similar is the conclusion reached by Harrison et al. (2002) in case of Brazil. The study shows that the MERCOSUR (regional trade agreement among Brazil, Paraguay, Uruguay and Argentina), FTAA (Free Trade Agreements of the Americas), and free trade with EU could be expected to result in gains in Brazil. The agreement with the EU seemed 1.5 times valuable to that of FTAA due to access to highly protected agricultural markets in the EU. The combined gain from both agreements was estimated greater than the gain obtained from the sum of the separate agreements due to a reduction of trade diversion. In most of the trade policy options, the authors evaluated either regional or multilateral or unilateral trade liberalization could result in a progressive distribution of the gains to different households. More specifically, the poor households could experience the greatest percentage increase in their incomes because the change in trade policy tended to shift resources from capital intensive manufacturing toward labor intensive agriculture, thereby inducing an increase in the wage of unskilled labor relative to the returns to other factors of production. This, in turn, could result in an increase in the incomes of the poorest households three to four folds relative to that of the richest. Authors concluded that Brazil could optimize its choice of trade policies by combining regional arrangements with both the Americas and the EU under multilateral trade liberalization; and if tariff uniformity is added to the regional and multilateral liberalization, further gains would be realized.

In CGE analysis of Egypt, Lofgren (2001) disclosed that there was no contradiction between more rapid growth, rapid productivity growth, and improved welfare for the poor. The results indicated that pro-poor redistribution of land and human capital assets could have been an effective tool if Egypt had prioritized the welfare of the poor more strongly. Such policies could have been implemented without any noticeable negative impact on growth or aggregate welfare. The results confirmed the findings of earlier analyses that pro-agricultural policies have a more positive impact on household welfare in general and the poor in particular as compared to pro-manufacturing policies. There is a significant synergy between a pro-agricultural shift in productivity growth, improved market access for agricultural exports, and reduced transactions costs in foreign trade to reduce the inequality.

El-said, Lofgren and Robinson (2001) addressed the longer-term issues of economic development in Egypt using a dynamic CGE model to assess the outcomes associated with two types of development approaches over the period 1998-2012. One was a targeted sector development approach; and the second more broad-based development approach. Under the first approach, technological advancement targeted to three sectors: agriculture, food processing, and textiles. The results indicated that, when agricultural exports remained relatively low, promoting the Egyptian textile sector was a win-win scenario in terms of rapid growth and equity. A crucial policy objective for achieving rapid and egalitarian growth for the Egyptian economy was considered the ability to secure improved access to international textile markets and the successful expansion of agricultural exports.

Thurlow and Seventer (2002) tested a standard International Food Policy Research Institute (IFPRI) CGE model for South Africa. This model used to simulate the economy-wide impact of a range of hypothetical policy levers including increased government spending, the elimination of tariff barriers, and an improvement in total factor productivity. Results indicated that assumptions regarding the mechanisms of macroeconomic adjustment are important in determining the expected impacts of these policies. Firstly, despite mixed results concerning changes in household income distribution, the impact of expansionary fiscal policy appeared to be growth enhancing with the Keynesian adjustment mechanism producing the most positive results. Secondly, a complete abolition of import tariffs also appeared to generate higher GDP growth, with negative and positive consequences for aggregate manufacturing and services, respectively. Finally, an increase in total factor productivity was growth enhancing, with the most positive results derived under neoclassical assumptions of the macroeconomic adjustment mechanisms. These simulations were meant to demonstrate the usefulness for economy-wide policy modeling and the paper concluded by highlighting areas of policy analysis that might benefit from more detailed applications with this framework.

IFPRI (2003) measured the impact of various macro policy reforms on household welfare along with many macroeconomic indicators for Zimbabwe. The counterfactual simulations included trade liberalization, changes in government expenditure and tax policies, maize marketing reform, and land redistribution. Simultaneously implementing trade liberalization, maize price decontrol, and income tax adjustment, there were substantial growth in GDP, foreign trade, and household income distribution relative to the scenario of zero fiscal deficits. Thus, the real effect of a contractionary fiscal policy could be effectively swamped by the economy-wide impact of the trade liberalization package. This scenario when compared with the results of involving only the trade liberalization package showed identical GDP effects but a more favorable equity effect. These comparative results from counterfactual simulations based on the Zimbabwe CGE model has illuminated the greater effectiveness of trade policy reform in promoting overall growth of the Zimbabwean economy and of fiscal and sectoral reforms in improving income equity among the five household groups. The significant improvements in aggregate household income and its distribution accompanied by a large increase in agricultural GDP are indicative of the central role of agriculture in achieving equitable growth in Zimbabwe. These results are consistent with the strong linkages observed in the SAM analysis, which suggested that the distribution of income would benefit from agricultural growth and overall GDP growth from stimulating smallholder productions.

Going beyond trade liberalization and dealing with internal liberalization reforms, some earlier studies revealed the anti-poor effects of structural reforms, at least for the short-run, Thiele (2001), Psacharopoulos et al. (1992); and continuing poverty to a large chunk of the population in developing countries, Musinguzi and Smith (1993). Downsizing the government's regular expenditure and devaluation of the domestic currency are known to make the lives of poor even poorer in many developing countries. Despite these anti-poor effects of the earlier structural reforms, the developing countries had little policy autonomy due to huge foreign debt and assistance not only from the developed world but also from the global financial institutions which basically work with liberal economic policies. Moreover, a non-globalizing country not only fails to participate in the benefits of an expanding world volume of trade but actually sees a deterioration in its position compared with the pre-globalizing era, Milanovic and Squire (2005), p. 4.

In addition to the trade reform, fiscal and labor market reforms are also emphasized as some of the major policy agenda in many developing countries and assessing their effects on unemployment and poverty; the latter are key issues in designing and sequencing of adjustment programs. In turn, assessing these effects requires understanding not only how the labor market operates but also how fiscal variables (taxes and expenditure) interact with the labor market. Because most taxes have an effect on the functioning of the economy, they also affect the labor market -- both directly and indirectly -- through changes in the level and distribution of wages, labor supply decisions, and the level and composition of employment. For instance, taxing the profits of small firms (which tend to be more labor intensive) may affect their ability to create jobs, whereas income taxation and the existence of an unemployment benefit system may affect the propensity of the unemployed to seek employment, Agénor (2003), p. 1. In case of the trade liberalization, these issues also become important because reduction of the custom duties is mostly compensated by the increase in the value added tax not to allow government revenue to decline.

Reimer (2002) made a comprehensive literature survey of the evidence on the impact of trade liberalization on poverty. He could not find a simple generalization about the relationship between them. However, Cororaton (2003), using data from 24,797 households from the Philippines, carried out a comprehensive poverty and income distribution analysis and concluded that poverty falls in the Philippines after a complete tariff reduction but income distribution worsens.

According to Hertel et al. (2003), the short run impact of trade liberalization on different household groups varies and not always be positive. However, the overall impact on poverty depends on the structure of poverty in each country. Combining the detailed household survey data with a global economic model in order to measure the poverty impacts of trade liberalization on the five different household strata in each country, the study concluded that as countries become wealthier and the labor market becomes more developed, it is mostly common to observe households specializing in wage labor. Accordingly, these households also become a larger part of the data base in the overall poverty picture. Since the poorest households tend to be heavily reliant on unskilled labor, the key earning variables for reducing poverty is the wage paid to unskilled labor. In most of the cases, this wage falls relative to average earnings, but it rises relative to skilled wages. Therefore, the impact of trade liberalization on this group of households is mixed, with the poverty increases more frequent than the decreases.

The findings of the paper have emphasized the differential short run impacts of multilateral trade liberalization on poverty across countries, across strata, and within strata, thereby highlights the links between the structure of poverty and the national impacts of trade liberalization. In the long run, when self-employed workers, land and capital investments are able to fully adjust to the trade policy shock, the results can be significantly altered.

The popular saying "a rising tide lifts all boats" does not apply sometimes. While it is generally true that countries experiencing a per capita gain also experience a reduction in poverty, Thailand offers an important exception (Ibid, p. 10). Here, the very sharp rise in staple grains prices following global trade liberalization pushed more non-agricultural households into poverty and that dominated the overall poverty picture. On the other side, in the case of Mexico, poverty fell despite the decline in per capita welfare following global trade liberalization. This was due to the decline in food prices that resulted from lower cost imports.

Decomposing social welfare into real income level and variance components, and emphasizing Gini and Atkinson indexes, Francois and Rojas-Romagosa (2005) analyzed general equilibrium relationships between trade policy and the household distribution of income. Embedding these inequality adjusted social welfare functions in a general equilibrium structure and mapping from tariff protection to household inequality, this study yields predictions regarding the linkages among trade protection, country characteristics and inequality within a broad general equilibrium framework. In addition, the efficiency and equity effects of tariffs on welfare are also separated. The study also examines the endogenous tariff formation when policy makers care about both equity and special interests.

For a representative democratic system, this study finds that positive optimum tariffs can be sustained in capital-abundant countries even when the policy-maker assigns a low or zero weight to the contributions of special interests groups. In this case, the positive distributional effect of import protection can offset or compensate the efficiency losses of reduced trade. In poor countries, characterized by the relative abundance of labor, positive tariffs are explained by the influence of special interest groups (i.e. capitalists) that heavily lobby for higher tariffs.

Most importantly, the study concluded that import protection in developing countries not only diminishes social welfare through efficiency and equity considerations, but also signals the economic and political weight of the capital-owners (p. 17).

Chitiga, Kandiero, and Mabugu (2005) used micro-simulations with a computable general equilibrium model to study the impact of trade liberalization on poverty in Zimbabwe. They worked with data from 14006 households derived from 1995 Poverty Assessment Study Survey (PASS). They conclude that complete removal of tariffs favors export-oriented sectors along with the rise in imports. The unskilled labor used intensively in agriculture, mining and services benefit from this policy. Most manufacturing sectors shrink leading to a fall in demand for skilled labor and capital. Returns to land increase as agricultural export expand. Overall consumer prices fall and consumption expenditure also falls in the economy. Simulations show the reduction of poverty in the economy, more in urban than in rural areas. However, the income distribution pattern reveals an insignificant changes (pp. 20-21).

Boccanfuso and Savard (2005) used a micro-simulated multiple household computable general equilibrium method, such as proposed by Decaluwé et al. (1999), for analyzing the impacts of the trade liberalization of groundnut production in Senegal. Tariff reforms and external shocks were simulated, and the impacts were measured at the macroeconomic, sectoral and household levels to establish a link between these economic reforms, poverty and income distribution. The model focused on the price effects linked to recent and ongoing tariff changes affecting the groundnut industry directly or indirectly. In conclusion, they stated that the removal of specific import taxes would be positive for the households since the price effect used to dominate the income effect.

Some primarily focus on the agricultural productivity growth and labor market to assess the impact of trade liberalization on distribution. Zhai and Hertel (2004) used a household-disaggregated recursively dynamic CGE model of the Chinese economy to evaluate the impacts of several key labor market distortions in China on rural-urban inequality and income distribution. The simulation results showed that the reforms in rural land rental market and increasing off-farm labor mobility would reduce the urban-rural income ratio dramatically. The reform associated with the land rental market had a significant impact on rural-urban inequality. Introduction of a fully functioning market for agricultural land permitted agricultural households to focus solely on the differential between farm and non-farm returns to labor in determining whether to work on- or off-farm and it increased the off-farm labor mobility in Chinese economy, boosted the GDP growth, and caused more labor moving out of agriculture and reduced rural-urban inequality. Furthermore, the combined impact of WTO accession and labor market reforms reduced rural-urban income inequality quite significantly.

Hertel et al. (2004) made another assessment of the impact of trade liberalization on poverty in a case-by-case basis and also developed a tractable methodology for the estimates of the global impact on poverty in a range of different countries. They considered three tools of analysis: (1) detailed earning data from household surveys, (2) an econometrically estimated demand system that reflects the changes in consumption patterns across the income spectrum and provides a natural vehicle for analysis of household welfare and poverty, and (3) a micro-macro consistent framework for projecting the price impacts of global trade liberalization.

Focusing on the case of Indonesia, the study concluded that the aggregate reduction in Indonesia's national headcount poverty index had masked a more complex set of impacts among different groups. In the short run, the poverty headcount rose slightly among the self-employed and agricultural households as the rise in farm profits was outpaced by consumer prices. However, in the long run, the poverty headcount fell for all strata in Indonesia since the increased demand for unskilled workers raised incomes of the formerly self-employed, some of them had moved to the wage labor market.

Valenzuela et al. (2005) using data on the predictions in agricultural productivity growth, price changes, and household income composition, confirmed that historically observed annual growth in agricultural productivity had a positive effect on poverty reduction for all of the eleven developing countries used in the study. Nonetheless, this growth could be redirected into different production sectors in agriculture for additional poverty reduction in the range from 4% in Bangladesh to 59% in Indonesia. Changing the momentum of the historical trend in the growth of productivity in agriculture could be a viable instrument to fight against poverty.

Valenzuela and Hertel (2006) proposed the application of a stochastic simulation framework to put the poverty impacts of trade policy reform by comparing them to the impacts of price variability in agricultural markets on the poor. According to this study, for developing countries targeting a decrease in poverty, international trade and openness are valuable means of economic improvement for the lowest income households. In countries exhibiting increase in poverty in the short-run, but expected to face a reduction in the medium-term, the policy implication would be to devise some sort of safety net mechanisms oriented to help the lowest income households for the adjustment to trade reform. For countries showing a discernable increase in poverty in the short-run, and for which there are predictions of increase in poverty in the medium-term, trade liberalization may not be the best alternative. In these instances, the policy implication is to allow for longer phases of reform implementation in combination with specifically targeted support of low-income households.

Under these circumstances a general system approach should be considered a more reliable and comprehensive tool of analysis to study the distributional impacts of trade reform. More recent literature is also surging with CGE models to trace the relationship between trade openness, liberalization, growth and distribution.

4. Recent Trends in International Development Policy on Liberalization and Poverty

4.1. From SAP to PRGF

For the last five decades, the direction of development policy, especially for the small and medium-size developing countries, has been remarkably dominated by policy views and development initiatives of the IMF and the World Bank. The two agencies started in 1986 with the Structural Adjustment Program (SAP). Thereafter, their development policy has undergone basic changes over time, culminating more than two decades later in the form of Poverty Reduction and Growth Facilities (PRGF).

The first phase of the SAP 1986–1989 mainly focused on macroeconomic adjustment and economic growth. This phase consisted of Structural Adjustment Fund facilities of the IMF and Structural Adjustment Loan facilities of the World Bank. Controlling money supply by cutting down the public expenditure remained the major strategy of the Fund while the World Bank involved itself to the identification and funding for major growth potential areas in the economy. Controlling the money supply and price, maintenance of competitive exchange rates, withdrawal of subsidies, privatization of state owned enterprises, simplification of custom duties and internal taxes were the major policy instruments of IMF/World Bank's SAP. This program believed that these measures could help the integration of domestic economy with the world economy so that there will be the creation of immense opportunities to the factors of production in developing world to get employed in most productive areas and get higher returns. Subsequently, the real wages of labors in developing countries would get increased which could help reduce poverty in these countries.

Late 1990s witnessed increasing realization that IMF and World Bank policies on stabilization and structural adjustment were anti-poor and they should be modified in favor of the poor. There were two basic ways in which the initial SAP made the lives of the poor people miserable. Firstly, the devaluation of the local currencies of many developing countries deteriorated their international terms of trade; consequently, income of the labor working in exportable sectors declined. Secondly, the liberalization of markets and withdrawal of subsidies again made the lives of poor people more difficult, especially those of industrial and agricultural labor whose products could not compete at the international market. Furthermore, reductions in development expenditure made many poor people destitute. In this way, the earnings and living conditions of poor declined faster than ever expected. With due realization of these facts, the IMF slightly modified its stabilization program.

Subsequently, the second phase of the extended SAP - named ESAP (Extended SAP) - started in 1992. This emphasized more revenue collection rather than expenditure cutting for balancing the state budget. Therefore, the development expenditure started increasing in many developing countries, which mitigated the adverse effects of the first phase program to some extent.

Both the first and second phases of the SAP have their deep-rooted affiliation with the neo-liberal development thinking. The thrust of the IMF policies was that the increase in the money supply should be seen as the major destabilizing factor in the economy, both internally and externally. The channel of reactions is through the higher rate of inflation (internally) and decline of the exports at fixed exchange rates (externally). Both of these notions originate from the neo-classical quantity theory of money. Furthermore, the liberalization strategies followed by the World Bank also believed that free and unfettered markets are the most growth inducing, and this has trickle down effects to reduce poverty. Therefore, there was no question of inequalities to be addressed so long as higher rates of economic growth are attained.

Ended in 1994, the second phase SAP has raised some important issues. Most prominently, poverty has multi-dimensional facets and economic aspect is one of them. Therefore, mere economic policies are not sufficient to address this problem. The other aspects that should also be equally addressed in this connection are good governance; participatory approach in development planning, project implementation and evaluation; empowerment of women and socially deprived classes of the societies; political commitment and stability of the government. Not withstanding the importance of these issues, the core question remains: which development policies and which economic structures would enhance income of the poor?

The Key features of PRGF-supported programs are:

- Broad participation and greater ownership. Basing the PRGF program on the country's PRSP should ensure that civil society is involved and that the country authorities are in the driver's seat.
- Embedding the PRGF program in the overall strategy for growth and poverty reduction. PRGF staff reports will show how IMF programs derive from the poverty reduction strategy and are complementary to World Bank activities and conditionality.
- Budgets those are more pro-poor and pro-growth. Government spending should shift toward activities that demonstrably benefit the poor, while tax reforms should improve both equity and efficiency.
- Social impact analysis of major reforms. Where there are expected to be major reforms, analysis of the impact on the poor - normally by the World Bank - will need to be conducted and countervailing measures incorporated in the PRGF program.
- Ensuring appropriate flexibility in fiscal targets. There should be scope to react to commonly experienced shocks, such as deteriorating terms-of-trade or poor harvests, or to spend newly-available aid when it is clear that it could be used productively
- Emphasis on measures to improve accountability for public resource management. Strengthening fiscal governance to improve public services and ensure proper use of debt relief and other government resources is to be a key objective of PRGF programs.
- More selective conditionality. With greater ownership expected, PRGF conditionality can and should be more selective, focusing on measures central to the success of the country's strategy.

Source: (http://www.imf.org/external/np/prgf/2000/eng/key.htm

Various studies revealed that the liberalization policies – the most importantly, trade liberalization -- recommended by the IMF and World Bank marginalized many poor people in developing countries. With due realization of the facts enumerated above, the Fund and the Bank initiated and implemented a newly formulated Poverty Reduction and Growth Facilities (PRGF) program in 1999.

The implementation of PRGF accommodates the following major steps:

- Discussion on macroeconomic framework has become more open and iterative between members and the Fund. Key macroeconomic policies in this regard are on growth and inflation, and the thrust of fiscal, monetary and external policies, as well as structural policies to accelerate growth.
- There is more exercise in the reallocation of government spending in support of the poverty reduction strategy. In the process of PRGF, the feasibility of mobilizing additional domestic fiscal revenues should be considered early on. Likewise, a judgment is needed at this stage on the scope of additional domestic financing taking into account the need to maintain macroeconomic stability and avoid unduly crowding out of the private sector.
- Donors are presented, during the formulation of a PRSP, with macroeconomic scenarios that give clearer indications what financing would be needed to meet program goals agreed with the country, particularly with respect to poverty reduction, in the context of the longer term international development goals.
- The emphasis on improvements in governance as a fundamental underpinning for macroeconomic stability, sustainable growth and poverty reduction is through the management of public resources, achievement of greater transparency, more active public scrutiny and generally increasing government accountability in fiscal management.

Source: IMF (1999), pp. 4-5.

The Interim Committee of the Policy Development and Review Department of IMF endorsed, on September 26, 1999, the replacement of the ESAP by the PRGF program, which aimed at making poverty reduction efforts among low income members a key and more explicit element of a renewed growth-oriented economic strategy.[2] The Bank and Fund, consequently, started adopting more pro-poor policies while supporting liberalization policies.

---

[2] The purpose of this new facility is "to support programmes to strengthen substantially and in a sustainable manner balance of payment position and to foster durable growth, leading to higher living standards and a reduction in poverty. PRGF-supported programmes, like those of IDA, will stem from and be consistent with Poverty Reduction Strategy Papers (PRSPs) prepared by the borrowing country and endorsed in their respective areas of responsibility by the Boards of IMF and World Bank.

The participatory process in the implementation of the program starts from the very beginning of the preparation of Poverty Reduction Strategy Paper with joint efforts of the country and the World Bank. This paper should incorporate the programs and strategies on enhancing economic growth, civil service reform, privatization, women empowerment, infrastructure development, provision of the safety nets, the conservation of environment, and most importantly trade liberalization. Henceforth, poverty alleviation efforts were meant to deserve much more microeconomic color and attention than was usual in the past.

This is how trade liberalization was considered along with other economic reforms in developing countries within the broader framework of structural adjustment program.

4.2. Is There Something New in PRGF?

Getting PRGF facilities requires the preparation of Poverty Reduction Strategy Paper (PRSP) by the country in consultation with the World Bank. PRSP is a professedly comprehensive approach to address poverty. It combines powerful econometric and ethnographic approaches to poverty policy with a battery of 'participatory' technique to a sharp neo-liberal economics and preparedness to innovate, ultimately linked to reproduce a four-pronged approach to poverty reduction. The approaches it uses are, Craig (2001), p.1:

(1) Broad-based growth: It is most recently understood as 'pro-poor' growth focusing on employment creating growth.
(2) Investment in human capital: typically on health and education sectors.
(3) Good governance: This issue has grown from anti-corruption and public accountability measures to embrace macro-economic fiscal management and decentralized governance, and
(4) Social safety nets: It is special purpose financing arrangements for those who are adversely affected by the adjustment process or are unable to participate in the growth.

A quick look on SAP/ESAP and PRGF shows that the former facilities of the IMF and World Bank were completely based on the adoption of neo-liberal development approach. The sole ideology of the programs was that competition raises economic efficiency, which is conducive to economic growth, and the benefit of latter automatically trickles down in the free market economy. These programs believed that integration of the poor people into the world market through trade liberalization provides them immense opportunities for more employment, which is the ultimate solution to alleviate poverty in developing countries. However, direct anti-poverty measures were not incorporated in SAP; it was weakly addressed within the periphery of broad-based growth objective of ESAP, but has now become the sole objective of PRGF.

PRGF seems trying to integrate macroeconomic policies with social and sectoral objectives to ensure that plans are mutually supportive and consistent with a common set of objectives to spur growth and reduce poverty. Key sectoral and social policies, infrastructure projects, institutional reforms, and other measures are costed, prioritized, and incorporated within the macroeconomic framework. This is a new feature in PRGF. However, the issue of good governance has been vaguely incorporated in PRGF and it is very hard to relate good governance directly with poverty reduction/income equality. The operational aspect of the PRGF seems quite silent while relating these two aspects.

In PRGF, the issues on good governance and social safety nets have focused equally to broad-based growth and investment in human capital. In fact, the latter two were the sole concern of ESAP for poverty reduction. In this sense, PRGF seems more comprehensive and trying to accommodate different facets of poverty dimension. Consequently, the convergence of broad-based growth and investment on human capital has got equal attention in PRGF phase similar to that of ESAP. Moreover, this new program has embedded in practice a plural, wide ranging set of techniques for identifying, mapping, measuring and reporting poverty as popularized by the publications like 'Voices of the Poor'. Likewise, non-government sector's role has become more important now because they are promoting the partnership with third sector organizations to secure participation of the community which are the primary sites for decentralized approach of governance. And, in confidently projecting values and ideals well ahead of their demonstrated capacity to deliver, they seem to have a special facility for re-spinning new progressive outfits for old conservative policy, or building what Perry Anderson described as "the best ideological shell of neo-liberalism today". However, critics say that the link between the liberalization/openness and the poverty reduction still needs to be clarified with clear transmission mechanism. According to them, promotion of the faster growth and poverty reduction by improving the climate for the private sector, thereby, generating more jobs at higher wages, reforming state enterprises to improve efficiency and free up the fiscal resources for poverty reduction program, restructuring the banking system to reduce the risk of financial crisis, and integrating their labor-intensive exports with the world economy are more rhetoric than in practice, Craig (2001), p. 4.

4.3. Appraisal/Evaluation Methods of PRGF

PRGF tries to work as a macroeconomic framework to sustained poverty reduction in developing countries. By virtue of its nature, it should review economic management (inflation, financial sector stability, fiscal management, exchange rate and trade regimes, and income and employment trends) and assess whether these policies are coherent with the anti-poverty policy. If the government does not have any anti-poverty policy, do these policies produce pro or anti-poverty biases? What is the impact of fiscal policy on domestic prices and financial stability and how are the poor affected? Do monetary, foreign exchange, investment, and/or trade policies erode the domestic goods and industries, particularly those which affect the poor? Who are the main beneficiaries of policy prescriptions? Are policies silent or explicit on issues of discrimination and/or access of the poor to resources and services? And if they are explicit, what roles they can play? Are policies, which are particularly pro-poor, actually implemented? These are some of the basic issues that PRGF should address to make the program instrumental.

As we can see, the constant emphasis of IMF and World Bank programs is on economic growth. Here we should be clear about the efficacy of the programs on the ground of the composition and distribution of growth. It is because, although economic growth and trade are the engines of poverty reduction, they work more effectively in some situations than in others as shown by the studies reviewed in sections 2 and 3. In this connection, it is necessary to highlight two important aspects of growth: nature of economic growth and its distribution.

If the benefits of growth are translated into poverty reduction through the existing distribution of income, then more equal societies will be the most efficient transformers of growth into poverty reduction. A number of empirical studies have found that the responsiveness of income poverty to growth increases significantly if inequality is lowered. This is also supported by a recent cross-country study which found that the more equal the distribution of income in a country, the greater is the impact of growth on the number of people in poverty. Others have suggested that greater equity comes at the expense of growth and there is a trade-off between growth and equity when it comes to poverty reduction. However, a large number of recent empirical studies have found that there is not necessarily such a trade-off and that equity in its various dimensions is growth enhancing, Ames et al. (2001), p. 5.

Regarding the sectoral economic growths, various country-specific and cross-country studies have shown that growth in the agricultural and tertiary sectors has had a major effect on reducing poverty while growth in the manufacturing has not.

This reinforces the case for duty-free access for agricultural exports from low-income countries to markets of industrial countries. However, the links may be more complex over the long run. More importantly, faster growth in agriculture may address rural poverty in the short-term, reliance on agricultural activity may also intensify output variability, which, in turn, would contribute to increasing rather than decreasing poverty in the long-run. A more diversified economy with a vibrant manufacturing sector might offer the best chances for a sustainable improvement in living standards in the long-run, (Ibid, p. 6).

5. Conclusion

To summarize, economic liberalization – more importantly trade liberalization -- bring both pro-poor and anti-poor growth effects as well as economic expansionary and contractionary forces in motion. The effects in the long and short run periods may differ. The relative strengths of these forces determine the change in economic welfare of different income groups. Review of the substantial empirical research during the past two decades does not lead us easily to robust conclusions regarding the relationship among liberalization, growth and inequality. In most of the cases, as the literature shows, liberalization leads higher growth but not necessarily pro-poor. As was apparent from review of cross-country regression analysis, the combination of complex but partial phenomena, choice of variables, and data inadequacies have rendered the empirical works both hazardous and partial. In-depth country specific studies are more helpful in giving insight on the particular conditions that generate positive or negative redistribution effects of more trade. In this respect, the general system approach is more useful than a partial approach. A general system approach allows a study to incorporate more facets of the trade-distribution phenomena in a constrained framework of the whole economy and makes it possible to appraise alternative policy levers towards achieving pro-poor growth under trade openness.

Sustainable poverty alleviation requires the removal of two important trade-offs that are almost bound to occur in a free market economy. These two possible trade-offs are (i) Economic growth rate does not automatically trickle down to the desired sector/group/income strata. There is always a trade-off between the income growth at the higher income group and at the lower income group. Anti-poverty measures should try to translate the economic growth more to the lower income group and less to the higher income group. This can be interpreted as constrained equality effects of poverty reduction policies due to circular flow mechanisms. (ii) There is also the other trade-off between more government expenditure and the macroeconomic stability. More government expenditure is always necessary in favor of pro-poor growth, but it may also destabilize the economy. This can be interpreted as constrained equality poverty policies due to required macroeconomic balancing conditions.

To be more specific, the possible avenues through which these conflicts can be addressed are two: circular flow mechanisms and macroeconomic balancing conditions. With regard to circular flow mechanisms there are (i) micro foundational restructuring and policies, and (ii) income/employment/growth foundational restructuring and policies: growth of those sectors in which bulk of the poor are concentrated. More importantly, the macroeconomic balancing conditions need to be imposed on the circular flow before their final results are realized, and they may deviate from the original intention. Effective macroeconomic policies with due focus on trade openness and distribution must be at the core of these policy making endeavors.

References

Agénor, P. R. (2003). "*The Mini-Integrated Macroeconomic Model for Poverty Analysis: A Framework for Analysing the Unemployment and Poverty Effects of Fiscal and Labour Market Reforms*". The World Bank working paper, Washington DC.

Aghion, P., Caroli, E. and Garcia-Penalosa, C. (1999). "Inequality and Economic Growth: the Perspective of the New Growth Theories". *Journal of Economic Literature*, 37: 1615-60.

Alsenia, A. and Rodrik, R. (1994). "Distributive Politics and Economic Growth". *Quarterly Journal of Economics*, **109**(6): 1203-28.

Ames, B., Brown, W., Devrajan, S., and Izquierdo, A. (2001). "Macroeconomic Policy and Poverty Reduction". *Source Book for Poverty Reduction Strategies*. IMF and World Bank, Washington DC.

Atkinson, A. (2003). *"Income Inequality in OECD Countries: Data and Explanations"*, revised version of the paper presented at the CESIFO conference on "Globalisation, Inequality, and Well-Being" in Munich, November 8-9, 2003.

Barro, R. (2000). "Inequality and Growth in a panel of Countries". *Journal of Economic Growth*, **5**(1):5-32.

Bayer, H., Rojas, P. and Vergara, R. (1999). "Trade liberalization and wage inequality". *Journal of Development Economics,* **59**:103-23.

Berman, J., Birdsall, N. and Szekely, M. (2003). *Economic Policy and Wage Differentials in Latin America*. Mimeo, University of Pennsylvania.

Bhalla, S. (2002). *Imagine There is No Country*. Washington, D.C: Institute for International Economics.

Boccanfuso, D. and Savard, L. (2005). *"Impacts Analysis of the Liberalization of Groundnut Production in Senegal: A Multiple Household Computable General Equilibrium Model"*. Working Paper 05-12, GREDI, University of Sherbrooke, Canada.

Bourguignon, F. and Morrisson, C. (1989). *External Trade and Income Distribution*. OECD, Paris.

Bruno, V., Hanshom, D. and Aoshipala, J. (2004). *"Economic Reform Programmes, Labour Market Institutions, Employment and the Role of the Social Partners in Namibia"*. Economics Working Paper, Namibian Economic Policy Research Unit (NEPRU). Economics Department of Washington University, USA.

Chitiga, M., Kandiero, T. and Mabugu, R. (2005). *"Computable General Equilibrium Micro-Simulation Analysis of the Impact of Trade Policies on Poverty in Zimbabe"*. Poverty and Economic Policy (PEP) Research Network (www.pep-net.org), Working Paper 2005-01.

Cline, W. R. (1997). *Trade and Income Distribution*. Institute for International Economics, Washington D.C.

Corroraton, B. (2003). *"Analysis of Trade Reforms, Income Inequality and Poverty Using Microsimulation Approach: The Case of the Philippines"*. Philippines Institute of Development Studies (PIDS), Discussion Paper Series No. 2003-09.

Craig, D. (2001). *Poverty Reduction Strategy Papers: A New Convergence, paper presented at Regional Conference on National Poverty Reduction Strategies*. World Bank, IMF and ADB, Hanoi, Vietnam, 4-6th December 2001.

Decaluwé, B. P. and L. André Savard (1998). *Income Distribution, Poverty Measures and Trade Shocks: A Computable General Equilibrium Model of a Archetype Developing Country*. University of Laval, Canada.

Decaluwé, B., Dumont, J. C. and Savard, L. (1999). *"How to Measure Poverty and Inequality in General Equilibrium Framework"*. Université Laval and CREFA Working Paper No. 9920, Québec, Canada.

Deininger, K. and Squire, L. (1996). "A New Data Set Measuring Income Inequality". *World Bank Economic Review*, **10**(2): 565-91.

Devarajan, S. and Van der Mensbrugghe, D. (2000). *"Trade Reform in South Africa: Impacts on Households"*. Paper presented at the conference on Poverty and the International Economy, organised by the World Bank and the

Parliamentary Commission on Swedish Policy for Global Development, held in Stockholm, October.

Dollar, D. and Kraay, A. (2002). "Growth Is Good for the Poor". *Journal of Economic Growth*, **7**(3):195-225.

Edwards, S. (1997). "Trade Policy, Growth, and Income Distribution". *American Economic Review*, **87**(2):205-10.

El-said, M., Lofgren, H. and Robinson, S. (2001). *The Impacts of Alternative Development Strategies on Growth and Distribution: Simulations with a Dynamic Model for Egypt*. IFPRI, Washington DC.

Francois, J. F. and Nelson, D. (1998). "*Trade, Technology, and Wages: General Equilibrium Mechanics*". Tinbergen Institute Discussion Paper, Erasmus University, The Netherlands.

Green, F. and Dickerson, A. (2001). "A Picture of Wage Inequality and the Allocation of Labour through a Period of Trade Liberalization: The Case of Brazil. *World Development*, **29**(11): 1923-1939.

Hanson, G. H. (2004). *Globalisation, Labour Income, and Poverty in Mexico.* University of California, San Diago and National Bureau of Economic Research (NBER), USA.

Hanson, G. H. and Harrison, A. E. (1999). "Trade, Technology, and Wage Inequality in Mexico". *Industrial and labour Relations Review*, **52**(2): 271-288.

Harrison, G. W., Rutherford, T. F., Tarr, D. G. and Gurgel, A. (2002). *"Regional, Multilateral and Unilateral Trade Policies of MERCOSUR for Growth and Poverty Reduction in Brazil"*. IPEA Seminar in Brazil.

Harrison, G. W., Rutherford, T. F., Tarr, D. G. and Gurgel, A. (2002). *"Regional, Multilateral and Unilateral Trade Policies of MERCOSUR for Growth and Poverty Reduction in Brazil"*. IPEA Seminar in Brazil.

Hertel, T., Ivanic, M., Preckel, P. and Cranfield, J. (2004). *"The Earnings Effects of Multilateral Trade Liberalisation: Implications for Poverty in Developing Countries"*. GTAP Working Paper No. 16-Revised.

Hertel, T., Ivanic, M., Preckel, P. and Cranfield, J. (2003). *"Trade Liberalisation and the Structure of Poverty in Developing Countris"*. GTAP Working Paper No. 25.

Hertel. T. W., Preckel, P. V. and Cranfield, J. A. L. (2000). *"Multilateral Trade Liberalisation and Poverty Reduction"*. Purdue: Centre for Global Trade Analysis.

Hosoe, N. (2001),"A General Equilibrium Analysis of Jordan's Trade Liberalisation". *Journal of Policy Modelling*, **23**: 595-600.

Ianchovichina, E., Nicita, A. and Soloaga, I. (2001). "Trade Reform and Household Welfare: The Case of Mexico". *Working Paper* **2386**, The World Bank, DECRG-Trade.

IFPRI (2003). *"Effects of Policy Reform"*. IFPRI Research Report No. 128, Washington.

Johansen, S. (1988). "Statistical Analysis of Cointegration Vectors". *Journal of Economic Dynamics and Control*, **12**(2): 231-254.

Lofgren, H. (2001). *"Less Poverty in Egypt?"*. TMD Discussion Paper 72, IFPRI, Washington DC.

Löfgren, H., El-Said, M., Robinson, S. (1999). "Trade Liberalization and Complementary Domestic Policies: A Rural-Urban General Equilibrium Analysis of Morocco". *Discussion Paper* **41**, International Food Policy Research Institute (IFPRI), Washington DC.

Londono, J. L. (2002). *"Capital for Equity in Latin America"*. Fourth World Bank ABCDE Conference, Oslo, June.

Londono, J. L. (2002). *"Capital for Equity in Latin America"*. Fourth World Bank ABCDE Conference, Oslo, June.

Lundberg, M. and Squire, L. (2003). "The Simultaneous Evolution of Growth and Inequality". *Economic Journal*, **113**: 326-344.

Milanovic, B. (2005a). "Can We Discern the Effect of Globalization on Income Distribution: Evidence from Household Surveys". *World Bank Economic Review*, **19**(1):21-44.

Milanovic, B. (2005b) *Worlds Apart: Global and International Inequality 1950-2000*. Princeton University Press.

Milanovic, B. and Squire, L. (2005), "Does Trade Liberalisation Increase Wage Inequality? Some Empirical Evidence", (NBER), *Working Paper* **11046**, Massachusetts Avenue, USA.

Milanovic, B. and Squire. L. (2005). "Does Trade Liberalisation Increase Wage Inequality? Some Empirical Evidence". (NBER), *Working Paper* **11046**, Massachusetts Avenue, USA.

Musinguzi, P. and Smith, P. (2003). Structural Adjustment and Poverty: A Study of Rural Uganda. Department of Economics, University of Southampton, *Working paper series* **9813**, UK.

Psacharopoulos, G., Morley S., Fiszbein, A., Lee, H. and Wood, B. (1992). Poverty and Income Distribution in Latin America: The Story of the 1980s". World Bank, *LAC Technical Department Report* **27**. Washington, D.C.

Rajas-Romagosa, H. (2005). *Essays on Trade and Equity*. PhD dissertation submitted to Erasmus University Rotterdam, The Tinbergen Institute, The Netherlands.

Ravallion, M. and Lokshin, M. (2004). "Gainers and Losers from Trade Reform in Morroco. *Working Paper series* **WPS3368**, The World Bank.

Reimer, J. J. (2002). *"Estimating the Poverty Impacts of Trade Liberalization"*. GTAP Working Paper No. 20, Centre for Global Trade Analysis and Purdue University.

Robbins, D. and Gindling, T. H. (1999). "Trade Liberalization and the More-Skilled Workers in Costa-Rica". *Review of Development Economics*, **3**(2): 140–154.

Robertson, R. (2000). "Wage Shocks and North American Labour Market Integration". *American Economic Review* **90**(4): 742-764.

Sala-i-Martin, X. (2002). *"The Disturbing 'Rise' in Global Income Inequality"*. National Bureau of Economic Research (NBER) Working Paper 8904, Massachusetts, USA.

Spilimbergo, A., Londono, J. and Szekely, M. (1999). "Income Distribution, Factor Endowments, and Trade Openness". J*ournal of Development Economics*, **59**: 77-101.

Stolper, W. and Samuelson, P.A. (1941). "Protection and Real Wages". *Review of Economic Studies*, **9**(1): 58-73.

Thiele, R. (2001). *The Social Impact of Structural Adjustment in Bolivia*. Kiel Working Paper No. 1056, Kiel Institute of World Economics, Germany.

Thurlow, J. and Seventer, D. E. (2002). *A Standard Computable General Equilibrium Model for South Africa*, Discussion Paper no. 100. Trade and Macroeconomics Division, International Food Policy Research Institute 2033 K Street, N.W., Washington, D.C.

Valenzuela, E. and Hertel, T. (2006). *"Trade Reforms and Poverty: Are the Impacts Discernable?"*. Paper presented at the 9th Annual Conference on Global Economic Analysis, Addis Ababa, Ethiopia.

Valenzuela, E., Ivanic, M., Ludena, C. and Hertel, T. (2005). *"Agriculture Productivity Growth: Is the Current Trend on the Track to Poverty Reduction?"*. Paper presented at the American Agricultural Economics Association Meetings, 2005.

Vos, R. and Jong, N. de. (2000). *"Rising Inequality During Economic Liberalisation and Crisis: Macro Or Micro Causes In Ecuador's Case?"*. Working Paper, ISS, The Netherlands.

Wei, S. J.and Wu, Y. (2001). *"Globalization and Inequality: Evidence from Within China"*. NBER Working Paper No. 8611.

Wood, A. (1994). *North-South Trade, Employment and Inequality: Changing Fortunes in a Skill-Driven World*. Clarendon Press, Oxford.

World Bank (2002). *Globalisation, Growth, and Poverty: Building an Inclusive World Economy*. Oxford University press, New York.

Zhai, F. and Hertel, T. (2004). *"Labour Market Distortions, Rural-Urban Inequality and the Opening of China's Economy"*. Paper presented at the 7th Annual Conference on Global Economic Analysis, Washington DC, United States.

In: Trade Liberalization and Protectionism
Editors: B. Hahn et al, pp. 61-94
ISBN: 978-1-60876-837-0

Chapter 3

EVIDENCE OF MERCOSUR'S WELFARE EFFECTS: OVERVIEW AND ANALYSIS

Mario Klein
Georg-August Universitaet Goettingen
Inmaculada Martínez-Zarzoso*
Universitat Jaume I and Georg-August Universitaet Goettingen

1. Introduction

The MERCOSUR (Mercado Común del Sur, Southern Common Market)[1] agreement is a Regional Integration Agreement (RIA) among two of the largest states of Latin America, Argentina and Brazil, and two of the smallest, Paraguay and Uruguay. Besides its four original members, six other Latin-American countries are associate members of the agreement: Bolivia, Chile, Peru, Colombia, Ecuador and Venezuela.[2]

The core agreement (Argentina, Brazil, Paraguay and Uruguay) comprises a population of approximately 200 million people, encompasses an area of 12 million square kilometers, had a gross domestic product (GDP) of about US$ 670 billion in 1996 and accounted for about 50 percent of Latin American industrial output and total exports.[3] Despite the fact that MERCOSUR is the second largest

---

* The author acknowledges the support and collaboration of Proyecto SEJ 2007-67548.
[1] The MERCOSUR agreement is also known as MERCOSUL (Mercado Comum do Sul).
[2] Cf. MERCOSUR (2009).
[3] Cf. Diao & Somwaru (1999), p. 27.

RIA in the Western Hemisphere (after NAFTA) and that Argentina and Brazil are sufficiently large trading countries to influence world prices in some markets, the Common Market of the South is a relative small international trader accounting for only 1 percent of world markets.[4]

Besides the economic agreements with its associate members (comparable to FTAs), MERCOSUR also negotiated numerous agreements with several other countries and RIAs, for example a free trade agreement with Israel or framework agreements with Egypt, the EU, India, South Africa, Turkey and the Andean Community in order to intensify integration.[5]

Figure 1 displays the GDP (in PPP[6] international $) of Latin America & Caribbean[7], MERCOSUR and its biggest member countries Brazil and Argentina.

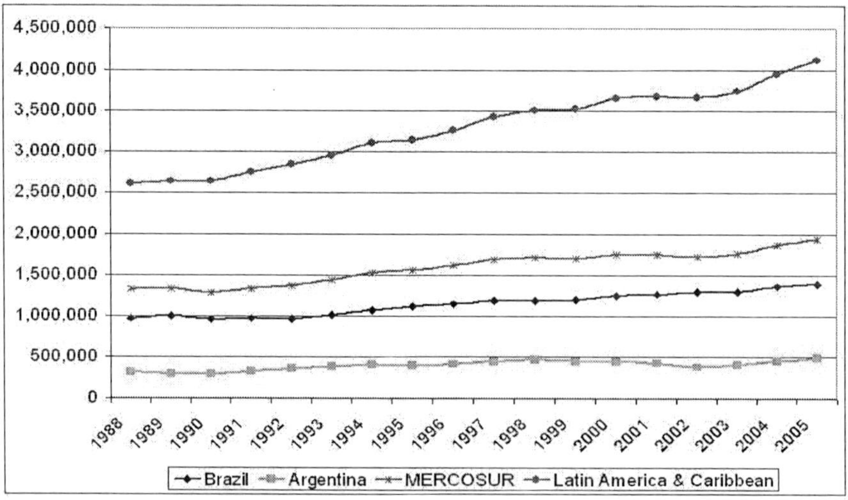

Source: World Bank (2007).

Figure 1. MERCOSUR and Latin America: GDP in millions, PPP (constant 2000 international $).

---

[4] Cf. Olarreaga, Soloaga & Winters (1999), pp. 2 ff.

[5] Cf. MERCOSUR (2009).

[6] Purchasing power parity (PPP).

[7] According to World Bank (2007) Latin America & Caribbean countries are: Antigua and Barbuda, Argentina, Aruba, The Bahamas, Barbados, Belize, Bolivia, Brazil, Cayman Islands, Chile, Colombia, Costa Rica, Cuba, Dominica, Dominican Republic, Ecuador, El Salvador, Grenada, Guatemala, Guyana, Haiti, Honduras, Jamaica, Mexico, Netherlands Antilles, Nicaragua, Panama, Paraguay, Peru, Puerto Rico, St. Kitts and Nevis, St. Lucia, St. Vincent and the Grenadines, Suriname, Trinidad and Tobago, Uruguay, Venezuela, Virgin Islands (US).

The Common Market of the South accounts for almost half of the region's GDP (Mexico accounts for approximately one quarter, thus the remaining quarter is divided between the remaining 33 countries). Among MERCOSUR member countries, the important role of Brazil becomes clear, it accounts for about 70 percent of the agreement's GDP while the Argentinean GDP represents nearly 25 percent, leaving the remaining 5 percent for Paraguay and Uruguay.

However, Figure 1 is not showing massive slumps in its overall positive trend, there are no huge indications for serious economic crises or an improvement of the situation with the creation of MERCOSUR. This picture changes when watching the PPP GDP per capita in Figure 2. No common tendency can be made out here with the exception of the negative impacts of the economic crisis in 2001-2003. The GDP per capita of Argentina and Uruguay increased with the establishment of MERCOSUR whereas it decreased in Brazil and remained nearly stable in Paraguay. Only the Argentinean and Uruguayan GDP per capita situate always above the MERCOSUR average. The MERCOSUR average is situated on such a low level because of the heavy weight Brazil has in the agreement, comprising about 80 percent of MERCOSUR's population.

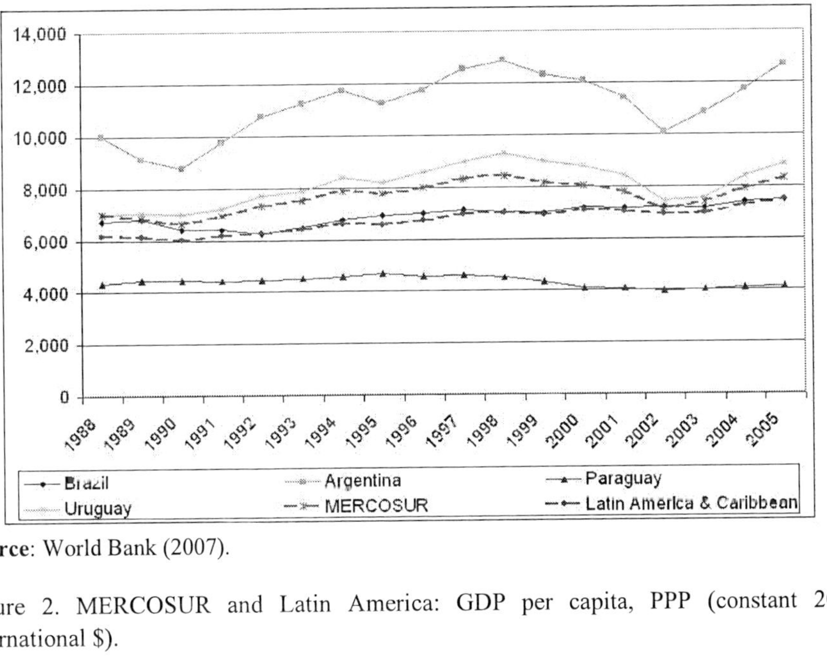

Source: World Bank (2007).

Figure 2. MERCOSUR and Latin America: GDP per capita, PPP (constant 2000 international $).

However, three of the MERCOSUR member countries have a GDP per capita above the Latin American average pushing the MERCOSUR average above the per capita GDP of the region, only Paraguay remains on a very low level, in recent years even decreasing, of per capita GDP.

The integration process preceding the foundation of MERCOSUR was mainly initiated by Argentina and Brazil. Both countries began with a stepwise deepening of their relations before they where joined by Uruguay and Paraguay and created the Southern Common Market. The bilateral approach between Brazil and Argentina took place mainly between 1985 and 1990. This approach was mostly designed to substitute import goods (mostly capital goods) from cheaper sources implying minimal, if any, welfare gains.[8]

The origins of MERCOSUR can be traced back to 1985, when the presidents of Argentina and Brazil declared their will to deepen bilateral integration between their countries in the Iguazú Declaration. This declaration was followed by an Integration and Economic Cooperation Program in 1986 in order to create a CU between both countries. More agreements followed until 1990 when the Buenos Aires Act was signed which aimed to create a common market between Argentina and Brazil by 1995. Finally, Paraguay and Uruguay joined the initiative in pursuing a common market and the MERCOSUR was founded in 1991 by the Treaty of Asunción.[9] Later on, MERCOSUR was notified under the GATT's Enabling Clause at the end of 1991.[10]

The Treaty of Asunción aimed to create a common market with free movement of goods, services and persons; to establish a common external tariff (CET); to coordinate trade policy towards nonmembers; to coordinate macroeconomic and sectoral policies and to harmonize the law in sectors affected by the integration.

The common market was planned to be established by the end of 1994, an unrealistic goal given that the European process to establish a common market took more than 20 years.[11]

Indeed, this proved to be political impossible and the ambitious objectives set by the Treaty of Asunción were only partially achieved with the Protocol of Ouro Preto which was signed in 1994. The protocol gave legal personality to MERCOSUR, defined the institutional framework and approved the CET. Under the Protocol, the CET was to be introduced in 1995 allowing an exception list for each member. Brazil, for example, named about 200 product lines in this list,

[8] Cf. Nogués & Quintanilla (1993), p. 294.
[9] Cf. Wehner (1999), pp. 49 ff.
[10] Cf. WTO (2008).
[11] Cf. Wehner (1999), pp. 63 ff.

mainly sensitive industries such as computers, electronics, chemicals, agroindustry, textiles, capital goods (machinery) and the automotive industry. Unilateral liberalization efforts followed by the Protocol of Ouro Preto reduced tariffs considerably in MERCOSUR member countries, from an average of 50 percent in 1988 to a CET average of 12 percent in 1995. However, since then the trade policy has been subject to vigorous debates and several changes to meet short-run political objectives have been made. Tariffs on textiles, toys and motor vehicles (a special issue within Brazil), for example, were increased to 70 percent for nonmembers in 1995.[12] These disputes lead to a sharp increase in tariffs in 1998 with an average MERCOSUR tariff of around 14 percent.[13]

Table 1. Products excepted from MERCOSUR's CET in June 2001

Exemptions	N° of Products	Deadline / Countries	Situation *	Decision
1. Capital goods	1.140	31.12.00 / Arg & Bra 31.12.05/ Pry & Ury	Not accomplished	Dec. 07/94
2. Information Tech. & Telecomm goods	435	31.12.05 / All members		Dec. 07/94
3. Sugar	04	31.12.00 / All	Not accomplished	Dec. 19/94
4.Automotive sector	95	31.12.99 / All	Not accomplished	De. 29/94
5. Exception list	300 399	31.12.00/Bra, Arg & Ury 31.12.05 / Paraguay	Not accomplished	Res. 07/94
6. Presence in the Final Adjustment List	Argentina (212) Brazil (29) Paraguay (432) Uruguay (958)	31.12.98 / Arg & Bra 31.12.99 / Pry & Ury	Accomplished Accomplished	Res.48/94
7 Supply Shortage	50	31.12.00 / All	Not accomplished	Res.22/95
8.Subject to Special Concessionary Regimes	Variable	31.12.00 / All	Not accomplished	Dec. 21/98
9. Bilateral Trade Agreements	Variable	31.12.94 / All	Not accomplished	Res. 35/92
10. 3% Increase in CET	All with CET	31.12.00 / All	Partially Accomplished	Dec. 15/97

*situation in June 2001

Source: de Azevedo (2004), p. 9.

The CET is collected by each member state and the state is the one that appropriates the revenues. It is still unclear how the duties are going to be redistributed among members or whether they will create a common budget. Any distribution mechanism has to consider the various asymmetries within the agreement and its special situation. Paraguay, for example, is a country with a high fiscal dependency on the duty revenues collected from imports. It is landlocked and has the lowest per capita income of all members. Furthermore,

[12] Cf. Chang & Winters (2001), pp. 17 ff.

[13] Cf. De Azevedo (2004), p. 10.

Brazil, the largest country with the largest market size, is not among the richest countries in the Southern Common Market.[14]

The situation for MERCOSUR changed dramatically following the Brazilian currency devaluation in 1999 and Argentina's default crisis in 2001 and intra-bloc trade shrunk below its peak in 1997. However, the strong commitment to revive the integration process along with the recovery of the Argentinean economy and the realignment of the bloc's main partners exchange rates led to new hope.[15]

The numerous exceptions from the CET still constitute a serious problem; its situation in 2001 can be seen in the exception list displayed in Table 1. The efforts to align the tariffs by 2001 for Argentina and Brazil and by 2006 for Paraguay and Uruguay were mostly unsuccessful.[16] Hence, in 2003 the new date established for the elimination of the CET exceptions was 2010.

Thus, despite the progress to complete CU and common market there are several significant remaining problems to be solved:

- Non-tariff trade barriers are still creating frictions among MERCOSUR members hindering intra-bloc trade;
- MERCOSUR still has no common external trade policy and no completely free circulation of imported products;
- The free circulation of factors of production and services is not yet implemented. MERCOSUR's legislation intended to put this in place but is still blocked by the national parliaments.[17]

However, besides all the obstacles and setbacks, MERCOSUR became a dynamic economic region, its area is the biggest emergent market in the region appealing many states on the Latin-American continent and even though the Common Market of the South could not achieve all of its goals, it reached a high degree of integration in a remarkably short time, considered nowadays as an incomplete CU. Orientating itself at the principles of free trade, the Southern Common Market seems to have further potential to deepen its integration and include new members.[18]

---

[14] Cf. Vaillant (2005), pp. 31 f.
[15] Cf. De Azevedo (2003b), p. 22.
[16] Cf. Chang & Winters (2001), p. 17.
[17] Cf. European Commission (2007), pp. 16 f.
[18] Cf. Wehner (1999), p. 237.

2. Static Welfare Effects

To evaluate the welfare effects of the MERCOSUR agreement, its trade creating and trade diverting effects have to be quantified. This is either carried out ex-ante on the basis of simulation methods or ex-post on the basis of an analysis of the development of intra-bloc and extra-bloc trade. Each method has its advantages and disadvantages.

Ex-ante simulation methods, such as computable general equilibrium (CGE) modeling, try to predict welfare effects under alternative assumptions about market structures and elasticities. CGE models are fully articulated computer (mathematical) models of economies that include, for example, tariff rates, factor markets, product supplies and demands as well as welfare indicators. These models typically contain a large quantity of microeconomic detail and can be used to predict sector-specific changes in production or changes in factor prices and real incomes.[19] However, many restrictive assumptions have to be made concerning market structure and elasticities of substitution.

Ex-post estimations are the most common method to quantify the costs and benefits of regional integration. They compare average trade shares among RIA members before and after the implementation to try and identify any changes.

However, these estimations have to make simplifying assumptions about what trade pattern would have occurred in the absence of the RIA. The most common "anti-monde" or counterfactual assumption is essentially that trade would have increased equally across partners in the absence of the RIA.

One approach to building an "anti-monde" consists on estimating a gravity model of trade. In this model, bilateral trade flows are explained as a function of a number of variables (e.g. GDP, population, transport costs, common border, common language, etc.). To these factors, variables are added to represent the additional trade that occurs if countries are members of a given RIA and, sometimes, the ways in which RIA members' imports from and exports to the rest of the world differ from trade patterns of countries with no membership in a regional agreement. This approach, the gravity model of trade (GM), is more specific about likely trade patterns in absence of the RIA. GMs are estimated on the basis of data from many countries and years and are the most commonly used framework to estimate trade creation and trade diversion effects.[20]

---

[19] Cf. Schiff & Winters (2003), pp. 47 f.

[20] Cf. de Melo (2004), p. 12.

2.1. Ex-ante Studies

For ex-ante policy analysis scholars normally are bounded to use CGE techniques in different variants. According to Schiff and Winters (2003) they are even "...about the only tool available for predicting the likely effects of an RIA before it is implemented."[21] The impacts of RIAs on welfare in both member and nonmember countries as well as the existence of trade creation and trade diversion are evaluated relying on CGE modeling.

CGE models have become increasingly sophisticated as the technique has been refined over the years. First-generation models assume perfect competition and ignore dynamics. The costs and benefits of RIA membership arise only from trade diversion and trade creation. Second-generation models include increasing returns and imperfect competition. They incorporate scale and competition effects. The third generation models allow for some dynamics, capital accumulation and sometimes also technical progress.[22] Broadly, these models conclude that there are gains from regional integration but that these gains are small and vary between 1 and 5 percent of GDP depending on the generation of the model that is used.[23]

Table 2. Welfare Results of the Full Implementation of the MERCOSUR CU (1995 US$ million)

Regions	Allocative Effects	TOT Effects	I-S Effects	Aggregate Welfare Effect	Share of GDP
Arg	-9	-86	0	-96	-0.037%
Bra	852	-446	-89	318	0.045%
Ury	-22	10	5	-7	-0.041%
NAFTA	33	125	33	191	0.002%
EU	107	135	12	255	0.003%
Andean	8	35	1	44	0.019%
Asean	8	66	19	93	0.002%
ROW	46	159	19	224	0.004%
Total	1,024	-2	0	1,021	0.004%

Source: de Azevedo (2003a), p. 16.

[21] Schiff & Winters (2003), pp. 48 f.
[22] Cf. Baldwin & Venables (1995), pp. 1629 f.
[23] Cf. Schiff & Winters (2003) p. 48.

Table 3. Breakdown (in Percent) of Welfare Gains in MERCOSUR's Imperfectly Competitive Sectors

Sector	*Lower Trade Costs*	*Lower Markups*	*Diversity*	*Diversion*	*Export Prices*	*Import Prices*	*Total*
Steel	45.2	71.2	−9.2	−3.1	−5.0	0.9	100
Machinery	28.5	82.2	−1.2	−0.4	−9.4	0.3	100
Automobiles	48.5	69.5	0.0	−11.3	−7.2	0.5	100
Other vehicles	50.5	78.1	−2.3	−8.8	−18.0	0.5	100
Chemicals	37.5	73.2	−1.0	−4.4	−6.8	1.5	100

Source: Flôres (1997), p. 9.

De Melo (2004) suggests three broad conclusions of some ex-ante exercises. First, all else equal, an RIA is likely to be welfare-enhancing if the abolishment of protection favors, on average, industries with increasing returns to scale. Second, small developing countries involved in South-South RIAs are not likely to gain from market access to the protected partner's market as this is probably not compensating for the trade diversion effects resulting from switching to a less efficient partner. Third, unilateral trade liberalization is always better than equivalent trade liberalization within the agreement. The same applies for an additive regionalism, which is always preferable to bilateral engagements.[24]

In what follows, ex-ante simulations for MERCOSUR using different CGE approaches are investigated more in detail. A first-generation CGE model with constant returns to scale and perfect competition in production activities was used by de Azevedo (2003a) to infer directly the impact of MERCOSUR on welfare in both member and nonmember countries as well as the existence of trade creation and trade diversion. His simulations on the impacts of MERCOSUR's CET that was scheduled for 2006 are displayed in Table 2. He predicts that the negative allocative and terms of trade (ToT) effects can not be outweighed by the efficiency effects for Argentina and Uruguay (Paraguay was considered too small and was not included in the analysis) resulting in negative effects of respectively 0.037 percent and 0.045 percent of world GDP. Brazil, on the other side, benefits form the implementation of the MERCOSUR CU. The net effect prediction for the region and nonmember countries is positive with a total gain corresponding to

[24] Cf. de Melo (2004), p. 11.

0.004 percent of world GDP. De Azevedo's modeling suggests overall positive but small trade creating effects from the formation of MERCOSUR.[25]

Flôres (1997) calculated the potential gains that might be expected from competition and scale effects of MERCOSUR. He used a CGE model with key sectors that are partly perfectly and partly imperfectly competitive (comparable to a second-generation model mentioned above). Three scenarios were examined, varying from increased world regionalism to an optimistic multilateral situation. For the basic scenario, the "union case" in which the MERCOSUR CET is equal to a weighted average of the members' tariff, he estimated GDP gains of 1.8, 1.1 and 2.3 percent for Argentina, Brazil and Uruguay. In this case, Uruguay gains more than the larger countries because advantages in the perfectly competitive sectors enable it to expand its market share. Table 3 shows the sources of welfare benefits he determined for imperfectly competitive sectors.

The most important effects identified are the direct resource savings resulting from reduced trade and transport costs and the decrease in firms' markups. Increased variety, trade diversion and changes in export and import prices have only minor negative effects on the welfare of the Southern Common Market. The predictions show, that especially the steel industry and the automobile and other vehicles sectors will benefit from integration in this area. Summarizing, Flôres' predictions suggest a potential net trade creation effect due to the competition and scale effects triggered by integration between Brazil, Argentina, Paraguay and Uruguay.[26]

Finally, Diao and Somwaru (1999) used dynamic general equilibrium (third-generation) modeling to simulate both short-run and medium-run transitional effects of trade reforms in the context of MERCOSUR and the US economy, the largest trading partner of the Southern Common Market. Their simulation results indicate that the RIA raises MERCOSUR member countries' economic welfare by stimulating investment, production and consumption. The major reason for the increase in total trade for the agreement is the growth of intra-regional trade, an expected outcome of regional integration. However, reducing the CET would allow MERCOSUR members to expand both intra- and extra-bloc trade and hence benefit more. Negative effects for nonmembers, such as the US, are considered to be marginal. Furthermore, members and nonmembers are expected to benefit more if MERCOSUR countries reduce the CET. Hence, Diao's and Somwaru's

[25] Cf. De Azevedo (2003a), pp. 18 f.

[26] Cf. Flôres (1997), pp. 7 ff.

findings support the view that positive trade creation effects will prevail when MERCOSUR cuts its external protection rate further.[27]

2.2. Ex-post Studies

The most straightforward approach to evaluate trade diversion and trade creation effects ex-post consist on comparing the evolution over time of internal and external trade flows before and after the agreement. The main shortcoming of this approach is that changes in trade figures may also be due to other factors different from the elimination of trade barriers. Figure 3 shows intra- and extra-MERCOSUR import shares before and after 1995.

It shows that intra-bloc trade shares increased strongly about 5 percent since MERCOSUR was founded. This result seems quite positive as strong international trade performance is one of the main determinants of economic prosperity. However, this development does not distinguish trade creation from trade diversion. Hence, intra-bloc imports and extra-bloc imports as a share of GDP have to be analyzed, too. If the share of imports in the GDP increases, the economy becomes more open and there has been a net trade creation effect. If the share of nonmember imports in GDP falls, a net trade diversion effect can be observed.

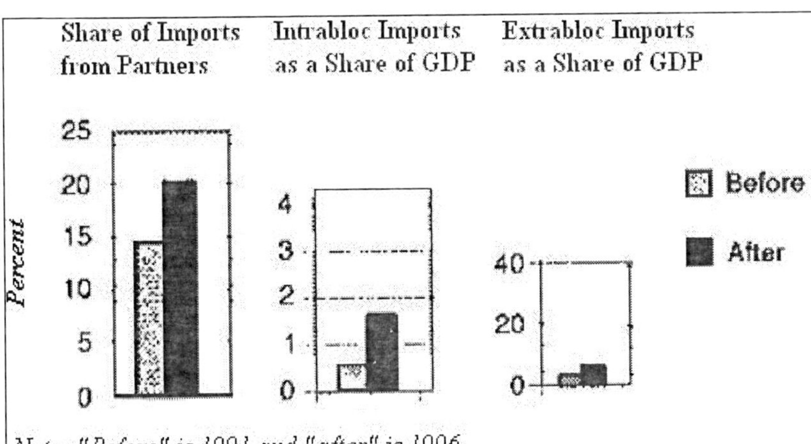

Source: Schiff and Winters (2003), pp. 32 ff.

Figure 3. Evolution of MERCOSUR imports.

[27] Cf. Diao & Somwaru (1999), pp. 39 f.

Table 4. Trade Effects of MERCOSUR, One Year before and Five Years after Implementation

	Import Shares		Trade Intensity		Import/GDP Ratio			Trade Propensity	
RIA	Intra-bloc	Extra-bloc	Intra-bloc	Extra-bloc	Intra-bloc	Extra-bloc	Total Imports	Intra-bloc	Extra-bloc
MERCOSUR									
1990	14.5	85.5	10.52	0.87	0.57	3.34	3.91	0.41	0.03
1996	20.2	79.8	14.12	0.81	1.64	6.48	8.10	1.15	0.07

Source: Schiff and Winters (2003), p. 59.

Table 4 shows the changes in openness (defined as imports over GDP), summing up intra-bloc and extra-bloc imports: MERCOSUR imports as a share of GDP more than doubled between 1990 and 1996, from 3.9 to 8.1 percent. One can see in these numbers, presented in Table 4, that intra-bloc imports as a share of GDP as well as extra-bloc imports as a share of GDP show trade creation.

But, would the observed changes have occurred also in the absence of the MERCOSUR agreement? To answer this question an "anti-monde" has to be identified. Some authors calculate indices in order to consider external changes, whereas others focus on the estimation of gravity models of trade. Both approaches are discussed.

First, trade intensity indices are needed to consider that countries growing faster tend to absorb more of world trade. Trade intensity indices allow determining whether one country's imports are biased towards another country. Such bias might exist, for example, because of geographic proximity, common language or commodity composition. However, since those factors tend to evolve relatively slowly, a causal relationship might only be inferred if sharp changes in trade intensity are observed with the creation of an RIA. Table 4 displays the trade intensities of MERCOSUR. Intra-bloc trade intensity has increased and extra-bloc trade intensity has decreased. Since the increase in intra-bloc trade intensity is higher than the decrease in extra-bloc trade intensity, net trade creation can be found.

Second, trade propensity indices are used in order to consider also domestic sales. Trade propensity is the product of trade intensity and the ratio of one country's imports to its GDP and reflects both the biases in trade patterns and the impacts of RIAs on overall trade volumes. Figure 4 and Table 4 illustrate that intra-bloc as well as extra-bloc trade propensities more than doubled between

1991 and 1996. Thus, the MERCOSUR agreement shows an increase in the share of GDP spent on imports from members and nonmembers that is larger than the increase in member and nonmember shares of world trade.

In summary, these ex-post observations suggest an increasing progress toward opening the economies of RIA members and indicate that regional integration in MERCOSUR has been associated with net improvement in economic performance.[28]

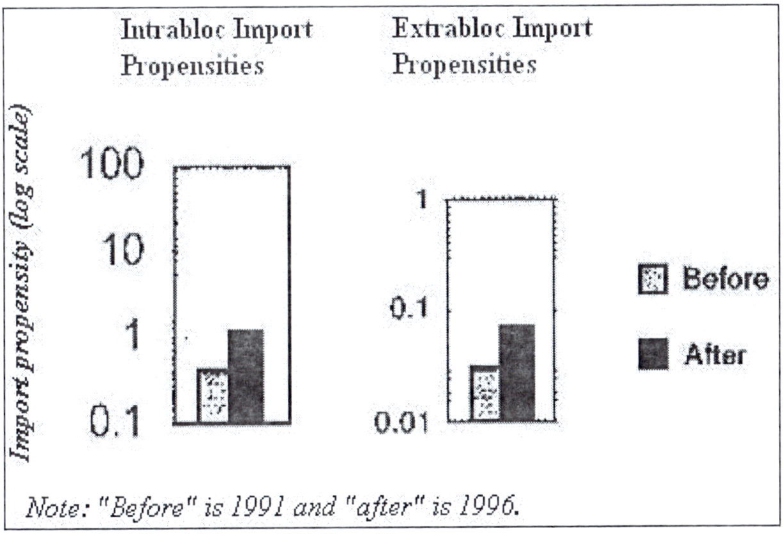

Source: Schiff and Winters (2003), p. 39.

Figure 4. Figures on MERCOSUR Import Propensities.

Yeats (1997) used trade figures and indices to determine the static trade effects of the MERCOSUR agreement. By analyzing the trade intensity ratios for MERCOSUR countries he documented increasing trade between MERCOSUR members and inferred a major reorientation of exports towards regional markets. These results are shown in Table 5. With the exception of Paraguay (for which the quality of the data is poor), the bilateral intensity index ratios for MERCOSUR intra-trade are higher in 1994 than in any previous period. For example, Argentina's index for exports to Brazil rose fivefold from 1979-1981 to 1994 and Brazil's index for exports to Argentina more than doubled over the same period. He then calculated a "regional orientation" index for MERCOSUR exports to analyze shifts in the direction of trade. This index was compared with a

[28] Cf. Schiff & Winters (2003), pp. 32 ff.

"revealed" comparative advantage index in order to provide an indication of the extent to which the agreement distorted exports from patterns consistent with the comparative advantage.

Table 5. Trade Intensity Ratios for MERCOSUR members: Intra-Trade and Trade with North America

		Trading Partner						
		MERCOSUR				North America		
Exporter	Year	Argentina	Brazil	Paraguay	Uruguay	Canada	Mexico	USA
Argentina	1979-1981	---	7.4	86.8	27.5	0.3	6.0	0.7
	1986-1988	---	14.0	40.5	49.2	0.2	2.8	0.8
	1994	---	39.2	92.7	89.4	0.1	1.5	0.7
Brazil	1979-1981	9.0	---	80.7	19.0	0.6	3.2	1.4
	1986-1988	9.9	---	56.0	31.6	0.6	1.4	1.7
	1994	21.7	---	71.5	36.7	0.3	2.1	1.3
Paraguay	1979-1981	41.7	11.2	---	45.1	0.0	3.4	0.5
	1986-1988	48.6	41.9	---	48.8	0.0	0.2	0.3
	1994	25.2	67.2	---	27.7	0.0	0.4	0.4
Uruguay	1979-1981	22.7	14.6	52.2	---	0.4	0.6	0.7
	1986-1988	36.0	33.1	22.2	---	0.2	1.7	0.8
	1994	44.7	43.7	36.8	---	0.2	2.1	0.4

Source: Yeats (1997), p. 9.

Several product groups where matched with results that strongly suggest that MERCOSUR was becoming less, rather than more, internationally competitive in products where trade was most rapidly reoriented towards the RIA. The regional orientation for exports was growing more rapidly for products where there was little evidence that the agreement has a comparative advantage.

Yeats' results suggest that a significant amount of the increased trade within MERCOSUR is a result of trade diverted from more efficient nonmembers to less-efficient producers within the agreement. As a cause for these findings he suggested the high external tariffs and NTBs of the Southern Common Market.[29] Yeats' conclusions where reconsidered, among others, by Hudgins (1997). He criticized the non-consideration of special reasons for shifting exports (e.g. the fall of communism), the simplicity of the calculations and the specific situation of the MERCOSUR agreement (it began with some of the world's highest tariff rates). Nagarjan (1998) also evaluated the methodology used by Yeats. Yeats based his study on comparing shifts in intra-regional exports with a measure of relative efficiency in production. Nagarjan argues that he should have instead focused on imports.

He remarks that the growth in intra-regional as well as nonmember imports reflects the increased openness of the MERCOSUR economies and adapts Yeats methodology to examine trends in imports. The observed results indicate that the growth in intra-MERCOSUR imports has been accompanied by growing trade with the rest of the world.[30] Furthermore, he argues that: "trade diversion has undoubtedly occurred for some products, but the increasing multilateral openness of the MERCOSUR countries coupled with the dynamic effects of the growth in their economies' may have outweighed any static welfare losses."[31]

Using an approach comparable to those used by Nagarajan and Yeats, de Azevedo (2003b) examines changes in MERCOSUR's trade patterns based on descriptive statistics. He concludes that the most likely effect associated to the implementation of the Common Market of the South is related to "export-diversion". Using different methods, he finds signs of a decline in exports to nonmembers ("export-diversion") Still, only a small fraction of sectors out of the 238 sectors studied show signs of diversion. Furthermore, he notes that the descriptive statistics he used are only a first step towards a more detailed analysis.

A major drawback of this approach is the inability to isolate the impact of the RIA from the other variables influencing trade patterns, thereby attributing too much to the bloc effect, an issue that is addressed below.[32]

The trade changes discussed above suggest, except for Yeats' study, mostly beneficial outcomes of regional integration in the MERCOSUR agreement. However, their no-change anti-monde calculations do not allow concluding that regional integration is beneficial. Member countries can improve their trade policies and performance over time and RIAs may implicate large distortions relative to the members' economic potential in multilateral free trade or relative to trade patterns elsewhere in the world. The key question is whether the changes are due to nondiscriminatory trade liberalization that RIA members undertook around the same time or to regional integration per se. A more sophisticated way of representing the counterfactual is needed to answer this question.[33] The most popular of the more elaborated ex-post approaches is the gravity model. In the

---

[29] Cf. Yeats (1997), pp. 8 ff.
[30] Cf. Nagarajan (1998), pp. 23 ff.
[31] Nagarajan (1998), p. 21.
[32] Cf. De Azevedo (2003b), pp. 21 f.
[33] Cf. Schiff & Winters (2003), p. 40.

following, selected GM applications regarding regional bias to trade and trade effects in the Southern Common Market are surveyed.

Frankel, Stein and Wei (1997) used a GM with five basic variables: size, per capita income, bilateral distance, common borders and common language in addition to dummy variables for intraregional trade (bloc effects that account for trade creation). If higher levels of trade were not associated to the RIAs, then the five basic variables would absorb all the explanatory power, however, he finds that these dummy variables account for at least some trade between countries. Their findings suggest a clear upward trend in the bloc effect for MERCOSUR. In 1990 it reaches the largest bloc effect from the eight RIAs examined, implying that the member countries trade among themselves almost seven times as much as otherwise-similar countries. A strong intraregional trade bias can be observed that is far higher than what would be explained by GDP growth and the distance between member countries ("gravity") or the remaining three variables. All in all, Frankel finds only little trade diversion for individual years and identifies MERCOSUR as an effective RIA.[34]

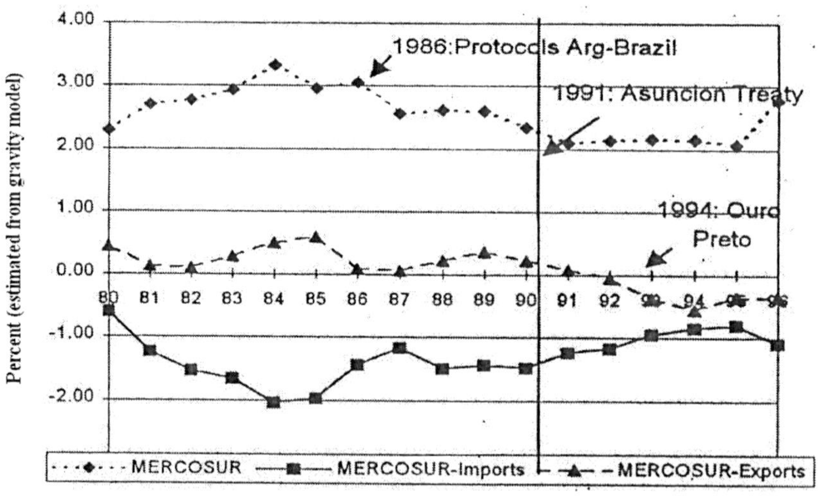

Source: Soloaga and Winters (2001), p. 20.

Note: The y-axes show values of coefficients on RIA dummy variables, in logarithmic equations. A coefficient of b implies that the RIA raised trade by {[exp(b) - 1] × 100}% above the "expected" value.

Figure 5. Effect of MERCOSUR on Trade within and among Blocs, 1980-1996.

[34] Cf. Frankel (1997), pp. 77 ff.

Soloaga and Winters (2001) estimate trade effects for every year during the period 1980-1996. They explicitly test whether the changes in the effects are statistically significant and extend the GM by looking for three separate effects on the trade of MERCOSUR and other RIAs: the effects on intra-bloc trade, on extra-bloc imports and on extra-bloc exports. These effects are plotted in Figure 5 over time. Figure 5 shows that MERCOSUR members have traded more with each other over the whole period 1980-1996 than with third countries. However, this fact could reflect pre-existing integration arrangements, geographical isolation, regional sentiment or idiosyncratic tastes.

With the implementation of the agreement in 1991 overall MERCOSUR imports rose while overall MERCOSUR exports decreased. These opposite movements suggest that MERCOSUR trade performance has been influenced more by competitiveness than by trade policy. In their paper, Soloaga and Winters do not find convincing evidence for trade diversion caused by the Common Market of the South. On the other hand, they observe a statistically significant positive trend in the estimated coefficients for MERCOSUR members' overall imports.[35]

Azevedo (2002) based his study on the works by Frankel (1997) and Soloaga and Winters (2001). He tries to identify differences between the post-integration (1995-1998) period and the pre-integration phase (1987-1990) of the Southern Common Market by introducing product-dummies associated with the bloc dummies in the post-MERCOSUR period. He finds that, after controlling for variables which determine bilateral trade flows, the surge in intra-bloc trade would have occurred in a similar fashion even if MERCOSUR had not been in force. Table 6 indicate that the Common Market of the South seems to have influenced members overall imports and exports. Trade between member countries was already above the expected level, according to the GM, even before the agreement's formation. De Azevedo estimates a reduction of 33 percent in the MERCOSUR overall export coefficient in the transition period (1991-1994) in relation to the pre-integration period, a decline of US$ 39.9 billion. This reduction is exacerbated even further in the post-integration period, with the overall export coefficient falling 52.5 percent in comparison with the base period bringing out a decline of US$ 55,364 million overall MERCOSUR exports. The impact of the agreement on overall imports is positive (an increase of 46.7 percent in the transition period in relation to the pre-integration period), expanding further in the period over 1995-1998 (56.7 percent).

[35] Cf. Soloaga & Winters (2001), pp. 23 ff.

The changes in the coefficients estimated for overall imports and exports show a structural break in both the transition and the post-integration period in relation to the pre-integration period. This suggests that, after the formation of the arrangement, MERCOSUR members became more open to imports from outside the agreement showing no signs of trade diversion. An increase in intra-bloc trade significantly above overall imports could not be found. What significantly affected MERCOSUR overall exports and imports was the liberalization on an MFN basis. Intra-bloc trade increases could not be explained by the regional agreement. The only effect he identifies as potentially harmful to non-member countries is "export-diversion" where the bloc's overall exports declined in the post-integration phase compared with the pre-integration period.[36] The latter was also determined by Soloaga and Winters (2001).

Table 6. Changes in Overall Trade due to bloc formation

Absolute (US$ million) and Relative Changes in Mercosur Overall Trade due to formation of bloc [/1]

Flow	Method	1991- 94		1995- 98	
		Rel Change	Abs Change	Rel Change	Abs Change
Exports	OLS[/2]	29.5%	-36,635	46.4%	-50,970
	OLS[/3]	32.6%	-39,538	51.7%	-54,808
	Tobit	33.0%	-39,903	52.5%	-55,364
Imports	OLS[/2]	32.0%	48,514	60.2%	298,668
	OLS[/3]	43.6%	66,101	55.6%	275,846
	Tobit	46.7%	70,801	56.7%	281,304

/1: Change in relation to Pre-Integration Period;
/2: OLS without zeros (white estimator);
/3: OLS with 0.001 instead of zeros (white estimator).

Source: de Azevedo (2002), p. 22

Carrère (2006) used an estimation method that takes into account the unobservable characteristics attached to each bilateral trade relationship, the endogeneity of some of the explanatory variables and a potential selection bias. She estimates two types of GM: one with cross-section data (corresponding to most uses of gravity modeling for ex-post evaluation of RIAs) and one with panel data in order to isolate more specifically trade diversion and trade creation effects. She found quite different results depending on the estimation method and infers

[36] Cf. De Azevedo (2002), pp. 22 ff.

that panel estimates show a far more plausible pattern of trade effects associated for RIAs. Figure 6 pictures the evolution of MERCOSUR regional dummies over time with all the non-significant estimated coefficients graphed as zero. The cross-section estimates (Figure 6.a) suggest large volatility throughout the years 1962-1996. The panel estimates (Figure 6.b), however, show the expected effects of an RIA around the time of announcement or implementation much more clearly: an increase in intra-bloc trade and a decrease in extra-bloc imports.

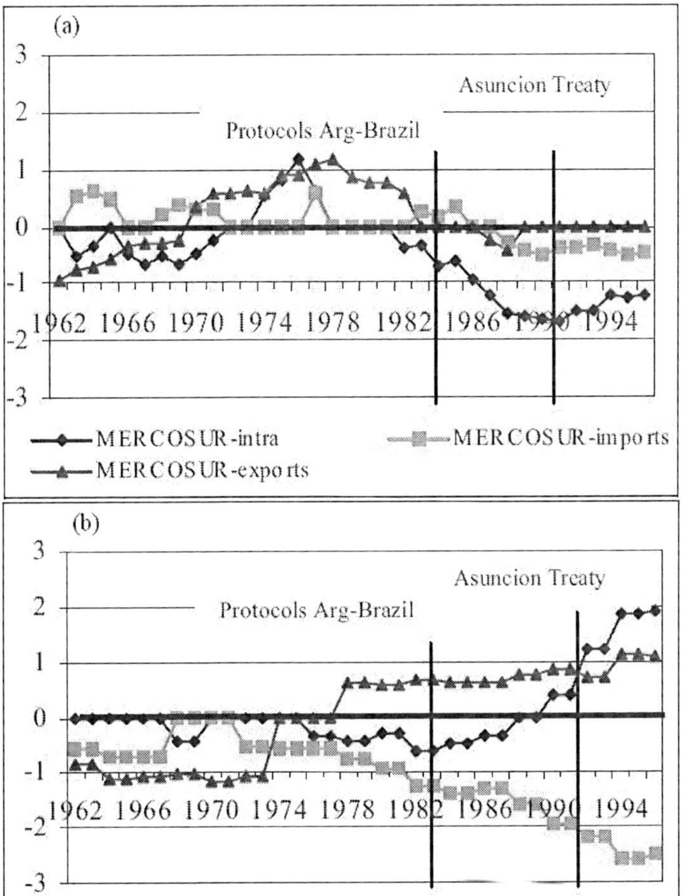

Source: Carrère (2006), p. 236.

Figure 6. Evolution of MERCOSUR Dummies over 1962-1996: (a) in cross-section and (b) in panel.

Furthermore, the panel estimates in Figure 6 suggest some evidence of an increase of MERCOSUR exports to nonmembers. Carrère ascribes this effect to non-discriminatory reduction in trade barriers that was taking place at the same time that the Southern Common Market was founded. Carrère (2006) finds evidence for import diversion for the MERCOSUR agreement as well as some export trade creation. With the signing of the Treaty of Asunción in 1991 the increases in intra-bloc trade and exports to nonmembers outweighs the decreasing imports of the agreement.[37]

Finally, Trotignon (2007) also estimated a GM with panel data and three sets of regional dummies. He used it to asses the effects of selected RIAs in Latin America and finds that all selected agreements generate internal trade creation. They also have in general (with the exception of one agreement) a positive impact on imports and exports with the rest of the Latin American region. For MERCOSUR he estimates that a significant positive intra-bloc trade effect is accompanied by a largest increase in extra-bloc trade. Even when recent periods are considered, including currency fluctuations in Brazil (1999) and the Peso Crisis in Argentina (2001-2002), Trotignon concludes that the Common Market of the South and other Latin American RIAs are net trade makers for the Latin American region. He also suggests that these results constitute an argument for a South American FTA developing into a Free Trade Area of the Americas (FTAA), a FTA to eliminate or reduce the trade barriers among all countries in the Americas.[38]

2.3. Summarizing the Findings - Trade Creation or Trade Diversion?

Before summarizing the findings mentioned above, a critical observation of the two main techniques mentioned is following.

Even though CGE models have sufficient microeconomic structure to allow a detailed view on the effects of a policy change and to calculate its real income effects, they have weaknesses and limitations that cast a more negative light on its outcomes. Unfortunately, many crucial variables can not be measured sufficiently, critical relationships are often specified lacking empirical justification, the level of sectoral detail is often rather low, the behavioral assumptions are usually very simple and the results are very sensitive to measurement error. These problems and the assumption of heterogeneous goods, a major feature of almost all CGE

[37] Cf. Carrère (2004), pp. 234 ff.

models, tend to bias the model towards finding benefits from RIAs. It is therefore important to recognize its limitations: CGE simulations are rather "thought experiments" about what the world would be like with the RIA in existence and fully operative in the base year and they are almost wholly theoretical, not empirical, with no possibility of testing against experience.[39]

Gravity models, on the other hand, have been frequently used over the last two decades. This approach has experienced a resurgence partly due to systematic efforts to reinforce its theoretical underpinnings and partly because of the availability of a growing number of "natural experiments" in the form of RIAs. However, increased theoretical sophistication implies further empirical challenges to separate regional trade effects from empirical specification errors. The debate about these econometric issues is summarized by Greenaway and Milner (2002): Estimation methods, data difficulties, model misspecifications and problems with dummy variables are still discussed. Despite these concerns, the prospects for extending the use of GMs in the context of investigating regionalism are substantial. Its role in both measuring and testing is likely to expand with more careful application of models allowed by panel data and stronger theoretical underpinnings.[40]

The findings of most of the studies suggest a positive net effect for the MERCOSUR agreement. Several studies found evidence for trade diversion outweighed by trade creating effects. Only Yeats (1997) finds net trade diversion from his results, even though he notes that MERCOSUR both created and diverted trade and that "...even trade diverting customs unions can improve economic welfare if they lead to declines in producer and consumer prices."[41]

The summary seems to indicate quite unanimously that the Southern Common Market causes trade creation effects that are larger than trade diversion effects even though it is characterized as a South-South agreement. However, the different limitations and problems with the methods applied for ex-ante and ex-post analyses have to be kept in mind as well as the fact that dynamic effects were not considered. Furthermore, it is worth noting that the abovementioned studies represent, to our knowledge, the most cited and the most recent studies investigating the trade effects of the implementation of the MERCOSUR agreement.

---

[38] Cf. Trotignon (2007), pp. 16 ff.

[39] Cf. Schiff & Winters (2003), pp. 48 f.

[40] Cf. Greenaway & Milner (2002), pp. 578 ff.

[41] Yeats (1997), p. 29.

3. Dynamic Welfare Effects

After dealing with the trade creation and trade diversion effects of the MERCOSUR agreement the focus is now on the dynamic effects of MERCOSUR's creation and progress.

3.1. Terms of Trade Effects

An RIA can cause a trade creation effect that is large enough to improve the ToT of the particular agreement. This occurs due to sinking prices of nonmembers' exports to the countries in the agreement. To trigger such an effect, the RIA has to be large enough to influence those prices. However, it is commonly believed that this ToT effect is not a big motivator of trade policy stances and that most RIAs, especially South-South RIAs, are too small to have noteworthy influence.[42] The question now is if these assumptions also apply to the MERCOSUR agreement.

Whereas the effect of RIAs on the volume and quantities of trade are frequently examined, studies focusing on the price (ToT) effects of an RIA on its trading partners are scarce. In what follows, two works are presented that analyze the mentioned impacts for MERCOSUR.

Olarreaga et al. (1999) analyze the dominant forces behind regionalism: the internalization of ToT effects or political-economy forces. ToT effects lead to price externalities among countries that trade similar goods. For example, assuming that when Brazil raises tariffs on extra-bloc imports this leads to a fall in international prices and causes a positive externality also for Argentina. If Brazil would have considered the effects of its tariffs not only on his own ToT, but also on Argentina's ToT, it would have set a higher tariff. The positive externality would have been negative if Argentina's export to the world would consist of mainly the same products as Brazil imported.

The creation of a CU raises the opportunity for the internalization of the ToT effect for all members. They would not focus any longer on their individual market power when deciding about their tariff, but on the market power of the whole bloc.

To identify the key forces behind regional integration Olarreaga et al. (1999) analyzed the ex-post structure of MERCOSUR's CET by regressing tariff levels on political economy variables. Their findings are contrary to the opinion of most researchers who neglected the ToT as a possible explanatory variable: ToT effects

[42] Cf. Schiff & Winters (2003), p. 65.

account for between 6 and 28 percent of the explained variance of the CET. Although political-economy powers seem to explain a large proportion of the CET, the ToT effect on tariffs can not be ignored.[43]

Chang and Winters (2001) also suggest that the ToT effect is important for the Southern Common Market. They examined the effect that the agreement has had on the prices of its imports from nonmembers in an imperfectly competitive setting with differentiated products. In their sample period (1989-1996) they concentrate on the Brazilian import market since it is, by far, the largest market for imports in MERCOSUR and good data is available. They show that regional integration does affect the prices of traded goods and that it matters significantly for nonmember exporters that supply an RIA. Furthermore they infer that even if an RIA aims only to liberalize trade between its members and even if, as with MERCOSUR, it undertakes general trade liberalization at the same time, other economies may still be affected negatively. This happens because nonmembers are forced to reduce their prices to meet competition from suppliers within the RIA. They conclude that MERCOSUR's preferential tariffs caused significant declines in the prices of nonmembers' exports to Brazil.[44] To summarize, the identified ToT effect has positive consequences for the MERCOSUR agreement and implies negative effects for the rest of the world.

The results of both studies seem surprising given that the Southern Common Market is relatively small in terms of world GDP. Despite its low trade volume (MERCOSUR accounts for only one percent of world markets) MERCOSUR trade policy seems to have significant influence on world market prices. Thus, the common belief that the ToT effect is not a big motivator for policy stance in small countries may be limited to a small number of cases.

Regarding the "beggar-thy neighbor" argument, Estevadeordal et al. (2000) state that the Common Market of the South is more a "Land of Cockaign" than a "beggar-thy-neighbor" agreement due to the finding that the MERCOSUR is a case of "New Regionalism" where preferential liberalization is accompanied (or preceded) by unilateral trade reforms in the member countries. Their results suggest that MERCOSUR would diminish possible "beggar-thy-neighbor" effects.[45]

---

[43] Cf. Olarreaga, Soloaga & Winters (1999), pp. 1 ff.
[44] Cf. Chang & Winters (2001), pp. 3 ff.
[45] Cf. Estevadeoral, Goto & Saez (2000), p. 33.

3.2. Foreign Direct Investment in the Southern Common Market

The MERCOSUR agreement undertook several actions to attract FDI and to create an attractive climate for investment (e.g. the 1993 Colonia Protocol on the Promotion and Reciprocal Protection of Investment within MERCOSUR and the 1994 Protocol on the Promotion and Protection of Investment from nonmembers). These are, however, mostly freestanding investment agreements independent of trade agreements which can be modified for other partners (e.g. cooperation projects regarding investment from Canada or from Europe).[46]

Table 7 denotes, after a steady increase in previous years, a high leap in foreign investment following the signature of the Treaty of Asunción in 1991. FDI in member countries increased from US$3.7 billion in 1991 to US$18 billion in 1996 and to US$53 billion in 1999. With the Brazilian currency crisis in 1999; Argentina's Peso crisis in 2001 and the recession in 2003, however, FDI dropped to US$20 billion in 2005. This can be attributed partly to the lack of coordination in macroeconomic policies, especially of the two major members, Brazil and Argentina, which has caused trade strains and interest conflicts in attracting FDI.[47] Brazil's preeminence in the agreement becomes clear once again when examining the table (e.g. in 1998 and 2005 it contributed around 75 percent of the bloc's FDI).

A constraint to these figures is that it is not sure whether it was MERCOSUR per se rather than better policies in general that boosted FDI, in the Southern Common Market both occurred more or less simultaneously. Furthermore, the welfare implications are ambiguous as some of the boost in FDI seems to be tariff-jumping FDI, caused by trade and industrial policy distortions such as very high tariffs, which was directing capital into the inefficient automotive sector.[48]

Regarding the current situation of MERCOSUR as an incomplete CU and the length of time the EU needed to complete its Single Market and achieve financial integration to deal with FDI provisions, it will take a long time until MERCOSUR can attract high amounts of FDI.

[46] Cf. MERCOSUR (2009).

[47] Cf. Baer, Calvacanti & Silva (2003), pp. 25 ff.

[48] Cf. Schiff & Winters (2003), p. 120.

Table 7. Net Inflows of Foreign Direct Investment, MERCOSUR, 1989-2005 (millions of current US$)

	1989	**1990**	**1991**	**1992**	**1993**	**1994**	**1995**	**1996**	**1997**
Argentina	1,028	1,836	2,439	4,431	2,793	3,635	5,609	6,949	9,160
Brazil	1,131	989	1,103	2,061	1,292	3,072	4,859	11,200	19,650
Paraguay	13	77	86	118	75	137	103	149	236
Uruguay	38	42	32	11	102	155	157	137	126
MERCOSUR	2,210	2,943	3,660	6,621	4,262	6,999	10,728	18,435	29,172
	1997	**1998**	**1999**	**2000**	**2001**	**2002**	**2003**	**2004**	**2005**
Argentina	9,160	7,291	23,988	10,418	2,166	2,149	1,652	4,274	4,730
Brazil	19,650	31,913	28,576	32,779	22,457	16,590	10,144	18,166	15,193
Paraguay	236	342	95	104	84	10	27	44	64
Uruguay	126	164	235	274	271	175	417	333	711
MERCOSUR	29,172	39,710	52,893	43,575	24,979	18,924	12,239	22,816	20,697

Source: World Bank (2007).

3.3. Rules of Origin and MERCOSUR – the Latin American Spaghetti Bowl

Rules of Origin (RoO) are important barriers to trade. They became more and more relevant with the rise of regionalism and the growth of overlapping and intersecting preferential trade agreements, each with its own and differing rules. Possible distortions and incompatibilities among those different RIAs appear. Latin America is not ranking behind Europe when looking at the numerous, crisscrossing trade agreements that have been negotiated among the countries of the South American continent.

Figure 7 shows the Latin American Spaghetti Bowl drafted by Antoni Estevadeordal in 2002. He differentiates between "First Generation" Agreements signed under the ALADI[1] using general RoO across the board for all tariff items and "Second Generation" Agreements, such as NAFTA, applying different RoO depending on the product in question. The RoO of the MERCOSUR agreement fall between those two types of agreements, they are involved in "First Generation" Agreements with different countries and RIAs in Latin America as well as reciprocal agreements between Chile and Bolivia.

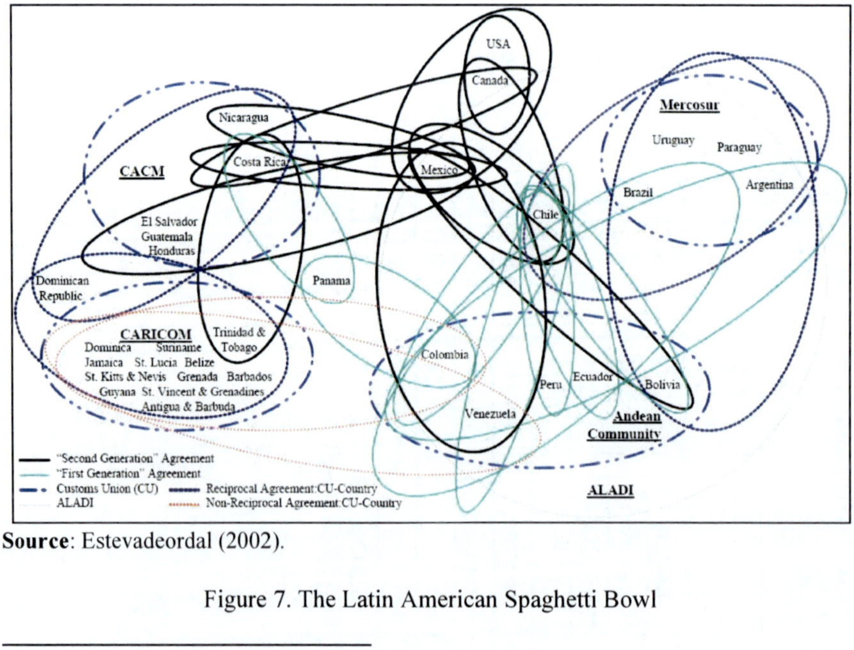

Source: Estevadeordal (2002).

Figure 7. The Latin American Spaghetti Bowl

---

[1] ALADI (Asociación Latinoamericana de Integración) is also called by the english acronym LAIA (Latin American Integration Association).

The development of the past two decades resulted in more than 40 bilateral or regional trade agreements within the Hemisphere. In fact every American country except Cuba has been part of at least one RIA.[2]

With regards to a "hub-and-spoke" situation Figure 7 suggests that Mexico, the Andean Community and MERCOSUR seem to be hubs for Latin America. One can see that MERCOSUR is not as well connected as Mexico and a possible FTA with the EU could effectively make it a spoke of the EU hub unless the FTAA is formed.[3] On the other hand it could become a hub for European and North American trade when successfully concluding agreements with the EU and the US.[4]

Thus, MERCOSUR is not an exception regarding the "spaghetti bowl" phenomenon. That becomes even clearer when considering the numerous agreements that MERCOSUR also has with countries and RIAs outside of the American continent. Therefore there is plenty of potential to manipulate RoO in order to protect domestic industries.

The exceptions from the agreement's CET are a major problem in this context (see Table 1 for the exception list in 2001). The holes in the CET have undermined two of the main advantages of a CU when compared with a FTA: the absence of a need for RoO to hinder intra-bloc trade deflection and the security of access to member markets.[5] As the MERCOSUR customs union is yet to be accomplished, the need for RoO spread to a large number of products. To be considered a MERCOSUR product, a good should have a intra-bloc content of at least 60 percent. Originally, there where only specific groups of products that would have been subject to these RoO in intra-bloc trade, but by 2000 all products where still underlying rules of origin examination and, as the removal of the goods from the exception list was unsuccessful, RoO remain. This created a lack of predictability in the future which deteriorated the prospects for both trade and investment in MERCOSUR.[6]

Thus, the numerous exceptions from the CET have to be reduced and the path to a complete CU has to be accomplished in order to avoid trade deflection and diminish protectionist tendencies resulting from RoO-use in intra-MERCOSUR trade.

---

[2] Cf. Hertel et al. (2004), p. 15.
[3] Cf. Schiff & Winters (2002), p. 490.
[4] Cf. Busse & Koopmann (2002), p. 237.
[5] Cf. De Azevedo (2004), p. 8.
[6] Cf. De Azevedo (2004), pp. 12 f.

Regarding RoO outside of the Common Market of the South, the FTAA efforts, started in 1994 by 34 democracies in the Western Hemisphere to prepare negotiations, may provide a way of simplifying the complex network of RIAs and unravel the Latin American "spaghetti-bowl".[7]

3.4. The "Domino-Effect" and MERCOSUR

The idiosyncratic event that triggered knock-on effects resulting in the formation of RIAs in Latin America is the creation of NAFTA, especially its US-Mexico trade provisions. The North American Free Trade Agreement, in turn, was most likely triggered by European regionalism (i.e. the EU) in order to create a countervailing trade bloc.[8] With the beginning of NAFTA negotiations Chile, Brazil, Argentina, Uruguay and Paraguay all approached the US, either formally or informally, with requests for trade agreements. These requests, though, where refused by the US.

MERCOSUR's connection with NAFTA is difficult to pin down. The reason for its formation, among others, was because the US administration trade officials suggested that Paraguay, Uruguay, Brazil and Argentina band together in their own RIA before pursuing bilateral agreements with the US. Regarding the Latin American affinity for regional integration and precedent Brazilian-Argentinean approaches it seems unlikely that this was the prime cause. However, the MERCOSUR agreement is seen as the most important of the overlapping RIAs in the Hemisphere triggered (partly) by NAFTA.

MERCOSUR soon generated another domino by creating its own incentives for inclusion. Chile became an associate member in 1996, seeing that MERCOSUR, unlike most S-S agreements, implemented preferential liberalization and affected trade patterns. The gravitational pull of MERCOSUR continued with Bolivia, Peru, Columbia, Ecuador and Venezuela becoming associate members and the negotiations of several other agreements in- and outside of Latin America.[9]

These observations and the findings obtained so far in this work suggest that a combination of "competitive liberalization" and "competitive regionalism" took place in the Latin American continent combining both unilateral and regional liberalization.

---

[7] Cf. Hertel et al. (2004), p. 15.
[8] Cf. Busse & Koopmann (2002), p. 235 and Bhagwati (1993), p. 541.
[9] Cf. Baldwin (1997), pp. 870 f.

A possible result of the "domino-effect" in Latin America could be the Free Trade Area of the Americas, a FTA covering all countries in the Americas except Cuba. This huge agreement is still under negotiation and debated,[10] but its implementation would most likely lead to positive welfare effects.[11] Furthermore, the realization of the FTAA, even though far away, would promote a world situation with less trading blocs. It remains to be seen, however, if such a world would result in a global free trade situation or a Krugman worst-case scenario with three trading blocs.[12]

4. MERCOSUR – An Effective South-South Agreement?

The gains from integration between countries with high levels of economic development depend on two criteria: they require both similarity in per capita income (so that the products demanded are similar) and a certain depth in consumption or input variety. In S-S RIAs, this is often not the case as they normally trade more with extra-bloc countries and have no broad variety in products. MERCOSUR is normally considered to be an S-S RIA among developing countries, even though Brazil and Argentina are members of the G-20 and bloc members are denominated "middle-income countries".[13] Furthermore, the treatment of the WTO suggests that the MERCOSUR agreement is about to "grow out" of being an S-S RIA.[14]

Figure 2 show that the first criterion to obtain gains from integration, similarity in per capita income, could not be achieved. Per capita GDPs in 2005 range between 4,000 international PPP-$ in Paraguay and 12,000 international PPP-$ in Argentina. Due to low per capita GDPs and the inequality between member countries, the Southern Common Market can still be considered an agreement between developing countries. Greater Inequality within MERCOSUR countries was also found by Lo Turco (2005) who even claimed that MERCOSUR seems to foster divergence, but finds no evidence

[10] Cf. Schiff & Winters (2003), pp. 88 f.
[11] Cf. Schiff & Winters (2003), p. 216 and Hertel et al. (2004), pp. 26 f.
[12] Cf. Krugman (1991), p. 18.
[13] Cf. Schiff & Winters (2003), p. 120.
[14] The MERCOSUR agreement is the only agreement that is certified by the WTO under the Enabling Clause but is being examined under the Committee on Regional Trade Agreements (CRTA) under both the Enabling Clause and Article XXIV.

for harmful localization effects.[15] Regarding the second criterion, a certain consumption depth and input variety may be assumed due to the status of member countries as emerging markets, Argentina's high per capita GDP and the amount of intra-bloc trade. However, there are certainly more effects to be considered when assessing the outcomes of MERCOSUR than the abovementioned two criteria.

Despite the fact that MERCOSUR can still be classified as an agreement among developing countries, differences from the typical S-S RIA classification can be observed. The figures even seem to suggest that the Common Market of the South benefits more in a North-South manner from regional integration. Therefore RIAs should be analyzed individually instead of categorizing them in a framework with only three possible classifications.

5. Conclusions

In this paper the economic effects of the MERCOSUR have been analyzed devoting special attention to the trade effects. Regarding the ex-ante and ex-post analysis of the static effects of the Southern Common Market, a positive net trade creation effect is found in the majority of the studies. Furthermore, MERCOSUR's commitment to democracy is a very important factor for stability and peace, not only for the agreement, but also for the whole Latin American continent, a feature that must not be underestimated.

However, MERCOSUR still has many obstacles to overcome. Policymakers in domestic institutions are still very susceptible to interest group's pressures, a point that can be seen in the numerous CET exceptions. Institutional problems and overdue reforms amplify the negative effects on members' welfare and the ambiguity and lack of enforcement of WTO rules gives the agreement practically carte blanche to design its trade policy.

These problems need to be faced, for example, by the implementation of a supranational institutional framework and more rigorous enforcement of WTO rules. Advancements on the supranational and the multilateral level can reduce the CET exceptions, elevate the gains from trade integration and help completing the MERCOSUR customs union.

Nowadays, MERCOSUR is an incomplete CU and the ambitious goal to create a common market between its member states is not likely to be reached in the foreseeable future. However, the rapidity of its formation is impressive

[15] Cf. Lo Turco (2005), p. 25.

regarding the history and difficulties the member countries and the whole region had to face in the past decades. After all, the Common Market of the South is an agreement constituted among developing countries and has to overcome the problems of inequality additionally to its integration agenda. The effects of the agreement, despite numerous insufficiencies, pose an important step towards enduring prosperity and development in the region.

The achievements of the MERCOSUR agreement and its progress show how regional integration can increase welfare and improve the situation of whole continents. It is already a domino creating incentives for other countries to join or to create RIAs and to liberalize trade. If the Western Hemisphere ultimately forms the FTAA, it will be partly due to efforts of the MERCOSUR agreement.

This study's findings highlight the need for further research on the individual characteristics of trade agreements. A detailed and individual examination of RIAs should undertake empirical research on static effects and consider dynamic as well as political effects in order to present a comprehensive understanding of the effectiveness of the particular RIA.

Abbreviations and Acronyms

ALADI	Asociación Latinoamericana de Integración; Latin American Integration Association (LAIA)
CET	common external tariff
CGE	computable general equilibrium (model)
CRTA	Committee on Regional Trade Agreements (WTO)
CU	customs union
FDI	foreign direct investment
FTA	free trade area
FTAA	Free Trade Area of the Americas
GATT	General Agreement on Tariffs and Trade
GDP	gross domestic product
GM	gravity model
MERCOSUR	Mercado Común del Sur; Common Market of the South
MFN	most-favored nation
NAFTA	North American Free Trade Agreement
NTB	non-tariff barrier
PPP	purchasing power parity
RIA	regional integration agreement

RoO	rules of origin
ToT	terms of trade
US	United States (of America)
USA	United States of America
WTO	World Trade Organization

References

Baer, Werner; Tiago Cavalcanti and Peri Silva (2003): *Economic Integration without Policy Coordination: The Case of MERCOSUR*, Working Paper, Bureau of Economic and Business Research, University of Illinois at Urbana-Champaign.

Baldwin, Richard, E. and Anthony J. Venables (1995): Regional Economic Integration, in: Gene Grossman and Kenneth Rogoff (ed.), "*Handbook of International Economics*", vol. 3: pp. 1597–1644, Amsterdam: North-Holland.

Baldwin, Richard, E. (1997): *The Causes of Regionalism, in: The World Economy,* Vol. 20, No. 7, pp. 865-888, Blackwell Publishers, Oxford.

Bhagwati, Jagdish (1993): *Regionalism versus Multilateralism, in: The World Economy,* Vol. 15, No. 5, pp. 535-556, Blackwell Publishers, Oxford.

Busse, Mathias and Georg Koopmann (2002): *Transatlantische Handelsbeziehungen zwischen Konflikt und Kooperation*, HWWA Forum 4/2002, pp. 235-238, Wirtschaftsdienst HWWA Hamburg.

Carrère, Cèline (2006): *Revisiting the effects of regional trade agreements on trade flows with proper specification of the gravity model*, in: European Economic Review 50, pp. 223-247.

Chang, Won and Alan Winters, L. (2001): *How Regional Blocs Affect Excluded Countries: The Price Effects of MERCOSUR*, World Bank Policy Research Working Paper No. 2157.

De Azevedo, André Filipe Zago (2002): *What has been the real effect of Mercosur on trade? A Gravity Model Approach*, Working Paper, Universidade Federal do Rio Grande, in:
http://www.ufrgs.br/ppge/pcientifica/2002_01.pdf.

De Azevedo, André Filipe Zago (2003a): *MERCOSUR: The Impact of Preferential Liberalization and Prospects for the Customs Union*, Working Paper, ANPEC, in:
http://www.anpec.org.br/encontro2007/artigos/A07A078.pdf.

De Azevedo, André Filipe Zago (2003b): *Mercosur's change in trade patterns*, Working Paper, Universidade Federal de Rio Grande do Sul, in:http://www.ufrgs.br/fce/rae/edicoes_anteriores/pdf_edicao41/artigo03.pdf.

De Azevedo, A. (2004), 'Mercosur: Ambitious Policies, Poor Practices'. *Revista de Economia Politica,* 24, 584-601.

De Melo, Jaime (2004): *Regionalism and Developing countries: A Primer*, University of Geneva and CEPR.

Diao, Xinshen and Agapi Somwaru (1999): MERCOSUR and the U.S.: An intertemporal General equilibrium evaluation of the regional integration, in: *International Economic Journal*, Volume 13, Number 1, pp. 27-43.

Estevadeordal, Antoni, Junichi Goto and Raul Saez (2000): *The New Regionalism in the Americas: The Case of MERCOSUR*, Working Paper 5, INTAL-ITD, Buenos Aires.

Estevadeordal, Antoni (2002): *Regional Integration and Regional Cooperation in Latin America*, LAEBA Annual Meeting, ADB Institute and Inter-American Development Bank, Singapore. http://www.adb.org/documents/events/2002/trade_policy/NRA_pres.pdf.

European Commission (2007): *MERCOSUR Regional Strategy Paper 2007-2013*, 02.08.2007 (E/2007/1640).

Flôres, Renato, G. (1997): The Gains from MERCOSUL: A General Equilibrium, Imperfect Competition Evaluation, *Journal of Policy Modeling* 19 (1), pp. 1-18.

Frankel, Jeffrey, A. (1997): *Regional Trading Blocs in The World Economic System*, Institute for International Economics, Washington.

Greenaway, David and Chris Milner (2002): Regionalism and Gravity, in: *Scottish Journal of Political Economy*, vol. 49, no. 5, pp. 574-585.

Hertel, Thomas, David Hummels, Maros Ivanic and Roman Keeney (2004): *How confident can we be in CGE-based assessments of Free Trade Agreements?* NBER Working Paper 10477, National Bureau of Economic Research, Cambridge.

Krugman, Paul (1991): *The Move Toward Free Trade Zones*, in: Policy Implications of Trade and Currency Zones, Kansas City: Federal Reserve Bank of Kansas City, pp. 7-41.

Lo Turco, Alessia (2005): *South-South Trade Agreements, Location of Production and Inequality in Latin America*, Discussion Paper No. 127, Ibero-America Institute for Economic Research, Göttingen.

MERCOSUR (2009): *Portal oficial*, in: http://www.mercosur.int (accessed on 19.01.2009).

Nagarajan, Nigel (1998): *MERCOSUR and Trade Diversion: What Do The Import Figures Tells Us?* In: Economic Papers, Number 129, European Commission, Directorate-General for Economic and Financial Affairs, Belgium.

Nogués, Julio, J. and Rosalinda Quintanilla (1993): *Latin America's integration and the multilateral trading system*, in: Jaime de Melo and Arvind Panagariya (Editors) "New dimensions in regional integration", pp. 278-313, Cambridge University Press, Cambridge.

Olarreaga, Marcelo, Isidro Soloaga and Alan Winters (1999): *What's Behind Mercosur's Common External Tariff?* Policy Research Working Paper 2231, The World Bank, Development Research Group, Trade.

Schiff, Maurice and Alan Winters, L. (2002): Regionalism and Development: The Implications of World Bank Research for ACP and Latin American Countries, in: *Journal of World Trade* 36(3), pp. 479-499, Kluver Law International.

Schiff, Maurice and Alan Winters, L. (2003): *Regional Integration and Development*, World Bank and Oxford University Press, Washington.

Soloaga, Isidro and Alan Winters, L. (2001): Regionalism in the nineties: What effect on trade? In: *North American Journal of Finance*12, pp. 1-29.

Trotignon, Jérôme (2007): *Les Groupes régionaux latino-américains : building ou stumbling blocks? Un modèle de gravité en données de panel*, Working Paper 07-19, Groupe d'Analyse et de Théorie Économique (GATE).

Wehner, Ulrich (1999): *Der Mercosur*, Nomos Verlagsgesellschaft, Baden-Baden.

World Bank (2007): *World Development Indicators CD-ROM,* Washington DC.

WTO (2008): *World Trade Organization Website*, in: http://www.wto.org.

Yeats, Alexander (1997): *Does Mercosur's Trade Performance Raise Concerns about the Effects of Regional Trade Arrangements?* Policy Research Working Paper 1729, The World Bank, International Economics Department, International Trade Division.

In: Trade Liberalization and Protectionism
Editors: B. Hahn et al, pp. 95-129 ISBN: 978-1-60876-837-0

Chapter 4

IMPACT OF TRADE ON SERVICE SECTOR EMPLOYMENT IN INDIA[1]

Arup Mitra[*]
Institute of Economic Growth, Delhi University Enclave
Delhi-110007

Abstract

This study makes an attempt to assess the impact of trade liberalization on services sector employment. Based on the time series macro data, the elasticity of organised services sector employment with respect to value added and exports and imports have been estimated. After controlling for growth it is difficult to identify a positive and significant impact of international trade on employment in the organized service sector. We have also tried to work out the direct and indirect effects of exports and imports on employment after deciphering their effects included in overall growth. However, the positive effects are mostly negligible. For the informal or unorganized services sector employment the impact does not seem to be greatly different from what is observed in the case of the organized services sector employment. Also as per the company level data

---

[1] The author is thankful to the National Commission for Enterprises in the Unorganised Sector (NCEUS) for sponsoring this study. He has gained enormously from the discussion with Dr Arjun Sengupta, Chairman, NCEUS, other members of NCEUS particularly Dr K.P. Kannan and Dr Ravi Srivastava, and several other experts including Dr Ajit Ghose and Professor B. N. Goldar. Mr. Shashi Bhushan Ray, Mr. Yashobanta Parida, and Mr. Nitesh Kumar Singh provided excellent research assistance.
[*] E-mail address: arup@iegindia.org. fax: 91-11-27667410

international trade does not seem to be an important determinant of employment in the services sector.

1. Perspective

In the present context of globalisation countries across the globe are pursuing vigourously a pro-growth approach. However, growth alone may not be sufficient to bring in any major improvement in economic and social wellbeing, particularly of those who are located at the lower echelons of the socio-economic ladder. The basic pre-requisite for this is rapid growth in productive employment opportunities by means of which the benefits of growth may be shared more equitably with the deprived lot. The cross-regional variations in growth and poverty are enormous (Minujin, Vandermoortele and Delamonica, 2002). To be specific, whether economic growth is able to generate employment opportunities on a large scale, particularly for the unskilled, semi-skilled and the less educated labour force is an important question that has been bothering the development economists since long. Second, what impact have the economic reforms in various sectors made on the employment front is another important dimension of the issue that needs thorough investigation.

From the historical experience of the present day developed nations it is evident that an important determinant of economic growth is industrialization. The role of industry is crucial in generating high productivity employment and in enhancing the standard of living of the population. In the process of development a structural shift both in the value added and in the work force composition takes place away from the primary sector first towards the secondary and later towards the tertiary sector. This structural change is accompanied not only by a rise in per capita income but also in an improvement in many other development indicators. It involves an upward mobility of individual occupations and incomes and a shift in rural-urban composition of the population (Kuznets, 1966).

Several developing countries are, however, deviating from this path. Either the agriculture sector continues to form a major source of livelihood for a vast section of the population or the shift in value added and/or work force structure is more towards the services or tertiary sector rather than industry. The rapid expansion of the services sector is easy to rationalize in the context of the developed countries because following the rapid progress in industrialization the demand for several services grows faster, which in turn reduces the share of the secondary sector in the total product and subsequently the work force. But in the case of the developing countries a dominance of the tertiary sector much before the secondary sector's relative size could increase to a reasonably high level does invite concerns. This is mainly because the high productivity tertiary/services sector does not have adequate openings for productive absorption of the work force pushed out of the agriculture sector. Sub-sectors like transport, communication and banking are seen to contribute significantly to the overall economic growth. The role of information technology (IT) and business process outsourcing services (BPOS) in enhancing the overall economic growth has been specially evident across countries, (World Bank 2004, Gemmel, 1986). All this has prompted some to view the tertiary sector as the engine of growth though traditionally manufacturing was seen as the driver of economic growth (Kuznets, 1966, Kaldor, 1967). However, most of these high income activities within the tertiary sector are not conducive to an absorption of the unskilled and semi-skilled work force, and hence, the mismatch between the labour demand and labour supply is expected to become unmanageably large instead of disappearing in the process of growth. A critical look at some of these issues would possibly help us deal with this situation of rapid value added growth in the high productivity sector while vast sections of the population remain at the same time engaged residually in low productivity informal sector activities.

Globalization has compelled countries to enhance growth. Several growth-oriented strategies, that include trade-openness, FDI-inflows and capital mobility, including technology transfer, have been adopted in a big way. The argument, which is usually given in favour of technology transfer, is that the wheel that has already been adopted does not require to be rediscovered if countries seek to be cost efficient[2]. But an important question that arises in this context is whether growth that is maximized through these strategies is conducive to poverty reduction or does it merely benefits those who are located in the higher echelons, thus excluding a sizeable lot. On the other hand, strategies that aim at improving human capital formation and social infrastructure are believed to have a direct and greater effect on the overall well-being of nations by reducing poverty while also in the long run enhancing economic growth.

One important view in the context of growth and globalization suggests that economic growth is a positive function of globalization, as the latter facilitates free mobilization of resources. Hence, low income and labour surplus countries by specializing in labour intensive exportable goods can accelerate growth, generate employment and reduce poverty. However, technological innovation can bring in

[2] It is argued that countries further from the frontier have lower R&D returns, implying that the cost of innovation is more in a poor country than in a rich country. Hence, it is still cheaper for a latecomer to buy the technology already invented by others than to re-invent the wheel though it is widely noted that international technology does not come cheap (UNIDO, 2005).

a shift in the demand for skilled labour and hence, can reduce wages of the less skilled, implying a rise in wage inequality (Feenstra and Gordon, 1996). Though this concern has been primarily expressed in the context of the developed countries, the same logic can be extended to the developing countries as well if they import technology from the former. Research for various Latin American countries is indicative of a widening impact of trade on wage inequality, and more importantly this is spearheaded by the notion of skill-biased technological change induced through trade. On the whole, though freer trade or trade openness is believed to enhance economic growth, the opponents of globalization view it as socially malign on several dimensions including poverty (Bhagwati and Srinivasan, 2002). However, highlighting the findings of Dollar (2001), Bhagwati and Srinivasan (2002) point out that countries, which registered significant declines in poverty, are also the ones which integrated faster into the world economy in terms of trade and direct investment, and hence according to them it would not be correct to suggest that trade openness bypasses poverty. Rivera-Baitz and Xie (1992) also argued that knowledge diffusion and trade in ideas trough a GATT-type patent system are needed for the whole world to grow faster, and thus argued for multilateral liberalization that comprises trade in goods and ideas both. United Nations Conference on Trade and Development (2007) urged that market opening has contributed to attracting foreign capital into the services sector, which has promoted the development and growth of the domestic service market and contributed to the training of local service providers. However, before drawing any conclusive statement in this regard it is important to assess the impact of trade liberalization on the service sector employment. Since the service sector is highly heterogeneous and comprises both a high productivity component and a low productivity informal segment, a careful analysis in this regard is indeed warranted to draw effective policy lessons for the Indian economy.

The study is organized as follows. In the next section we focus on the composition of organized service sector employment and the growth in employment in various components of the organized service sector over time. Section 3 focuses on the informal service sector employment. In Section 4 using the time series data the elasticity of organized service sector employment with respect to international trade has been obtained. Based on the cross-sectional data we estimate the elasticity of informal service sector employment with respect to organized service sector employment and using this cross-sectional estimate we work out the possible effect of trade on the informal service sector employment. An indirect method of this kind had to be adopted because there is no time series information on the latter. In Section 5 we use the company level data to capture employment growth in the more recent years, i.e. after 2005. Using some of the trade-specific variables at the company level, we assess the possible effect of the international trade on the service sector. Finally, section 6 summarizes the major findings. The database of the study is drawn from various rounds of NSSO's surveys on employment and unemployment (1999-2000 and 2004-05), DGET data on organised service sector employment, trade statistics on services from RBI Bulletin and Monograph of India's Balance of Payment, unit value index of exports and imports from Economic Survey, CSO's data on gross value added and the Capital Line data at the company level. Though DGET data on employment is said to be underestimated, the time series information is rich which helps undertake important exercises. Second, the problem of underestimation seems to be serious in the case of manufacturing rather than for the service sector, and that is the reason why in the previous part on trade liberalization and organized manufacturing we have considered the ASI data instead of DGET data. Similarly the Capital Line dataset has serious problems namely that it is not exhaustive and also it is not able to provide balanced panel information. Notwithstanding these limitations we make an attempt to utilize the firm level details to draw substantive patterns, which could not have been possible otherwise.

2. Organised Sector Employment

Of the total organized sector employment, that of the public sector constitutes a significant share. The only exceptions are manufacturing and wholesale and retail trade, hotels and restaurants – the activities which are dominated by the private sector. Since DGET data is collected on voluntary basis it is quite likely that organized private sector employment in these activities is underestimated. However, the ASI data on organized manufacturing sector employment are more comprehensive and have a better coverage, for which reason the previous section uses ASI data extensively. But for the different components of the services sector, the DGET data had to be used since they include time series information, as mentioned above. Except for the trade and hotel sector, the criticism of underestimation, however, does not seem to be applicable to other activities since they are largely located in the public sector (see Table 1).

Table 1. Share of Public Sector in Total Organised Sector Employment

Year	Manu-facturing	Utilities	Const-ruction	Trade, Hotel etc.	Transport, Storage & Communication	Finance, Business Services	Community, Social and Personal Services	Total
1975	19.86	92.87	88.27	14.64	96.77	75.15	86.20	65.43
1976	21.12	93.87	91.34	16.33	97.03	72.81	86.29	66.06
1977	22.74	94.15	92.40	21.65	97.20	74.17	86.17	66.72
1978	23.87	94.63	92.32	23.25	97.64	76.32	86.17	66.85
1979	24.21	94.91	92.56	26.05	97.34	76.30	86.12	67.06
1980	24.66	95.11	93.60	28.65	97.39	77.03	86.09	67.60
1981	24.84	95.13	93.80	29.70	97.83	79.24	85.75	67.68
1982	25.46	95.10	94.00	28.97	97.89	79.98	85.70	67.88
1983	25.96	95.11	94.28	30.03	97.95	80.83	85.88	68.54
1984	27.74	94.95	94.44	31.00	98.05	81.03	86.09	69.66
1985	28.49	95.12	94.24	32.11	98.17	81.78	86.12	70.26
1986	28.98	95.15	94.48	32.11	98.19	82.33	86.20	70.57
1987	29.69	95.17	95.33	32.60	98.28	82.18	86.26	70.99
1988	29.81	95.39	96.04	32.94	98.33	82.15	86.07	71.25
1989	29.83	95.70	94.32	34.40	98.31	82.76	86.04	71.22
1990	29.56	95.73	94.34	34.01	98.31	82.84	86.07	71.22

Table 1. Continued

Year	Manu-facturing	Utilities	Const-ruction	Trade, Hotel etc.	Transport, Storage & Communication	Finance, Business Services	Community, Social and Personal Services	Total
1991	29.24	95.77	94.03	33.33	98.28	82.46	86.14	71.28
1992	28.96	95.82	93.65	35.09	98.27	82.03	85.88	71.00
1993	28.94	96.08	94.05	32.96	98.23	81.88	85.81	71.11
1994	27.81	95.91	95.81	34.77	98.22	81.86	85.67	71.03
1995	27.17	95.90	95.65	34.47	98.17	81.41	85.57	70.72
1996	25.61	95.75	95.63	33.82	98.10	80.71	85.17	69.54
1997	24.07	95.89	95.45	34.10	98.00	80.07	85.57	69.25
1998	23.59	95.78	93.74	33.81	97.94	79.07	85.31	68.94
1999	23.25	95.91	93.97	33.54	97.81	78.34	85.21	69.06
2000	23.14	95.85	95.04	33.06	97.78	78.36	85.01	69.08
2001	22.19	94.73	94.99	32.47	97.56	77.59	85.01	68.87
2002	21.71	95.65	94.82	31.91	97.54	75.88	84.82	69.01
2003	20.99	94.81	95.56	33.58	97.38	76.37	84.55	68.81
2004	20.94	94.90	95.39	34.02	97.20	75.46	83.81	68.82
2005	20.11	94.61	94.90	32.92	97.00	72.92	83.56	68.06

Note: Total includes agriculture.
Source: Economic Survey, DGET Data.

Table 2. Composition of Public Sector Employment

Year	Manu-facturing	Utilities	Const-ruction	Trade, Hotel etc.	Transport, Storage & Comm.	Finance, Business Services	Community, Social and Personal Services
1975	7.91	3.94	7.42	0.41	18.35	3.97	50.02
1976	8.35	4.02	7.45	0.42	18.15	3.68	49.83
1977	8.91	4.09	7.33	0.55	17.92	3.88	49.17
1978	9.54	4.22	7.03	0.58	17.75	4.08	48.72
1979	9.65	4.32	7.03	0.67	17.70	4.41	48.18
1980	9.59	4.38	7.08	0.73	17.58	4.58	47.91
1981	9.70	4.41	7.03	0.76	17.50	4.83	47.50
1982	9.98	4.38	6.97	0.71	17.44	5.11	47.33
1983	9.90	4.38	6.82	0.72	17.21	5.32	47.54
1984	10.18	4.35	6.64	0.74	16.98	5.42	47.31
1985	10.20	4.40	6.64	0.76	16.76	5.69	47.04
1986	10.26	4.44	6.68	0.74	16.56	5.82	47.05
1987	10.33	4.38	6.57	0.74	16.48	5.86	47.32
1988	10.19	4.63	6.63	0.76	16.44	5.98	47.13
1989	10.10	4.71	6.21	0.81	16.12	6.09	47.76
1990	9.97	4.78	6.04	0.80	16.11	6.15	48.07
1991	9.72	4.75	6.03	0.79	15.88	6.27	48.42
1992	9.69	4.77	5.99	0.83	15.95	6.32	48.34
1993	9.58	4.82	5.97	0.77	15.81	6.48	48.52
1994	9.17	4.82	6.00	0.83	15.86	6.55	48.74
1995	9.02	4.80	5.98	0.83	15.96	6.59	48.82
1996	8.95	4.87	5.97	0.83	15.91	6.59	49.00
1997	8.49	4.89	5.80	0.84	15.81	6.62	49.83
1998	8.32	4.91	5.71	0.84	15.88	6.63	50.14
1999	8.08	4.95	5.70	0.84	15.88	6.67	50.45
2000	7.93	4.90	5.65	0.84	15.93	6.71	50.59
2001	7.47	4.89	5.65	0.85	15.90	6.69	51.36
2002	7.19	4.92	5.47	0.84	16.03	6.55	51.86
2003	6.78	4.91	5.10	0.98	15.82	7.41	51.72
2004	6.53	4.80	5.12	0.99	15.47	7.74	50.98
2005	6.28	4.78	5.06	1.02	15.28	7.82	51.38

Note: The percentages are taken relative to the row total. The percentage figures do not add up to 100 per cent because agriculture is not included in the table.

Source: See Table 1.

Table 3. Composition of Private Sector Employment

Year	Manu-facturing	Utilities	Const-ruction	Trade, Hotel etc.	Transport, Storage & Comm.	Finance, Business Services	Community, Social and Personal Services
1975	60.38	0.57	1.87	4.54	1.16	2.48	15.16
1976	60.75	0.51	1.37	4.19	1.08	2.67	15.41
1977	60.65	0.51	1.21	4.00	1.03	2.71	15.81
1978	61.35	0.48	1.18	3.89	0.87	2.56	15.76
1979	61.50	0.47	1.15	3.90	0.99	2.79	15.82
1980	61.12	0.47	1.01	3.79	0.98	2.85	16.15
1981	61.46	0.47	0.97	3.75	0.81	2.65	16.52
1982	61.76	0.48	0.94	3.67	0.80	2.70	16.68
1983	61.52	0.49	0.90	3.65	0.78	2.75	17.02
1984	60.89	0.53	0.90	3.76	0.78	2.91	17.55
1985	60.49	0.53	0.96	3.79	0.74	3.00	17.91
1986	60.32	0.54	0.94	3.76	0.73	3.00	18.06
1987	59.89	0.54	0.79	3.76	0.71	3.11	18.45
1988	59.46	0.55	0.68	3.83	0.69	3.22	18.90
1989	58.81	0.52	0.93	3.84	0.68	3.14	19.17
1990	58.78	0.53	0.90	3.84	0.69	3.15	19.26
1991	58.37	0.52	0.95	3.91	0.69	3.31	19.34
1992	58.20	0.51	0.99	3.77	0.69	3.39	19.46
1993	57.89	0.48	0.93	3.83	0.70	3.53	19.74
1994	58.39	0.50	0.64	3.81	0.71	3.56	19.99
1995	58.39	0.50	0.66	3.82	0.72	3.64	19.89
1996	59.32	0.49	0.62	3.72	0.70	3.59	19.48
1997	60.32	0.47	0.62	3.65	0.73	3.71	18.93
1998	59.82	0.48	0.85	3.67	0.74	3.90	19.17
1999	59.53	0.47	0.82	3.71	0.79	4.12	19.54
2000	58.81	0.47	0.66	3.82	0.81	4.14	19.93
2001	57.94	0.60	0.66	3.92	0.88	4.28	20.04
2002	57.72	0.50	0.66	3.97	0.90	4.64	20.66
2003	56.34	0.59	0.52	4.28	0.94	5.06	20.85
2004	54.44	0.57	0.55	4.26	0.98	5.55	21.73
2005	53.11	0.58	0.58	4.44	1.01	6.19	21.53

Note: The percentages are taken relative to the row total. The percentage figures do not add up to 100 per cent because agriculture is not included in the table.

Source: See Table 1.

The composition of the public sector employment shows that community, social and personal services constituted almost half of the total (Table 2). Though there was a declining tendency in the share of this activity in total public sector employment over the late seventies and the eighties, there seems to be a mild increase in the recent past. On the other hand, the composition of the organized private sector employment is indicative of a decelerating share of the manufacturing activity and a rise in the share of community, social and personal services (Table 3).

In terms of growth in employment in different activities in the organized sector we may note that except (a) wholesale, retail trade and hotel etc. and (b) financing and business services the other components within the services group have experienced a decline between 2001 and 2005 (Table 4). The total organized sector employment also registered a decline during the same period. Though both wholesale, retail trade and hotel etc. and finance and business services grew sluggishly at a little above one per cent per annum over the nineties they seem to have recovered in the recent past.

Table 4. Growth in Employment in the Organised Sector (% p.a.)

Period	Manufac-turing	Utilities	Trade etc.	Transport etc.	Finance etc.	Other Services	Total
1975-85	2.05	3.79	1.60	1.99	6.20	2.34	2.30
1986-91	0.2	3.05	2.10	0.6	2.83	2.04	1.33
1992-2000	0.8	0.5	1.11	0.13	1.33	0.80	0.53
2001-05	-3.64	-2.11	2.93	-2.53	4.54	-1.23	-1.27

Source: See Table 1.

3. Effect of International Trade on Service Sector Employment

Methodological Framework

In this section, we first estimate the responsiveness of organized service sector employment (from DGET data) to export and import and gross value added. Export and import figures have been deflated by the unit value index (the base converted from 1978-79 to 1999-2000) of export and import, respectively. Gross value added figures are also taken in constant prices (1999-2000 prices). The export and import figures for different groups of services sector are derived in the manner as follows: travel account from the composition of services exports is taken to match the group that comprises trade, hotel etc.; transportation account and communication services are kept in the category of transport, storage and communication; insurance, financial services, software services and business services are taken to correspond finance and business services group; and government, news agency, personal, cultural and recreational services and other services are put under the category of community, social and personal services. A similar grouping has been followed to derive the imports for four categories of services.

Since the value added includes the impact of export and import as well, we have tried to separate out their effect by regressing value added originating from a particular activity on total non-agricultural value added (a proxy for overall growth) and the exports and imports corresponding to that activity. After substituting the results into the first equation for organized employment we then derive the direct and indirect effects of exports and imports on employment.

In the next step we work out the elasticity of informal service sector employment with respect to formal service sector employment using NSSO's cross-sectional data on the informal sector employment for the year 1999-2000 and 2004-05. The elasticity of informal sector employment to formal sector employment has been estimated in the following manner: First, given the population figures from the censuses of 1991 and 2001 the average annual growth rates have been computed on the basis of which population for the year 1999-2000 and 2004-05 have been projected. Given the NSS estimates of worker (principal plus subsidiary) to population ratio, the absolute numbers of workers for these two years have been derived. In the next step, the NSS estimates of per thousand distribution of workers across different activities have been applied to derive the absolute number of workers in each of the activities. In the third step, NSSO's results of the survey on the informal sector workers in non-agricultural activities have been used to split the total workers in each activity into informal and formal components. NSSO's estimate of the per thousand distribution of workers in the informal sector is applied to the absolute number of workers in each activity to derive the absolute number of workers in the informal sector, which has been then deducted from the total number of workers in each activity to deduce the formal sector workers[1].

[1] For 1999-2000, NSS provided the absolute number of workers in the informal sector directly. The proportions have been calculated by considering the NSS estimate of population for the year 1999-2000. Since the NSS estimate of population is said to be grossly underestimated these proportions are then applied to the absolute number of workers derived from the projected population of 1999-2000 on the basis of the decennial census figures. The adjusted set of absolute number of workers in the informal sector is then used for further analysis.

Since time series information on informal sector employment is not available in the Indian context, the elasticity of informal sector employment with respect to formal sector employment had to be calculated in this manner from the cross-sectional data. These elasticity estimates are then used to derive the impact of export and import on the informal sector employment. The assumption is that the elasticity of organized service sector employment from DGET data with respect to export and import would be same as that of the formal service sector employment derived from the NSS data had the latter been available annually. The other assumption is that international trade affects informal service sector only indirectly, i.e., through the organized sector. This assumption may not be unrealistic as unorganized or informal services are not exposed to international trade in any significant way.

Broad Patterns

Before turning to the econometric work it may be useful to take a look at the value added growth and export and import growth in various components of the services sector. Besides, we may examine the share of informal sector in total employment across states and the growth rate of informal and formal sector employment across activities between 1999-2000 and 2004-05.

Service sector value added has been growing very rapidly for last two decades (Table 5). In fact in terms of value added the structural shift has taken place away from agriculture and largely towards service rather than manufacturing. All the four components within the service sector exhibit fast growth. Particularly, the growth rate in value added originating from transport, storage and communication shot up to 14.01 per cent per annum during 2001-05.

Table 5. Growth in Value Added (% p.a.)

Period	Value Added: Wholesale and Retail Trade, Hotels and Restaurants	Value Added: Transport, Storage and Communication	Value Added: Finance, Real Estate Ownership and Business Services	Value Added: Community, Social and Personal Services
1975-85	4.75	5.49	6.17	3.68
1986-91	5.29	5.52	9.00	6.02
1992-2000	8.48	8.25	7.58	7.12
2001-05	8.27	14.01	8.81	6.87

Note: Growth rates are based on figures in 1999-2000 prices.
Source: Central Statistical Organisation, Government of India.

Table 6. Growth in Export and Import (% p.a.)

Period	Export: Trade	Export: Transport, Storage and Commun-ication	Export: Finance, Business Services	Export: Community, Social and Personal Services	Import: Trade	Import: Transport, Storage and Communi-cation	Import: Finance, Business Services	Import: Community, Social and Personal Services
1975-85	10.630	1.51	11.48	12.20	23.25	11.44	6.40	13.42
1986-91	4.98	9.44	19.59	3.13	5.05	9.42	51.03	-13.24
1992-2000	6.97	12.77	29.46	22.47	23.63	9.49	7.75	32.63
2001-05	14.67	17.47	19.76	-3.69	12.47	16.11	31.33	13.87

Source: Monograph on India's BOP, July 1993; RBI Bulletin, January 2001, April 1999, Economic Survey, 2007-08, Government of India.

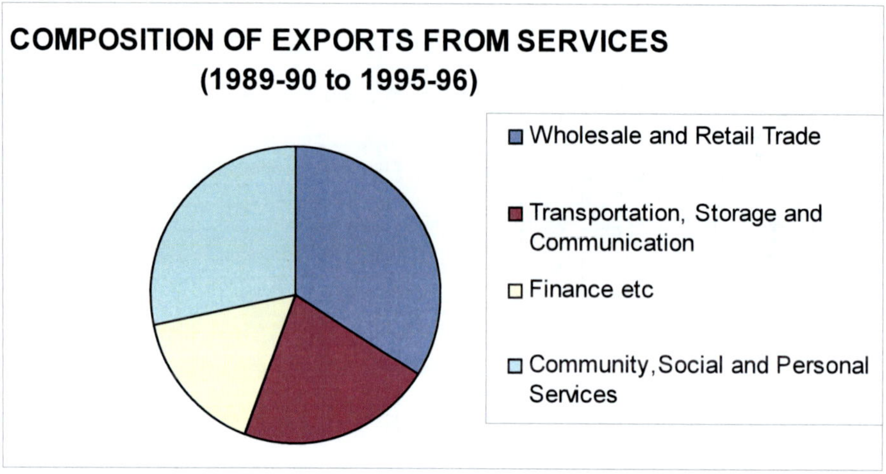

Figure 1.

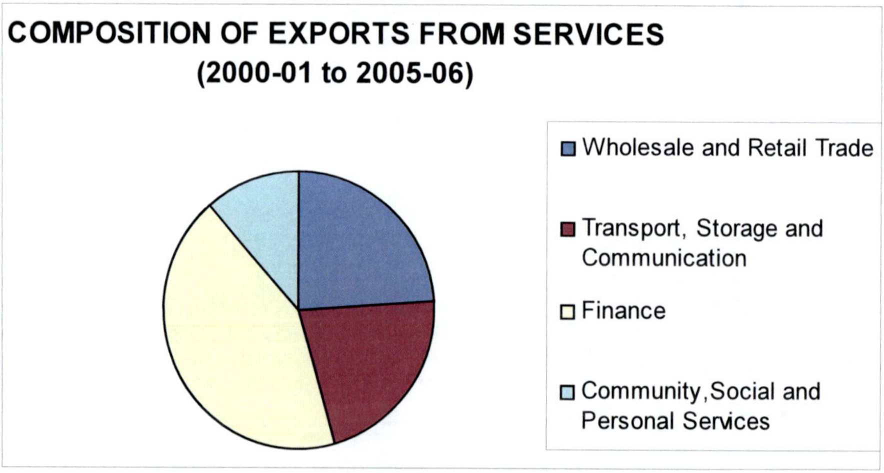

Figure 2.

Export and import growth in all the four broad groups of the service sector have been phenomenal (Table 6). However, because of the low base the growth rates turn out to be unusually high. Only community, social and personal services registered a negative growth rate in terms of exports over the period 2001-05 and imports over the period 1986-91. In terms of composition, exports from the service sector have undergone considerable changes. For example, Figures 1 and 2 suggest that the average share of finance and business services in total exports from the service sector has increased substantially over the years, while that of wholesale and retail trade and community, social and personal services has declined perceptibly. On the other hand, in terms of imports, the share of transport, storage and communication has declined over time while that of wholesale and retail trade and community, social and personal services has increased somewhat (Figures 3 and 4).

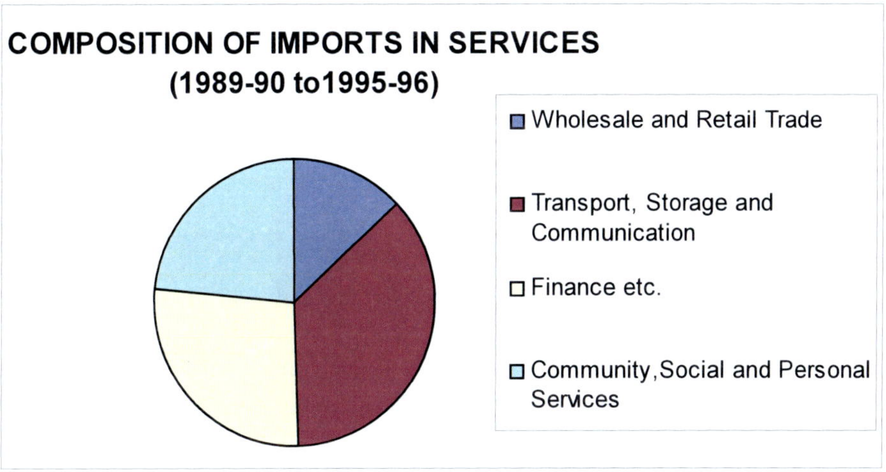

Figure 3.

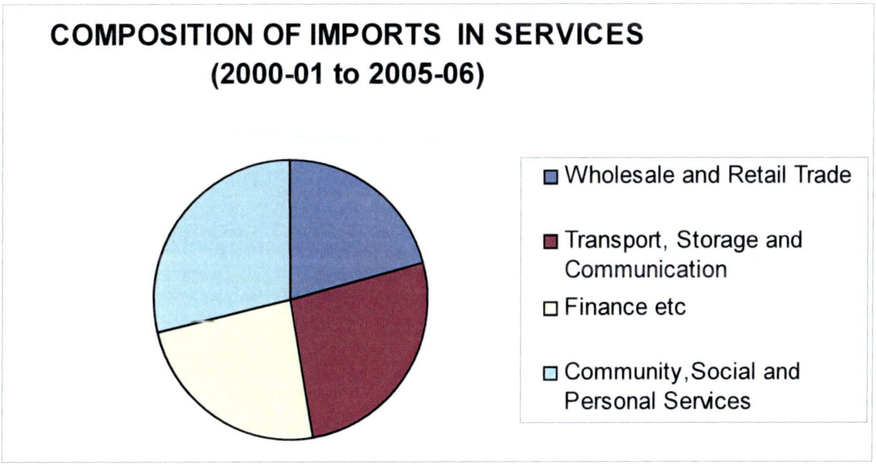

Figure 4.

The share of informal sector in total non-agricultural employment has been extremely high in both rural and urban areas. Across states considerable variations exist but the relative size in most of the cases is on the high side. At the all-India level, the informal sector constituted around 78 per cent of the work force in 1999-00 (in the rural and urban areas combined), which then increased to 84.5 per cent in 2004-05 (Tables 7 and 8).

Following the methodology explained above the exponential growth rate in employment in the informal sector and the formal sector has been calculated over the period 1999-00 to 2004-05 (Table 9). Much of the growth in total employment seems to have taken place due to employment growth in the informal sector. The formal sector employment growth in most of the non-agricultural activities has been negative during this period. At the all-India level only finance and business services experienced a positive employment growth in the formal segment (Table 10). Some of the service sector activities like trade, hotel etc., transport, storage and communication and community social and personal services which experienced a rapid value added growth do not however, reveal a positive employment growth in the formal component of these groups. In other words, the rise in value added in these activities seems to have come across through a rise in capital intensity in the formal segment. These findings tend to go against the common belief that the service sector is highly employment intensive. At least with regard to the formal segment of the service sector it is difficult to subscribe to such a view.

Table 7. Relative Size of the Informal Sector: 1999-2000 (%)

State	Inf. Mfg	Inf. Cons.	Inf. Trade, Hotel	Inf. Transport	Inf. Finance	Inf. Ser.	Inf. Agg.
Andhra Pradesh	73.41	76.52	91.89	67.90	58.76	47.87	71.15
Arunachal Pradesh	6.34	20.45	49.86	42.07	7.42	1.41	12.89
Assam	82.26	62.96	86.42	65.85	46.22	34.46	58.51
Bihar & Jharkhand	74.93	49.02	78.29	59.53	63.10	36.04	62.57
Goa	30.48	68.71	80.08	64.13	26.81	14.63	55.82
Gujarat	73.45	69.86	91.07	67.46	56.02	25.53	67.38
Haryana	63.84	71.93	82.48	66.13	39.93	25.30	62.83
Himachal Pradesh	66.93	59.79	85.41	70.25	34.21	11.50	52.13

Table 7. Continued

State	Inf. Mfg	Inf. Cons.	Inf. Trade, Hotel	Inf. Transport	Inf. Finance	Inf. Ser.	Inf. Agg.
Jammu and Kashmir	92.17	80.41	87.92	60.30	58.34	9.47	59.41
Karnataka	76.30	71.57	86.96	66.88	46.54	27.55	67.23
Kerala	82.60	85.08	79.72	76.05	54.03	34.63	72.38
Madhya Pradesh & Chattisgarh	71.00	53.78	90.28	66.25	54.88	26.91	62.94
Maharashtra	67.46	63.76	88.91	57.85	48.64	25.83	61.87
Manipur	90.60	91.81	87.79	79.80	34.55	12.39	54.47
Meghalaya	74.94	67.67	83.04	69.63	14.40	5.60	42.00
Mizoram	96.20	71.80	92.71	87.69	40.73	5.30	44.35
Nagaland	75.95	51.45	85.24	65.51	47.64	4.36	23.93
Orissa	83.88	60.31	89.35	57.20	47.95	33.83	68.92
Punjab	75.79	78.03	85.60	76.50	50.21	33.47	69.78
Rajasthan	85.76	76.93	93.93	73.27	54.39	28.06	72.54
Sikkim	76.50	66.59	96.63	79.74	39.68	4.66	41.24
Tamil Nadu	81.47	69.75	91.09	63.66	49.69	32.08	71.60
Tripura	76.65	57.00	72.96	79.35	37.00	28.61	47.57
Uttar Pradesh & Uttaranchal	82.88	74.15	91.73	75.67	59.04	44.79	75.51
West Bengal	84.22	73.16	90.83	74.13	53.86	36.77	74.95
Andaman	68.70	49.21	77.68	40.20	67.35	13.90	45.75
Chandigarh	62.03	77.92	89.13	80.89	60.44	17.89	57.21
Dadra	65.31	30.00	101.80	94.59	132.37	29.83	66.33
Daman	44.75	84.40	98.46	68.50	45.66	44.45	62.22
Delhi	80.21	66.54	89.55	68.95	51.53	15.18	62.81
Lakshadweep	23.53	35.49	10.89	24.29	0.00	0.33	12.64
Pondicherry	68.43	69.55	91.87	83.99	67.99	26.21	68.55
All-India	77.91	69.70	88.78	67.37	53.45	33.07	68.46

Note: Aggregate is the combination of all the non agricultural activities shown in the table.

Source: Informal Sector in India, 1999-2000, Report No. 459(55/2.0/2), National Sample Survey Organisation, Ministry of Statistics and Programme Implementation, May 2001.

Table 8. Relative Size of the Informal Sector: 2004-05 (%)

State	Inf. Mfg	Inf. Cons.	Inf. Trade, Hotel	Inf. Transport	Inf. Finance	Inf. Ser.	Inf. Agg.
Andhra Pradesh	87.66	92.59	95.56	80.18	68.39	79.66	87.13
Arunachal Pradesh	43.78	4.61	47.78	64.44	18.20	29.48	30.49
Assam	84.63	72.98	88.58	74.26	55.91	53.61	73.05
Bihar	93.67	76.98	89.85	78.41	83.55	77.87	85.95
Chattisgarh	80.16	78.96	92.91	69.51	95.39	59.50	78.08
Delhi	80.68	70.55	93.71	65.82	43.83	45.96	70.96
Goa	47.53	92.73	89.09	72.04	97.43	43.73	70.88
Gujarat	73.46	90.07	96.13	84.09	75.14	68.84	80.73
Haryana	65.54	61.35	92.12	84.41	76.65	65.77	73.73
Himachal Pradesh	59.41	45.59	92.28	56.22	76.54	55.18	60.01
Jammu and Kashmir	88.94	59.36	89.27	85.82	79.87	51.42	74.02
Jharkhand	70.18	69.96	88.43	68.29	75.59	68.83	73.88
Karnataka	87.22	85.98	95.98	83.36	52.37	68.39	83.76
Kerala	87.16	88.75	95.54	82.00	82.11	53.21	82.00
Madhya Pradesh	67.84	75.11	89.32	73.51	81.77	66.24	75.15
Maharashtra	77.14	80.16	94.51	70.24	72.29	66.10	78.49
Manipur	81.35	67.81	82.36	76.38	22.83	37.95	64.77
Meghalaya	81.35	83.12	83.08	65.77	100.00	14.31	50.56
Mizoram	87.13	56.26	80.71	77.97	63.38	34.66	55.38
Nagaland	84.28	39.99	75.70	44.23	19.98	30.94	51.99
Orissa	90.26	71.34	94.10	74.93	72.60	71.23	82.99
Punjab	88.39	86.60	95.00	78.07	93.48	56.01	82.81
Rajasthan	94.80	84.02	94.39	87.43	86.55	60.12	85.02
Sikkim	86.86	61.77	74.19	81.20	0.00	17.67	51.20
Tamil Nadu	89.40	91.11	96.88	72.32	58.42	69.94	84.92
Tripura	84.06	65.48	75.69	70.16	83.41	26.90	51.82
Uttaranchal	73.65	86.76	90.04	81.16	80.94	49.66	74.78
Uttar Pradesh	88.71	84.00	93.84	77.36	83.54	76.26	86.29
West Bengal	89.22	88.35	92.98	78.00	74.77	67.92	84.19
Andaman	74.44	62.11	86.41	69.31	53.70	12.07	51.61
Chandi	77.92	85.83	88.55	53.60	97.50	59.44	72.67

Table 8. Continued

State	Inf. Mfg	Inf. Cons.	Inf. Trade, Hotel	Inf. Transport	Inf. Finance	Inf. Ser.	Inf. Agg.
Dadra	63.98	87.84	86.93	10.00	100.00	50.54	64.22
Daman	18.33	17.35	58.90	93.73	90.83	70.31	50.32
Lakshadweep	83.36	73.39	53.81	37.73	55.20	42.09	59.52
Pondicherry	66.87	96.86	91.65	86.59	83.45	50.22	76.77
All-India	84.54	81.95	94.44	77.38	69.16	67.12	82.05

Note: Aggregate is the combination of all the non-agricultural activities shown in the Table.

Source: Informal Sector and Conditions of Employment in India, 2004-05, Report No. 519(61/10/7), National Sample Survey Organisation, Ministry of Statistics and Programme Implementation, April 2007.

Table 9. Growth Rate in Employment in the Informal Sector: 1999-2000 to 2004-05 (% p.a.)

State	Inf. Mfg	Inf. Cons.	Inf. Trade, Hotel	Inf. Transport	Inf. Finance	Inf. Ser.	Inf. Agg.
Andhra Pradesh	10.96	7.99	6.43	11.98	11.53	11.50	9.38
Arunachal Pradesh	26.71	-25.86	7.93	42.33	41.99	71.91	25.88
Assam	1.90	11.84	5.09	7.44	-7.22	3.22	4.72
Bihar & Jharkhand	4.61	24.45	10.60	14.25	14.94	13.18	11.12
Goa	9.07	2.72	4.74	3.21	27.13	33.59	7.31
Gujarat	9.88	7.19	3.99	7.36	10.76	21.01	8.60
Haryana	10.81	6.82	5.13	13.00	26.96	25.15	10.49
Himachal Pradesh	6.59	0.72	10.48	5.34	16.24	33.35	9.07
Jammu and Kashmir	20.31	-1.85	4.61	23.32	6.29	35.87	12.36
Karnataka	6.14	9.05	5.73	11.28	8.54	22.52	8.76
Kerala	2.29	4.43	2.57	5.54	15.37	13.92	4.86
Madhya Pradesh & Chattisgarh	5.04	17.86	5.53	4.49	20.70	22.62	9.73
Maharashtra	8.35	11.89	4.97	6.77	18.08	23.12	9.78

Table 9. Continued

State	Inf. Mfg	Inf. Cons.	Inf. Trade, Hotel	Inf. Transport	Inf. Finance	Inf. Ser.	Inf. Agg.
Manipur	6.77	13.56	8.38	9.58	-3.92	24.31	10.58
Meghalaya	32.29	7.66	5.91	4.81	39.67	25.76	11.96
Mizoram	6.37	-11.25	0.53	3.98	5.57	40.34	6.84
Nagaland	24.07	9.50	22.70	8.47	-8.91	36.78	23.14
Orissa	7.95	14.59	9.01	16.93	23.64	19.37	11.44
Punjab	10.20	12.35	4.59	2.06	23.39	14.39	8.66
Rajasthan	9.46	7.78	5.70	7.45	16.45	19.81	9.04
Sikkim	10.24	18.61	4.07	13.11		26.66	10.81
Tamil Nadu	5.73	11.06	3.63	4.81	16.33	18.55	7.25
Tripura	11.20	12.59	2.87	6.75	12.61	-0.95	4.89
Uttar Pradesh & Uttaranchal	7.13	14.64	4.65	6.27	15.64	10.81	7.88
West Bengal	2.72	13.11	4.07	4.66	17.36	17.00	6.11
Andaman	-1.40	12.76	11.70	18.87	10.86	9.46	11.23
Chandigarh	8.62	-2.22	-5.43	9.07	22.56	31.56	9.08
Dadra	8.72	24.24	23.73	-47.22	39.37	29.22	10.75
Daman	-23.57	-10.05	-10.42	17.03	37.56	10.08	-3.84
Delhi	4.61	7.74	3.97	6.88	10.93	23.71	6.77
Lakshadweep	38.92	40.06	3.44	16.57		97.71	35.95
Pondicherry	-2.30	9.07	-0.68	15.97	9.32	16.23	3.73
All-India	6.82	11.39	5.27	7.79	17.00	16.54	8.54

See Tables 7 and 8.

Table 10. Growth Rate in Employment in the Formal Sector: 1999-00 to 2004-05 (% p.a.)

State	FMfg	FCons.	FTrade, Hotel	FTransport	FFinance	FSer.	FAgg.
Andhra Pradesh	-7.95	-18.89	-6.41	-0.98	3.17	-17.50	-10.81
Arunachal Pradesh	-22.15	7.56	9.59	24.04	21.57	4.47	4.15
Assam	-1.52	2.58	1.14	-0.62	-15.00	-12.53	-8.35
Bihar & Jharkhand	-7.50	3.93	-6.56	0.07	-2.13	-20.20	-8.28
Goa	-5.45	-32.48	-9.44	-4.10	-65.69	3.35	-5.81

Table 10. Continued

State	FMfg	FCons.	FTrade, Hotel	FTransport	FFinance	FSer.	FAgg.
Gujarat	9.88	-20.10	-13.78	-11.36	-6.52	-16.25	-5.55
Haryana	9.32	16.39	-13.08	-7.40	-4.98	-9.56	0.35
Himachal Pradesh	13.07	12.19	-3.80	17.53	-20.49	-11.63	2.66
Jammu and Kashmir	27.92	18.82	1.95	-4.33	-14.54	-10.42	-0.96
Karnataka	-8.88	-8.75	-19.76	-6.90	3.88	-12.25	-9.67
Kerala	-4.87	-2.07	-31.36	-1.67	-11.89	-1.36	-6.20
Madhya Pradesh & Chattisgarh	5.74	-2.35	5.87	-1.30	-8.88	-9.50	-2.53
Maharashtra	-1.40	-4.74	-10.30	-4.07	-2.20	-11.33	-6.42
Manipur	22.61	47.00	17.03	13.58	7.66	-4.97	1.99
Meghalaya	24.74	-9.45	5.85	8.35		5.05	5.06
Mizoram	32.73	2.41	22.77	17.97	-12.90	-4.62	-2.02
Nagaland	13.48	18.77	35.05	25.94	16.95	-8.93	-1.58
Orissa	-3.61	4.72	-3.83	0.83	2.51	-12.17	-4.32
Punjab	-7.57	0.38	-18.64	0.28	-29.68	-4.18	-6.05
Rajasthan	-12.69	-1.33	4.02	-11.17	-17.26	-7.23	-6.25
Sikkim	-3.94	22.81	50.05	11.24	3.36	-2.94	2.77
Tamil Nadu	-7.29	-18.76	-18.56	-3.18	9.28	-13.35	-8.82
Tripura	1.73	5.42	0.00	16.58	-30.32	0.76	1.48
Uttar Pradesh & Uttaranchal	-1.84	2.27	-1.03	4.17	-9.33	-14.22	-5.41
West Bengal	-6.06	-7.35	-1.73	0.40	-1.27	-8.84	-5.42
Andaman	-7.05	2.25	-0.35	-5.37	22.37	12.71	6.53
Chandigarh	-6.79	-13.02	-4.26	35.04	-42.22	-6.55	-4.67
Dadra	9.88	-32.24		53.94	!	11.68	12.62
Daman	2.10	54.93	65.57	-21.52	-11.78	-11.63	5.89
Delhi	4.01	4.02	-7.08	9.73	17.11	-7.47	-0.62
Lakshadweep	-16.88	7.82	-41.65	3.85	-2.17	-10.35	-10.41
Pondicherry	-0.87	-42.97	-0.11	11.82	-7.97	-4.65	-4.60
All-India	-1.94	-2.21	-10.01	-2.30	3.61	-11.83	-6.35

See Tables 7 and 8.

4. Econometric Analysis

For estimating the elasticity of organized service sector employment with respect to export and import we have controlled for value added, that is, a proxy for growth. Log transformation of the organized service sector employment - each of the groups separately - has been regressed on the log transformation of value added from the corresponding group and the export and import figures derived for the corresponding group. Autoregressive distributed lag model (ARDL) has been applied and the Swartz Bayesian criterion has been followed to determine the appropriate lag length of the dependent variable. In most of the cases a one year lag is found to be suitable.

Then the long-run elasticity coefficients have been derived from the ARDL model[1]. However, to facilitate a simple interpretation of the results we have reported in the text the OLS estimates of the parameters obtained from the equation with no lag of the dependent variable (Table 11).

The time series estimates are not indicative of an invariably strong positive impact of exports and imports on the employment in the organized service sector, after controlling for value added. In the case of organized sector employment in wholesale, retail trade and hotels, etc. exports and value added both show a positive and significant effect while the impact of import is statistically insignificant. In the case of transport, storage and communication the value added turns out to be insignificant. On the other hand, while imports show a positive impact, exports exert a negative influence on the organized sector employment in this activity.

---

[1] Estimated Long-Run Coefficients Using the ARDL Approach (1977 to 2005): ARDL (1,0,0,0)

Explanatory Variables	Dep. Var: ln(Employment in Organised Wholesale, Retail Trade, Hotel etc.	Dep. Var: ln(Employment in Organised Transport, Storage and Communication	Dep. Var: ln(Employment in Organised Finance, Business Services etc.	Dep. Var: ln(Employment in Organised Community, Social and Personal Services
Ln(Exports)	0.09 (2.89)*	0.55 (0.30)	0.06 (0.29)	-0.03 (-0.82)
Ln(Imports)	002 (0.64)	0.61 (0.43)	-0.10 (-0.83)	
ln(Value Added)	0.07 (1.05)	-3.08 (-0.35)	0.27 (0.42)	0.63 (3.69)*
Constant	-2.64 (-4.62)*	26.27 (0.36)	-2.30 (-0.38)	-4.91 (-2.42)*

Note: Figures in parentheses are t-ratios. * represents significance at 5 per cent level.

Table 11. Regression Results based on Time Series Data (OLS Estimates)

Explanatory Variables	Dep. Var: ln(Employment in Organised Wholesale, Retail Trade, Hotel, etc.)	Dep. Var: ln(Employment in Organised Transport, Storage and Communication	Dep. Var: ln(Employment in Organised Finance, Business Services etc.)	Dep. Var: ln(Employment in Organised Community, Social and Personal Services)
Ln(Exports)	0.066 (3.21)*	-0.12 (-2.92)*	-0.17 (-4.63)*	-0.03 (-1.42)
Ln(Imports)	-0.0008 (-0.05)	0.14 (5.84)*	-0.07 (-2.25)*	-0.0007 (-0.02)
Ln(Value Added)	0.14 (3.32)*	0.03 (0.48)	0.99 (7.44)*	0.27 (4.38)*
Constant	-3.07 (-8.61)*	0.55 (1.63)	-9.36 (-8.30)*	-0.54 (-1.00)
No. of Observations	31	31	31	29
Adj. R^2	0.96	0.73	0.94	0.81

Note: Figures in parentheses are t-ratios.* represents significance at 5 per cent level.

Organised sector employment in finance and business services is not impacted positively either by exports or imports though value added unravels a positive effect. Both exports and imports take a negative sign in this case. Organised sector employment in community, social and personal services is not statistically responsive to exports and imports, while value added shows a positive effect. On the whole, exports and imports are not seen to impact organized service sector employment in a positive and significant way.

One may argue that the growth effect measured in terms of value added originating from a particular sector is not independent of export and import effects. Hence, there is a need to net out the export and import effects from growth so that the residue can be attributed to pure growth effect. Also these export and import effects included in the growth effect can be added to the export and import effects obtained after controlling for growth effect in the equations given in Table 11. The adjusted estimates of export and import effects will then represent the total (direct plus indirect) effects of export and import on employment. In order to separate out the export and import effects from the value added growth of a particular sector we have estimated first the following function. The log of value added originating from a particular activity i (ln VA(i)) has been regressed on the log of the total non-agricultural value added in the economy (ln

NAGVA) taken as a proxy for overall growth and the log of exports (ln E(i)) and imports (ln I(i)) corresponding to that activity: ln VA(i) = F(ln NAGVA, ln E(i), ln I(i))[2]. After getting the estimates of the parameters in this equation they are then substituted in the corresponding equations given in Table 11. The results reported in Table 12 represent the elasticity of employment in a particular activity i with respect to total non-agricultural GDP in the economy, and exports and imports corresponding to the ith activity. The effect of exports on employment is positive only in trade and hotel activity. However, the magnitude is nominal. In all other three activities export has a negative effect. On the other hand, though imports have positive effect on employment in all the three activities except finance and business services the magnitude is again seen to be nominal.

Table 12. Adjusted Elasticity of Organised Service Sector Employment

Elasticity with respect to	Elasticity of organized employment in various activities			
	Wholesale, Retail Trade, Hotel, etc.	**Transport, Storage and Communication**	**Finance, Business Services, etc.**	**Community, Social and Personal Services**
Exports	0.0688	-0.1097	-0.259	-0.034
Imports	0.00297	0.08	-0.0007	0.0039
Non-Ag Value Added	0.1218	0.649	1.168	0.2268

---

[2] Regression Results of Value added of a particular activity on total non-agricultural value added, and exports and imports corresponding to that activity.

Explanatory Variables	Dep. Var: ln(Value Added in Wholesale, Retail Trade, Hotel, etc.)	Dep. Var: ln(Value Added in Transport, Storage and Communication)	Dep. Var: ln(Value Added in Finance, Business Services etc.)	Dep. Var: ln(Value Added in Community, Social and Personal Services)
Ln(Exports)	0.025 (0.62)	0.019 (0.35)	-0.093 (-2.93)*	-0.15 (-1.08)
Ln(Imports)	0.027 (0.86)	-0.107 (-2.84)*	0.07 (4.26)*	0.017 (0.94)
Ln(Non-Ag Value Added)	0.0878 (11.26)*	1.18 (11.44)*	1.19 (10.69)*	0.84 (23.88)*
Constant	0.076 (0.010)	-3.34 (-4.38)	-3.50 (-3.13)	0.045 (1.32)
No. of Observations	32	31	32	30
Adj. R^2	0.99	0.99	0.99	0.99

Table 13. Elasticity of Informal Service Sector to Formal Service Sector Employment

	Dep. Var: ln(Employment in Informal Wholesale, Retail Trade, Hotel, etc.)	Dep. Var: ln(Employment in Informal Transport, Storage and Communication)	Dep. Var: ln(Employment in Informal Finance, Business Services, etc.)	Dep. Var: ln(Employment in Informal Community, Social and Personal Services)
ln(Employment in Formal Wholesale, Retail Trade, Hotel etc.)	1.13 (18.31)*			
ln(Employment in Formal Transport, Storage and Communication)		1.00 (22.56)*		
ln(Employment in Formal Finance, Business Services, etc.)			0.98 (15.21)*	
ln(Employment in Formal Community, Social and Personal Services)				1.24 (14.30)*
Constant	0.64 (0.98)	0.90 (1.92)	0.57 (0.90)	-3.61 (-3.39)*
No. of Observations	63	64	59	64
Adj. R2	0.84	0.89	0.80	0.76

Note: Figures in parentheses are t-ratios.* represents significance at 5 per cent level. Estimates are obtained based on the pooled cross-sectional data for 1999-2000 and 2004-05.

The elasticity of informal service sector employment – for each group separately - has been calculated with respect to the corresponding formal sector employment. These estimates are obtained from the cross-sectional data as time series information are not available. The rationale underlying this specification is as follows: There exist certain inter-linkages between the formal and the informal sectors. These can be conceived in terms of backward and forward linkages. As Papola (1981) pointed out, the informal sector grows in situations of both sluggish industrialization and rapid industrialization. When there is sluggish industrial growth a residual absorption of labour takes place within the informal sector. On the other hand, rapid industrialization opens up opportunities for the growth of ancillary activities, outsourcing and sub-contracting, etc. which are basically conducted within the informal sector. However, the former demonstrates a situation of supply-push phenomenon which reduces earnings in the informal sector while the latter throws up opportunities for demand induced activities to grow and result in increased earnings.

The relationship between the informal and formal sector employment is seen to be positive. For each of the four groups, the elasticity turns out to be almost unity (Table 13). In order to test the stability of the relationship between the informal and the formal sector we have estimated these equations from 1999-2000 as well as 2004-05 data (see Table in the Appendix) The results are more or less same. Table 14 gives estimates based on the pooled data for both the years.

Table 14. Effect of Export and Import on Informal Service Sector Employment

	Employment in Informal Wholesale, Retail Trade, Hotel etc.	Employment in Informal Transport, Storage and Communication	Employment in Informal Finance, Business Services etc.	Employment in Informal Community, Social and Personal Services
Exports	0.07	-0.12	-0.16	-0.04
Imports	-0.00089	0.14	-0.07	-0.0007

Based on these estimates the elasticity of informal sector employment with respect to exports and imports are shown below. One of the crucial assumptions in this exercise is that international trade (exports and imports) does not have any direct effect on the informal sector. The link is perceived through the formal sector. Thus the impact of export and import on the informal service sector employment is almost equal to the impact on the organized service sector employment (Table 14). The time series estimates did not show an invariably strong positive impact of exports and imports on the employment in the organized service sector. Similar conclusions can be drawn relating to the informal sector as well. Therefore we may conclude that exports and imports are not seen to impact the service sector employment – whether formal or informal - in a positive and significant way.

5. Analysis Based on Company Level Data

From the company level data (Capital Line) we have calculated the growth rate of employment in the service sector units for the recent years. It may be noted from Table 15 that a number of firms experienced rapid growth in employment during 2006-08. Similarly, between 2005 and 2007 several firms in the services sector registered a fast growth in employment (Table 15a). Though there are firms which experienced a decline in absolute terms, their number is quite limited. On the other hand, the magnitudes of the positive growth rates in several firms have been in double digit.

Table 15.a. Growth Rates of Employment in Different Companies in the Service Sector (% per annum)

Magnitudes and Sign	Period	Growth Rates
Negative	2006-08	-40.19, -26.53, -14.28, -5.43, -5.18, 5.01, -4.35, -4.28, -2.44, -2.22, -1.99, -1.92, -1.77, -1.77, -1.67
Positive but Low	2006-08	0.82, 2.41, 2.94, 3.66, 4.42, 4.84
Moderate and Positive	2006-08	6.21, 6.57, 6.72, 6.76, 7.90, 7.92
High and Positive	2006-08	11.73, 11.82, 11.98, 12.07, 12.12, 12.86, 12.98, 13.89, 14.45, 15.40, 17.07, 18.39, 18.61, 18.66, 20.52, 21.24, 21.34, 21.68, 21.95, 22.07, 22.34, 23.67, 24.91, 26.26, 26.66, 27.52, 29.79, 32.53, 34.71, 34.95, 35.06, 36.62, 37.20, 37.37, 40.35, 42.40, 42.90, 43.14, 45.81, 46.67, 53.85, 54.37, 58.90, 60.05, 61.1
One Negative, Another Positive	2007-08	-51.68, 24.0
Negative	2005-07	-15.11, -12.67, -5.38, -3.14, -1.80, -1.60, -1.56
Low/Moderate and Positive	2005-07	2.38, 5.68, 8.55, 9.27
High and Positive	2005-07	11.81, 12.92, 18.13, 20.42, 25.90, 26.11, 27.81, 30.79, 31.08, 44.84, 53.83
Negative, 0 & Positive	2006-07	-18.2, 0.00, 37.5
Negative	2004-06	-69.6, -22.6, -6.58, -2.67
Low/Moderate and Positive	2004-06	2.33, 7.66
High and Positive	2004-06	28.94, 31.21, 31.67, 45.81
High and Positive	2005-06	17.43, 26.86

Source: Capital Line Data.

Based on the data on employment for 256 firms in the service sector the growth rate turns out to be 7.1 per cent in 2003-04, 11.7 per cent in 2004-05, 18.9 per cent in 2005-06, 11.5 per cent in 2006-07 and 8.2 per cent in 2007-08. On the other hand, based on the wage bill reported by 510 firms in the service sector the employment figures have been generated by dividing the wage bill by the average wage rate. Employment growth in the service sector according to these estimates has been 7.7 per cent in 2002-03, 7.60 per cent in 2003-04, 15.80 per cent in 2004-05, 13.20 per cent in 2005-06, 15.30 per cent in 2006-07 and 11.60 per cent in 2007-08. However, based on the corporate sector data (Corporate Sector, CMIE, 2008) we have tried to calculate the employment growth rate for around 3000 firms in the service sector and these growth rates reported in Table 15(b) are not indicative of any substantive increase in employment opportunity in the service sector. For 2002-03 and 2005-06, the growth rates turn out to be negative and for 2003-04 it has been perceptibly low. The only exceptions are 2004-05 and 2006-07 corresponding to which the growth rates have been 6.9 per cent and 7.7 per cent, respectively. From the NSS 62nd round (2005-06) results it is again calculated that the total service sector growth has been only 1.58 per cent over 2004-05.

Table 15.(b). Estimated Employment Growth Rate (% p.a.)

	Growth rate based on data for firms that have reported employment	Growth rate based on data for firms that have reported wage-bill	Growth rate based on data for all corporate sector firms in services as reported in CMIE publication
2000-01			
2001-02			
2002-03		7.7%	-1.3%
2003-04	7.1%	7.6%	1.1%
2004-05	11.7%	15.8%	6.9%
2005-06	18.9%	13.2%	-1.7%
2006-07	11.5%	15.3%	7.7%
2007-08	8.2%	11.6%	
	Data for 256 firms used (Capital Line Data)	Data for 510 firms used(Capital Line Data)	data for about 3000 firms (CMIE, Data)

On the whole, we cannot therefore conclude equivocally that employment growth in the services sector has been rapid in the recent past when the output growth has accelerated significantly. So, economic growth does not seem to be generating employment in a significant way. In some of the service sector firms employment, however, seems to have shot up in last two two/three years. Production in terms of sales also accelerated in these firms. However, what needs to be assessed is the effect of trade liberalization on employment growth at the company level. More specifically we pose the question did exports raise the employable capacity of the firms. Similarly, what impact did import of capital goods and raw materials have on employment in the service sector firms is another important question.

Based on the company-level data the following equations have been estimated:

1. LnEMP = f(lnRSALES, lnRDCAP, lnRDRAWMAT, lnRIMCAP, lnRIMRAWMAT, lnREXP)

2. EMP/RESALES= g(DCAP/SALES, DRAWMAT/SALES, IMCAP/SALES, IMRAWMAT/SALES, EXP/SALES)

In the first equation, the log transformation of employees is regressed on the log transformation of the following variables: RSALES is real sales or operating income (in 1999-2000 prices) of the company derived from the nominal figures on sales/operating income deflated by the implicit price deflator. RDCAP is the real domestic capital defined as gross block minus imported capital expenditure, deflated by the same implicit price deflator. RDRAWMAT is the real domestic raw materials derived by deducting from the total raw materials the imported raw materials and deflating the series by the implicit price deflator. RIMCAP, RIMRAWMAT and REXP represent the real imported capital, imported raw material and exports. In the second equation, EMP/RESALES is the ratio of employees to real sales, DCAP/SALES is the proportion of domestic capital to sales, DRAWMAT/SALES is the domestic raw materials to sales, IMCAP/SALES is the imported capital to sales, IMRAWMAT/SALES is the imported raw materials to sales and EXP/SALES is the export to sales.

The equations have been estimated by OLS because not too many observations per firm are available over time (Table 16). For equation 1 in which the variables are considered mostly in log form the number of observations is only 100. Entries which have zero values cannot be included in the log form. However, in equation 2 the number of observations is 374. The results from the first equation indicate that the elasticity of employees with respect to sales is extremely high and positive. Exports and imported capital and imported raw materials do not have a positive and significant impact on employment. On the other hand, domestic capital has a complementary relationship with employment though domestic raw materials are indicative of a negative effect on employment. From the second equation again the positive effect of domestic capital and the negative effect of domestic raw materials on employment to sales ratio are evident. The ratio of imported capital or imported raw materials or exports to sales does not impact employment to real sales positively. All these findings are indicative of the absence of any positive effect of trade liberalization on employment in the service sector. We may further recall that these findings are quite consistent with the findings based on macro data.

Table 16. Regression Results Based on the Company-Level Data

Exp. Var	Equ. 1 (Dep. Var. lnEMP)	Exp Var.	Dep. Var. EMP/RESALES
lnRSALES	0.87 (12.67)*	DCAP/SALES	0.007 (1.96)*
lnRDCAP	0.55 (9.76)*	DRAWMAT/SALES	-0.04 (-3.45)*
lnRDRAWMAT	-0.34 (-8.85)*	IMCAP/SALES	-0.07 (-1.66)
lnRIMCAP	-0.03 (-0.96)	IMRAWMAT/SALES	0.03 (0.88)
lnRIMRAWMAT	0.06 (1.64)	EXP/SALES	-0.03 (-2.11)*
lnREXP	-0.107 (-4.15)*		
Constant	1.44 (6.37)*	Constant	8.71 (15.45)*
Adj. R2	0.93		0.07
	100		374

Note: Figures in parentheses are t-ratios.* represents significance at the 5 per cent level.

6. Summing-up

This study has made an attempt to assess the impact of trade liberalization on service sector employment. The service sector value added in the Indian context has been growing quite rapidly for the last several years. Hence, several researchers are of the view that the service sector could play the role of an engine of growth. In the backdrop of this view we therefore made an attempt to assess whether the service sector created employment opportunities on a large scale and if the service sector value added growth can be treated pro-poor. More importantly, the effect of trade liberalization on employment potential is judged from the past data because trade is indeed considered to be the engine of growth. Given the limitations of the data, these propositions, however, had to be examined quite carefully.

Based on the time series macro data, the elasticity of organised service sector employment with respect to value added and exports and imports have been estimated. These exercises have been pursued separately for four broad groups of services: trade and hotels, etc, finance and business services, transport, storage and communication and community, social and personal services. After controlling for growth it is difficult to identify a positive and significant impact of international trade on employment in the organized service sector. In other words, international trade does not seem to be contributing to employment growth in the organized service sector. We have also tried to work out the direct and indirect effects of exports and imports on employment after deciphering their effects included in overall growth. However, the positive effects are mostly negligible.

Since there is no time series information on the informal service sector employment NSS surveys on the informal sector employment for the years 1999-00 and 2004-05 were considered and the cross-sectional information were used to examine the relationship between the formal and informal sectors. Splitting the employment into formal and informal sectors across activities, the informal sector employment growth rate turned out to be positive whereas the formal sector employment growth rate was negative across several activities. Within the service sector only the formal component of finance and business services grew positively while the other three categories registered negative employment growth rates. The elasticity of informal to formal sector employment has been calculated and based on these estimates the impact of international trade on the informal services sector employment has been worked out. The impact does not seem to be greatly different from what was observed in the case of the organized service sector employment.

Since more recent data on employment were not available from the NSSO we had to use the company-level data in order to understand employment growth and its relationship with economic growth which has indeed shot up in the recent past. Though Capital Line data are indicative of a high employment growth in the service sector during the period 2005 to 2008, CMI data for around 3000 firms in the service sector do not unravel such a pattern. It would be, therefore, misleading to conclude that in the recent past the acceleration in economic growth is able to translate itself into employment growth as well.

Since some of the firms in the service sector as per the Capital Line data recorded an employment growth in double digit, suggesting possibility of close links between growth and employment, we have tried to assess the effect of international trade on employment in these units. However, as per the findings, international trade does not seem to be an important determinant of employment, implying that trade liberalization per se did not reveal any significant contribution to employment growth. However, in terms of policy issues this seems to have important implications. The question is how to make the service sector more responsive to international trade. Trade with developing countries will possibly hold brighter prospects of growth in employment intensive service activities. Second, several services in which India has a comparative advantage over other countries have to receive supportive measures for their expansion so that foreign demand and domestic demand do not conflict. For example, the health sector can be developed extensively to tap the demand potential for such services from several developing as well as developed countries. The price differences with respect to the developed countries can attract a great deal of foreign demand for health services in India. However, supplies often are too scarce even to meet the domestic demand. Similarly, in the education sector India has a great potentiality to attract foreign demand, particularly, from South and East Asia given her comparative advantages in terms of price differentials and medium of instruction.

More reforms relating to the financial institutions can invite foreign savings and this may result in employment growth as management of such savings will be employment intensive. Investment of such resources in productive activities will indeed open up new employment opportunities. The backward areas in India require massive infrastructural investment in order to get integrated with the rest of the world. Activities like business services which have been India's comparative advantage can expand further to create employment opportunities on a large scale. Instead of concentrating in a few million plus cities, foreign investment then can penetrate to other semi-urban areas. Skill up-gradation and human capital formation in the rural areas will enable the rural youth to take advantage of these new opportunities and thus international trade in services can be made pro-growth as well as employment-intensive. The other way to draw lessons from the findings is to strengthen and enhance the domestic demand so that economic growth and employment both can shoot up even when international trade does not contribute in a big way. This may result in a more equitable distribution of income.

Appendix

Elasticity of Informal Sector to Formal Sector Employment (1999-2000)

Explanatory Variable	Dep. Var: ln(Employment in Informal Wholesale, Retail Trade, Hotel, etc.)	Dep. Var: ln(Employment in Informal Transport, Storage and Communication)	Dep. Var: ln(Employment in Informal Finance, Business Services, etc.)	Dep. Var: ln(Employment in Informal Community, Social and Personal Services)
ln(Employment in Formal Wholesale, Retail Trade, Hotel, etc.)	1.34 (18.91)*			
ln(Employment in Formal Transport, Storage and Communication)		1.06 (14.24)*		
ln(Employment in Formal Finance, Business Services etc.)			0.93 (9.98)*	
ln(Employment in Formal Community, Social and Personal Services)				1.21 (15.02)*
No. of Observations	32	32	29	32

Note: Figures in parentheses are t-ratios. * represents significance at 5 per cent level.

Elasticity of Informal Sector to Formal Sector Employment (2004-05)

	Dep. Var: ln(Employment in Informal Wholesale, Retail Trade, Hotel etc.)	Dep. Var: ln(Employment in Informal Transport, Storage and Communication)	Dep. Var: ln(Employment in Informal Finance, Business Services etc.)	Dep. Var: ln(Employment in Informal Community, Social and Personal Services)
ln(Employment in Formal Wholesale, Retail Trade, Hotel, etc.)	0.99 (11.16)*			
ln(Employment in Formal Transport, Storage and Communication)		0.95 (18.20)*		
ln(Employment in Formal Finance, Business Services, etc.)			1.10 (19.84)*	
ln(Employment in Formal Community, Social and Personal Services)				1.33 (13.43)*
No. of Observations	31	32	30	32

Note: Figures in parentheses are t-ratios. * represents significance at 5 per cent level.

References

Bhagwati, J. and T.N. Srinivasan (2002), "Trade and Poverty in the Poor Countries", *American Economic Review*, Vol.92, No.2, pp.180-183.

Dollar, D (2001), "Globalization, Inequality and Poverty since 1980", Background Paper, World Bank, Washington, DC. (http://www.worldbank.org/research/global)

Dougherty, S. (2008), Labour Regulation and Employment Dynamics at the State Level in India. OECD Economics Department Working Papers no. 624, OECD publishing.Feenstra, Robert C. and Gordon H. Hanson, (1996), "Globalisation, Outsourcing and Wage Inequality," *American Economic Review*, Vol. 86, No.2, pp-240-245.

Gemmel, N. (1986), *Structural Change and Economic Development: The Role of Service Sector*. Hampshire: Macmillan Press.

Kaldor, (1967), *Strategic Factors in Economic Development,* Ithaca: Cornell University Press.

Krueger, A.O., H.B. Lary, T. Manson, and N. Akrasanee eds. (1981), *Trade and Employment in Developing Countries: Individual Studies*, Chicago: University of Chicago Press.

Kuznets, S.(1966), *Modern Economic Growth, Rate, Structure and Spread,* New Haven: Yale University Press.

Minujin, A., J.Vandermoortele and E. Delamonica, (2002), "Economic Growth, Poverty and Children", *Environment and Urbanization"*, Vol.14, No.2, pp.23-43.

Papola, T.S. (1981), *Informal Sector in a Developing Economy*, Vikas Publishing House, Delhi.

Papola, T.S. (2007), Employment Trend in India, in Kaushik Basu (ed.), *The Oxford Companion to Economics in India*, New Delhi: Oxford University Press, pp.131-136.

Rivera-Baitz, L.A. and D. Xie, (1992), "GATT, Trade and Growth", *American Economic Review*, Vol.82, No.2, pp.422-427.

Sundaram, K. (2007), Employment and Poverty in India, 2000-2005, *Economic and Political Weekly*, July 28, pp. 3121-3131.

Sundaram, K. (2008), Employment, Wages and Poverty in the Non-Agricultural Sector: All-India, 2000-05, *Economic and Political Weekly*, May 31, pp. 91-99.

UNIDO (2005), "Productivity in Developing Countries: Trends and Policies", United Nations Industrial Development Organisation, Vienna.

United Nations Conference on Trade and Development, (2007), *Challenging Conventional Wisdom: Development Implications of Trade in Services Liberalization, Trade, Poverty and Cross-cutting Development Issues*, United Nations.

World Bank. (2004), *Sustaining India's Services Revolution: Access to Foreign Markets, Domestic Reform and International Negotiations*, South Asia Region: India.

In: Trade Liberalization and Protectionism
Editors: B. Hahn et al, pp. 131-152
ISBN: 978-1-60876-837-0

Chapter 5

WHAT TRADE POLICY FOR THE DEVELOPED COUNTRIES TODAY: CLUSTERS LIKE ALTERNATIVE TO PROTECTIONISM?

Bertrand Blancheton and Bernard Yvars
University Montesquieu-Bordeaux IV

The traumatism associated with the closing trade of the 1930s led to ask for (in a more or less conscious) protecting the free trade debate in terms of binary choice. In the West, while tightening of trade policy is to resurface the idea of a drop-sufficient and is the subject of a condemnation in principle. The terms associated with the word protectionism are often charged with a negative connotation: temptation, spectrum, poison, trap, danger....

In these debates, it was largely forgotten in reality protectionism is a gradual concept. Free trade is an extreme case, that of a zero degree of protection. At the other extreme is the autarky absolute if the authorities avoid smuggling. Historically own in recent years, protection is the rule and free trade the except. However in economic theory, the reverse is true. Debate protection versus free trade should replace questions about the determination of trade policy relevant. Good policy depends heavily on the structures of the national economy, its specialties, its forward or its relative backwardness in terms of development.

The example of Great Britain in the nineteenth century shows that free trade is a policy relevant for a dominant economy, relatively early, with good specializations. The abolition of the Corn Laws in May 1846 as part of a broad package of trade liberalization (elimination of navigation's acts in 1849, repeal of many tariffs between 1846 and 1852) is generally considered like a success[1]. But always in the nineteenth century examples of the United States, Germany, Japan show the benefit of active trade policies to protect infant industries on relatively large national markets especially in the face of British competition, country then has absolute advantages in many manufacturing.

In general, economic history suggests that good policy must be active enough to maintain internal social cohesion, a balance between the social forces that control the speed of opening up trade, fostering the emergence of specializations, but also good enough to preserve an international opening vector of a gain in terms of welfare on a global scale.

Since the Second World War, the taboo has long led protectionist national authorities not to question the definition of a trade policy capable of promoting a pragmatic national interests and not be among the losers of globalization (case of an economy which, for example, specializes in one or more productions with the terms of trade are deteriorating).

In Europe and especially in France since the late 1990s, the controversies around the relocation of industrial enterprises and the technical unification process posed the problem of competitiveness of economies country's most advanced. While the international transmission of innovation is accelerating, the delay of wage growth on the growth of productivity in emerging countries seem to confer a competitive advantage in most manufacturing sectors. The phenomenon is accentuated by the retention by the emerging economies of a real under-valuation of their exchange rates like the Chinese yuan.

In the 2000s, some activism of trade policy has been observed. In France, rather than recognize the reality of a commercial activism that may well come under the definition of a protectionist policy, it was mentioned - in the wake of Prime Minister Dominique de Villepin - the implementation of "economic patriotism". The West is subject to a new challenge: how to bring benefits in

[1] The tariff allows the UK to open foreign markets to expand. The major European powers agree indeed steps to relax their policy like France, which since the early 1850s lowered the average level of tariffs. As expected, the British technical advance allows it to improve its positions. The growth of exports was already fast in the 10 to 15 years earlier (around 5% per annum) and the trend accelerated after 1846. From 1843-47 to 1857-61, the volume of British exports increased by just over 6% per annum. Growth is also exceptionally dynamic over the same period, the annual growth rate in volume of GDP is 2.4%.

terms of absolute cost of production in this environment of fierce competition from emerging countries?

In Europe, more precisely in the European Union, relations, particularly trade with the outside world is the common external trade policy. Upon the signing of the Treaty of Rome, the EU has stated its willingness to contribute to the removal of restrictions on international trade and development of world trade. Member States have vested exclusive jurisdiction to the Commission, which negotiates all trade agreements with third countries (export promotion - except refunds agricultural remaining with the Member States). The common commercial policy is based on uniform principles, particularly for changes in tariff rates, the conclusion of tariff and trade agreements, uniform measures of liberalization, export policy and measures to protect trade with those to be taken in case of dumping or subsidies (anti-dumping and anti-subsidy). It should be noted that tariffs contribute to the EU budget.. The Council of the European Union has complemented this by adopting in December 1994 a Regulation on trade barriers (ROC) which is a legal instrument giving the right to the firms, industries or their associations as well as Member States to act to open third country markets by eliminating trade barriers in the interest of EU exports. The ROC's mission is to ensure the effective application of rights conferred upon the Union by international trade agreements when countries adopt or maintain trade barriers[2]. The ROC is different from other trade protection instruments such as anti-dumping or countervailing measures, which require that the complainant represents a major proportion of the Community industry. Indeed, it is the only instrument of trade protection which allows a single company to file a complaint with the European Commission. With regard to trade barriers that affect the European Union market, a complaint may be filed by an industry of the Union or by a professional association recognized / accredited acting on its behalf, who has suffered injury caused by obstacles to trade that have an effect on the market. The rule is that this facility be restricted to producers who represent a major proportion of the total Community production of goods or services identical, similar or directly competitive and are affected by the obstacle to trade.

In applying these principles, the Council of Ministers shall act by qualified majority (unanimity required for agreements relating to services and intellectual property rights).

---

[2] For example, a third country introduced a barrier to trade which has adverse effects on exports from EU Member States or third countries introduced a barrier to trade which has adverse effects on the EU market . This applies, for example, when a trade barrier preventing the EU to get a basic product that it needs.

The European Union wants to keep a specificity with a common external tariff (which supplies the EU budget) and a common commercial policy. However, the GATT and the WTO and the mosaic of European preferential agreements with third countries have lowered the level of tariff protection community, resulting in increased vulnerability to fluctuations in exchange rates of countries. Moreover, at the time of the signing of the Treaty of Rome, the economy and foreign trade of the Community were primarily based on production and trade in industrial products. Today, the service sector is the main source of employment within the European Union and a substantial part of its international trade. This was due to the strong competition from emerging Asian and Latin American in traditional sectors and the economic changes brought about by new information technologies and communication. Services now represent 70% of employment and added value in developed countries and a fifth of world trade[3]. It is therefore an area known to play a major role in future international trade. The common external trade policy, very free-trading and characterized by a minimal regulatory framework, is it suitable for competitive context and relocation governing the European Union today because of globalization which leads entrepreneurs to invest in areas with low labor costs and social protection? What leeway national have they States to introduce distortions in trade or to make the emergence of specialization?

I. The Constraints of Globalization on European Union

The main lessons of international trade theory based on a hypothesis now contradicted by the facts: the international immobility of factors of production. As a result, nation states, sheltered behind tariff barriers and non-tariff, no longer represent the framework for production and trade of developed countries. One consequence is that the Ricardian model of comparative costs is largely inadequate to account for international specialization. The terms of trade between the nations have evolved considerably and contribute to the polarization of activities and employment in the lowest areas on a fiscal, social or environmental. Two arguments deserve to be further discussed today:

[3] The contribution of services to international trade is constant over the long period of around 20%, the development of the service sector leads structurally down the coefficients of opening of the economies (exports to GDP).

- The relevance of Ricardian comparative costs as founders of international specialization and the superiority of free trade on any organized exchange;
- The scope of the argument of the continuing rise in the range or uninterrupted access to higher value added for the production apparatus competition from developed countries, particularly those which may incorporate intensive research and development. An international exchange hierarchy would be in place with a specialization in which developed and developing countries will be winners by developing international exchange.

The differentiation of products continues to lead to a trade capacity development theoretically infinite. The development of intra - industry characterizes such a situation, and indeed it records a progress in international trade.. Consider each of the two arguments.

A. Comparative Advantage versus Absolute Advantage in Present International Specialization

While we are not yet in a world economy completely decompartmentalized but the trend is towards increased trade liberalization in two ways:

- The progress of multilateral negotiations under the GATT and now the WTO;
- Progress of regionalism with the creation of free trade areas or customs unions.

These are two complementary access to free trade, free trade is the generalized solution in the neo-classical analysis which sets the gains in welfare for the highest trading nations. Participation "suitable" in the international exchange relies on specialization according to comparative advantages in the institutional framework of exchanges completely open. This approach has been relativised by the American economist P. Samuelson (Samuelson, 2004). The demonstration is conducted within the framework of a model with two goods and two factors (according to the analysis of J. S. Mill) and taking the case of China and the United States with complete specialization in one of two goods for each country. If China has a productivity gain in the good of specialization from the United States until the equalization of the ratio of relative costs between the two countries, then trade has not interesting for the United States which appear losers in the international trade. How such a gain in productivity is possible for China? Simply because the international diffusion of innovation and research is developing rapidly and is made possible by the capacity of absorption of a workforce increasingly educated, skilled and mobile across the world. Even if one can believe that research and development progresses mainly in the more developed countries in the years ahead, catching up is at work and will reduce the gaps between nations. However, new processes, inventions and innovations will be further in the short-term mainly the fact of United States, Japan and the European Union and will be increasingly used in countries with lower social costs of production. The temptation of protection may then be stronger in developed countries. Economists such as J. Bhagwati (Bhagwati, 2003) stigmatize the protectionist temptation emphasizing the reciprocal gain in the exchange that would result from cheaper supplies from countries with low labor costs, thereby facilitating the productive processes of the developed countries by incorporating these inputs. This movement would be accompanied by an increase in product range of more advanced countries, thereby perpetuating a model of international cooperation where the countries leaders have always a time of technological advance on the followers. This pattern of economic development seems a little too mechanical and does not probably will check in any case and it can not meet the needs socially necessary jobs in developed countries. This is especially true that the relocation of companies, remaining micro – economically justified, is contributing to desertification industrial in developed countries (industries and businesses upstream and downstream suffer the negative effects). These are industries of Fordist mode of production which are mainly involved in this process of relocation to Asia (non-tradable goods, the new activities related to health or the environment, even information technologies, escape from this regulation ruthless).

B. The Final Stalemate in the Up-Market and in Product Differentiation

J. Bhagwati suggests to the developed countries, with labor relatively more costly, an increase in range to keep the gain to trade (Bhagwati, 2003). But with what limit? What can be said that this increase in range can be a continuous motion? The mechanical scheme of a rise in permanent range of production in developed countries while the lower-end products would be relocated in countries lagging behind, with the social cost of production lower and with a workforce relatively less skilled than that of advanced countries, is a model whose relevance can only be in a short period (this short period is consistent with the one we currently live). This assumes that there is definitely a technological advance of today's countries more advanced on others. Moreover, trade based on product differentiation could rise less sharply because of the speed of technology transfer, contributing to the similarity of product lines and strategies of firms in a position of monopolistic or oligopolistic market. Ultimately, these products, initially differentiated and substitutable, will become products competing because of the narrowness of differentiation, which disrupt the development of production and exchange. Today, the European Union is facing a process of "deterritorialization" of activities which concern particularly the European Western Union towards both directions: one in the intra - European countries towards the Eastern countries whose cost of labor is relatively lower and the other, towards the Asian region (especially India and China) because we find there low labor costs and a lack of social protection. To some extent, we can say that employees of the developed countries (countries with a high level of social protection) are injured, the profits are shared by labor abroad and the capital. This division is also unequal because the owners of real and monetary capital are recovering a large portion of profits in emerging countries, including China. D. Rodrik (Rodrik, 1997) points out that the legitimacy of the globalization process requires a fair distribution of global earnings that it generates. The idea that international trade could be developed based on the differentiation infinite of products is not in doubt since the transfer of technology and know-how is increasingly rapid with the progress of information technology and the raising in the qualifications of the work. It could ultimately lead to a poor differentiation which means that the products are more substitutable than competitive. Moreover, this type of trade can cause the appearance of external diseconomies (congestion of waterways with rising costs[4], rising energy costs and thus costs of road transport and shipping, resulting in pollution, etc).

Simultaneously, a new geography of economies of scale is being established. We can highlight it on two levels:

- at European level transiently;
- at Asian level tendentially.

The increasing returns activities have developed in old Europe (area named "European blue banana"). The rest of the European Union is a productive second choice, with lower economic development, where incomes and employment are

[4] Avatars of freight traffic in the Channel show it unambiguous.

lower skilled. The countries of Eastern recently members of the European Union, are an area of relocation of activities for companies in search of a factor work less expensive than in the rest of the European Union with the conditions of production socially and fiscally more beneficial. These arbitrations can be only transitory because the Eastern European countries quickly will present less competitive advantages than the countries of Asia, except adopting the social norms of the Asian countries. The Asian markets of production and in the long term of consumption represent today the best expression of exploitation of the remote economies of scale. Of course, the deterritorialization of the activities towards the Asian zone will benefit more and more with labour from this zone and the holders of real or monetary capitals (American, European, Japanese, etc). A shift in the geography of industrial specialization is in progress. The mastery of the most developed products-systems and the research remain temporarily located in countries currently leaders. The consequences could be significant in regard to the level of employment in these countries. Finally, recall the statistical current report: the intra-industrial trade, anywhere in the world including the most developed countries of the European Union, is primarily an vertical intra-industrial trade and not an horizontal intra-industrial trade as it was implicitly considered for several decades because of its measurement with the standard Grubel-Lloyd ratio (Grubel, Lloyd, 1975). So, we are confronted with a problem of economic adjustment costs because the inter-industry trade and the vertical intra - industry trade are leading both to specialization, and thus to social shocks by loss of activity.

In such a context of international competition, one might wonder whether a more proactive strategy of the European Union both in the direction of its relations with third countries and in respect of its domestic production is not necessary today. What are the ways of adaptation options?

II. The Current Margin for Action in the European Union

E. Laurent and J. Le Cacheux wrote in July 2005: "At least two contemporary developments must now be seriously considered: the first is the massive competition from Asia in manufacturing and industry; and the second is the comprehensive nature of this competition, which exercises (and will exercise more tomorrow) as well as at the top to the bottom of the ladder of comparative advantage. Unfortunately it is significant that Europe hangs in the trade negotiations at the idea of liberalization when the United States aggressively combine trade policy and exchange rate policy to maintain the momentum of their comparative advantages. The Union is able to change the theory when the facts change?". Can we consider an evolution of the common external trade policy without abandoning the necessary openness to international trade, a factor of peace and generally gain of welfare? How states can intervene? What flexibilities have?

A. A Possible Change of the External Trade Policy and / or a Tightening of State Intervention

Today, in general, any measure of import protection would contravene the rules set by WTO and is not relevant, if only because it exposes the State protectionist retaliatory measures commercial. However, we can legitimately consider that the arguments against protectionism are not always unquestionably founded. We will use some examples to illustrate our point. First, the case of the optimal tariff. We know that the imposition of a tariff by a large country leads to a lower world price and thus to support a portion of the tariff by the rest of the world. For the large country, an overall net surplus may occur. In this case, the tariff is optimal and creates a more advantageous position than before the introduction of customs duty. Then, we can take the example of agricultural levies who have disappeared following the GATT agreement, signed in Marrakesh in 1994, and were replaced by tariff equivalents with a timetable for lowering the level which quickly eliminated the community preference. At first, referring to the traditional analysis of the effects of a customs duty in a situation of partial equilibrium and for a small country, the new regulation from the agricultural Marrakesh Agreement established a more advantageous situation for the European Union and the rest of the world. In fact, the European gain is not certain at all. If to the short term, the intra - European net surplus generated by this new situation is positive (net gain for European consumers), however in the long term, the net result is more ambiguous. Indeed, agricultural products meet market mechanisms in spider webs (spider or cobweb model). As a result, fluctuations in prices and quantities can be large and in turn harm consumers and producers and/or third countries. It is precisely to limit such fluctuations which are harmful to the community that the European mechanism to support agricultural prices has been designed around a market price between two institutional prices, a price ceiling and a floor price (specific mechanisms of regulation are triggering at these price limits to maintain the market price in the desired range). European consumers have been able to benefit from stable prices (although generally higher than world prices). The Marrakesh Agreement put an end to this mechanism of stabilization of agricultural prices in Europe by performing the removal of agricultural levies. The European agricultural markets are now largely open and internationalized and thus subject to international economic vagaries. European consumers have been injured in 2008 by the rising international grain prices which have impacted particularly on the price of bread (a situation detrimental to the poorest). European markets, including those from agricultural commodities, are in direct contact with international markets without any tool similar community which can now absorb the fluctuations in price and quantity characteristics of agricultural spider models. The European Union is no longer immune to situation more chaotic than the year 2008 and it is not clear that the gain in the short term due to the abolition of agricultural tax offsets losses caused by variations in surplus of producers and consumers resulting from spider mechanisms which have not been stabilized (situation induced by the Marrakech Agreement). We therefore advocate for regulation of agricultural markets by ranges of administered prices with market prices released within these ranges because it is essential to stabilize agricultural spider cycles, the source of gains in the long run (domestic products being treated the same way as imported products).

More generally and with reference this time to industrial production, it can be shown in the same way that the abolition of tariff and non tariff has immediate positive net effects for the economy (net gain in consumer surplus). However, the loss of activity induced by a more efficient foreign competition can generate a range of costs that can reduce or eliminate gains initial lack of protection (increase of industrial desertification, especially in regions lagging behind, which could lead to loss of comparative advantages of other firms or sectors of activity).

Several solutions are available to States to seek support for certain areas: the definition of strategic sectors and the establishment of investment funds dedicated. Consider the actions that have been conducted in France.

Financial relations between France and abroad, in principle, are entirely in accordance with Article L 151-1 of the Monetary and Financial Code (MFC). This principle is confirmed by Article 56 of the Community Treaty. But this freedom is framed to allow the defense of national interests. In 2000, an awareness of the vulnerability of certain companies has produced, especially following the participation of U.S. fund TPG Gemplus Company (manufacturer of smart cards) and the appointment to head the an American company, a director of a fund linked to the CIA.

In order to preserve national interests Decree No. 2005-1739 of 30 December 2005 regulates the financial relations with foreign countries. It stipulates that foreign investors wishing to acquire control or a blocking minority of 33.33% must seek authorization from the State French. This text is not confined to taking control in the context of a takeover bid but to companies large and small, listed and unlisted companies, whatever the views of shareholders in place. Eleven sectors are defined as strategic by the government of Dominique de Villepin:

- gambling (on behalf of money laundering);
- private Security;
- research or development of means to cope with the illicit use in the course of terrorist activities pathogens (biotechnology: production of antidotes);
- equipment designed for interception of correspondence and conversations;
- the evaluation and certification of safety systems;
- the production of goods or services in the field of security systems;
- dual-use technologies (ie can be used for both civilian and military applications);
- cryptology (the science of secrecy whose purpose is to hide information from a message, she now has applications in the areas of Internet banking systems, telephony, multimedia ...);
- the activities of the depository business national defense;
- research, production or trade of arms;
- activities carried out by companies which have concluded a contract of study or supplying equipment to the Ministry of Defense, directly or through subcontracting.

On this basis the scope of the decree appears relatively large, the area of dual use technologies will be very large, most of the technologies may have uses in both civilian and military (communication ....). Furthermore, large groups of which a subsidiary operates in a sensitive area can be protected.

The European Commission initiated in April 2006 an infringement procedure against the decree of France; it considers incompatible with the free movement of capital within the zone (Article 56 of EU Treaty) and the principle of freedom of establishment (Article 43). The decree is "discriminatory and protectionist" in the words of European Commissioner Charlie McCreevy. The Commission sent on 12 October 2006 a "reasoned opinion" against the decree. But the position of the European authorities in fact testifies to a certain unease about this issue. They recognize the merits of the objectives of public security and defense of France, but consider the authorization associated with the decree disproportionate compared to the objectives. France responded in December 2006 that the case of companies with low share of turnover is made in a strategic activity, the decree provides for a review of the sector strategic and not referred to the entire company. The French government can consider a change of control without blocking the investment by asking for the engagements limited to the only establishment concerned. Since then, the procedure against France is "frozen". This position reflects the ultimate European concern to preserve against sensitive sectors such as equity participations massive sovereign wealth funds and the fact that Europe has no alternative to replace the States for this purpose.

This control of investments in key sectors is fairly widespread internationally. In the United States, the CFIUS (the Committee on Foreign Investment in the United States) is responsible to approve acquisitions of U.S. firms by foreign companies including from Allied countries. Germany in 2008 finalized its draft law on the control of sovereign investment funds. This project provides that the government could consider any equity participation of at least 25% of a Sovereign wealth funds in a German company belonging to a sector "sensitive".

Also in France, a Strategic Fund of Investment was created to support the development of future industry leaders to serve the country's competitiveness. On 20 November 2008, Nicolas Sarkozy announced the creation of a Strategic Fund of Investment (SFI). This announcement marks the start the willingness to develop a kind of sovereign funds in the French in reaction to the rise of such players in international financial relations. Sovereign wealth fund can be defined as funds of public investments having for mandate to remunerate resources actively, coming mainly from a surplus of foreign exchange reserves (Chinese funds ...) and oil or gas revenues (Gulf funds, funds of Norway ...). These funds have strategies for traditional investors and diversify their portfolios globally. The SFI is moving away from this definition. Its funds do not come from current account surpluses or rents energy and should only invest in French companies.

The SFI is a French limited company whose capital is held up to 51% by the *Caisse des Dépôts et Consignations* (the financial arm of the State) and 49% directly by the State. It appears as a subsidiary of CDC pursuing specific objectives in support of French companies likely to occupy dominant positions in the global marketplace for the competitiveness[5] of the national economy.

---

[5] The competitiveness of a national economy can be defined as the capacity of its manufacturing sector to meet domestic demand and foreign background, the clear objective to ensure a rising standard of living of residents and level of development the economy. Competitiveness must be distinguished from the attractiveness. The attractiveness of a national site depends more about its image and its ability to attract foreign investors in particular (FDI and portfolio investment).

The SFI aims to assist companies in mainly medium-sized companies which have greater potential for value creation, are likely to become leaders or actors in their reference segment on a global scale in particular because they control innovating technologies. It aims to invest in existing companies and not to finance creations of companies. It should not invest in financial services, distribution, real estate or non-competitive sectors. The SFI must be attentive to cover by its interventions the whole of the field of the industrial activities, by attaching a particular importance to the consolidation and the development of sectors with technological strong potential. To do this it must take account of the concept of industrial fixtures. It acts according to transparent principles:

- it invests in profitable projects;
- it is a strategic investor for the long term, socially responsible;
- it intended to take minority stakes but to raise co-investment by seeking the involvement of other investors;
- it is involved in the governance of the company (by participating in Board and of shareholders);
- it aims to invest in strategic enterprises with regard to the competitiveness of the economy, ie firms which have the skills, technologies and jobs irreplaceable for the national and European areas (industry, growth potential, technological, industrial know-how, employment and export potential, leadership in its markets, value of brands).

The SFI provides from an allocation of 20 billion euros, 14 billion in securities and 6 billion in cash. It is too early to conduct a review of its action. The SFI made his first investment in the firm Valéo on February 25 2009 (18.7 million euros, or 2.3% of capital). The automotive supplier is in crisis. It made a loss of 207 million euros in 2008 and saw its sales fall by 26.6% in the fourth quarter of 2008. It may be noted that the *Caisse des Dépôts et Consignations* already held 5.98% stake in Valeo.

On 1st April 2009, the SFI is investing 20 million euros in Farinia (french leader of materials processing (casting, forging, machining) for the construction, material handling, automotive and agriculture (firm founded in 2002, CA in 2008 142 million, 1100 employees, 9 manufacturing sites). The investment of the SFI makes it possible to consolidate the resumption of the Setforge company.

After being reluctant to engage in the firm Heuliez, the government announced that the SFI eventually support the automotive group to the tune of 10 million euros or more. This company, which develops and manufactures turnkey niche vehicles as well as modules and sub-body, is in great financial difficulty. The intervention in the Heuliez firm obey seems more politically motivated than purely strategic considerations: it illustrates the dangers that await action by the SFI in the future. In June 2009, the SFI has entered the capital of Gemalto (specializing in smart cards) up to 8%, partly replacing the fund TPG American.

The analysis of these experiments shows that it becomes essential to question the foundations of comparative advantage. They appear as a result of grants from state aid or proven practices of dumping? In this case, the European Union has at present the tools necessary to preserve the market for this type of unfair competition. But note that in general, trade with, for example, the Asian region is not affected by this type of problem, in particular there are few cases of dumping. In the future, costs of production in this part of the world are expected to rise (rising wage rates and progressive development of social protection), but for now, they give it a competitive advantage, particularly for many industrial products. Cancel this advantage by imposing on the border of the developed countries to a tax of social equalization would be a protectionist measure, a source of loss of well-being. It seems preferable to improve production in the most developed countries in maximizing the gains from economies of scale internal and external firms: competitive clusters can form such efficient production strategies while does not impede the development of international trade.

B. The Use of an Efficient Spatial Organization of Activities: Clusters (or Pole of Competitiveness)

On a domestic level, the production community, failing to be regulated by common policies, can create new sources of comparative advantage by developing production strategies focused on the formation of industrial districts. Some European Union countries are attempting experiments of this type that are still essentially national (Spain, Denmark, etc) without direct involvement of the Community public authorities. In France it is represented by the poles of competitiveness defined recently by the government. What are the advantages of such an organization of production?

On a theoretical level, one of the first analysis on the geographical dimension of the industry is due to A. Marshall (Marshall, 1920) which develops the idea that a company benefits from three positive effects by locating near other industry of the same sector: cost savings of transport in the production and distribution, a local labor market specialized and effective, and intensive exchange of information between producers. It is localized economies of scale. More recently,

M. E. Porter (Porter, 1998 and 2000) developed the theory of clusters that defines the clusters as a geographical concentration of firms and institutions whose activities are interconnected and interdependent in a particular economic sector. The success of a cluster will be based on competitiveness resulting from the interconnection between businesses and institutions in a given space. The sector will nevertheless have one or more advantages, ie the strengths that make a dominant sector in a specific area. There are four determinants in this competitive advantage: the factors of productions, including the specific factors, market demand, and related upstream industries, strategy and business structure. To explain the development of clusters, economic theory emphasizes the concept of economy of scale or increasing returns, ie the existence of gains to the concentration of production in a given space. There is a second element in any analysis of geographical economics is the emergence of transaction costs when officers are not at one location and they interact in their economic activities to exchange goods or services. These two conditions are necessary to explain the issue of geographic concentration. Thus the interaction of the forces of concentration - the exploitation of economies of scale localized- and transaction costs can explain the existence of clusters.

Today, the analysis of such clusters must take into account the evolution of imperfect competition induced by globalization activities that tend to bring more forms of monopolistic competition than oligopolistic. Indeed, the sharpness of competition between firms, due to the international mobility of factors and knowledge, is such that it leads to continuous efforts and increasingly important for product differentiation. Simultaneously, within the clusters the most efficient firms will benefit from significant effects of spillovers from particular technological externalities and social interactions (information exchange in education and employment).

This new productive context leads us to propose below an analysis of situations of equilibrium in the cluster in a monopolistic case. To the extent that production processes will face global competition increasingly fierce, the continued differentiation of the products will be the rule and will designate the monopolistic market structure as dominant. The activities meet increasing returns in a growth stage of the cluster, that of the cluster efficiency (graph below). RM is the average income of the producers (or inverse demand function) and Rm, the marginal income of the producers. CM and Cm represent the average cost and the marginal cost of the producers. By producing in the efficiency area of the cluster, firms maximize their profit (equilibrium Po, Qo). However, the cluster will be characterized by a long term curve of average cost in U[6] due to inefficiencies in the initial phase of cluster growth (external diseconomies due to its small size) and at a later stage if it does not to avoid the traditional costs of urban growth but also the costs of the periphery.

Situations of equilibrium in the cluster in the presence of economies and external diseconomies

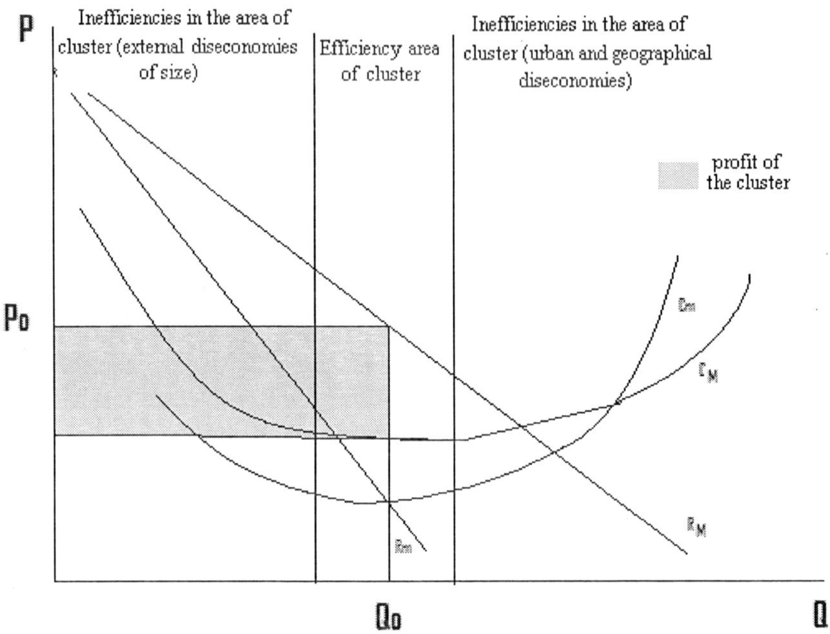

We can in particular stress that the distance of a port area is likely to make difficult its insertion in the international business which seems thus to condemn in the long term the poles of competitiveness, particularly in the European Union, those would be located outside the pentagon industrial community[7]. The zone of effectiveness of the cluster makes it possible to make emerge new competitive advantages that the firms will be able to exploit on the international markets: most frequently they will be activities intensive in research and development, innovation, qualified work.

---

[6] Even if each firm in the cluster benefit from increasing returns to scale.

[7] This is the productive zone to increasing returns to scale of the European Union bounded by the cities of London, Paris, Milan, Munich and Hamburg.

This strategy of building competitiveness cluster was developed in France since 2002. The government's goal is to create poles of excellence - in some cases, global poles - designed to enhance or bring out specializations within the French economy in the service of its competitiveness.

The policy of competitiveness clusters was decided in December 2002 (*Comité Interministériel d'Aménagement et de Compétitivité des Territoires* - CIACT). The CIACT of 14 September 2004 defines a method of implementation (call for projects on the basis of specifications). The government launched the first call for proposals on 2 December 2004, the procedure ended on 28 February 2005.

The government retains, in July 2005, 67 of the 105 submissions. The location of projects demonstrates that a target of spatial planning has guided the selection of projects and to a lesser extent the allocation of financial resources. The preliminary will of the government to concentrate on a reduced number of projects was inflected. However, a budget priority is given to clusters with a global scope (they are then six) or having a vocation to acquire it (nine).

The third call for applications for project funding clusters was closed in December 2006. It resulted in 224 deposits of projects. The results were announced in March 2007: 100 new projects from 47 poles will to receive funding by the *Fonds Unique Interministériel* (FUI). In total, in 2006, 339 projects have been assessed (143 were selected); they correspond to approximately one billion euros of investment in research and development.

In 2008, there are 71 competitive clusters of around 9000 researchers working in nearly 1,000 projects labeled. One billion of euros public were invested since the launch of the poles in 2005 on a total of 1.5 billion euros initially planned until 2008. One can observe that 50% of funding focuses on six areas of global competitiveness (see list attached). Mostly competitive clusters are associations of type Act 1901, ie the non-profit organizations. They can also take the form of economic interest groups (GIE) or scientific interest groups (SIG). The poles have a legal personality. The main principles on which the poles are:

- a funding mechanism for collaborative projects in R & D according to the principles of FUI current and with a sufficient financial size to attract and stabilize within clusters a critical mass of participants of any kind;
- a public support with local structures of animation of the poles, joining together great groups, SME, research organizations and training companies;
- coordinated action by local authorities and state policy in the poles.

The incentives associated with the projects labeled are substantial:

- tax exemptions and reductions in charges. A company participating in a research and development in an area recognized is exempt from corporate income tax during the first three years. The areas "zoned R & D" correspond in outline to the perimeter of the poles of competitiveness.
- credits from intervention including the Ministry in charge of industry and DIACT;
- preferential interventions from various agencies (National Research Agency established in 2005, the Agency for Industrial Innovation, which merged in January 2008 with Oseo and the *Caisse des Depots et Consignations*).

At the local level, local authorities are involved in financing.

The Boston Consulting Group and CM International led between November 2007 and June 2008, an assessment of competitiveness clusters and the accompanying policy established by the State. For these experts, the results seem very positive. The amounts pledged were actually used for the benefit of innovation. The clusters show a “promising dynamism”, the poles made it possible to make work actors whose activities were hitherto partitioned. The level of implication of SME is strong: they receive a big part of the financings dedicated to the projects. The high number of poles did not involve massive dilution of the financial resources thanks to a concentration of the means on the world poles.

According to the report, 39 poles have achieved the objectives of cluster policy, 19 have reached partly and should work on improving certain aspects of their work (their definition of strategy, governance arrangements, role of the team animation). 13 poles could benefit from a reconfiguration in depth. On this basis, the report recommends maintaining the main principles of poles and proposes five possible developments:

- consolidate and register in the duration the positive dynamics of cooperation around the innovation engaged since 2005 through to the poles of competitiveness;
- more highly-responsible actors of the poles of competitiveness by moving towards a logic of contracts and verification, in a simplified local environment;
- reaffirm the commitment of the State to the poles and develop the strategic dimension;

- maintain project funding collaborative innovation and pursue the optimization of circuits funding by enhancing their overall coherence;
- better integration of the cluster policy in research policies and support for R & D.

A report from CEPREMAP also published in 2008 is more reserved on the functioning of French poles. They would be inefficient compared to their high cost. The report recommends rather to reduce the obstacles to the creation of poles of optimal size. In this context particular attention should be paid to the functioning of the real estate market (lower transaction costs, increased supply of land at the local level ...) and to improve the quality of public goods. Furthermore, according to the rapporteurs, a specialization artificial and forced in some sectors makes vulnerable the economy to the sectoral shocks that globalization makes it more likely.

Nevertheless, the influence of these poles on the specializations of the national economy can be seen that over the long term: the benefits and costs can only be assessed on a distant horizon. The poles are now the most promising policy for the emergence of specialization in an environment increasingly open where technologies are spreading faster and faster.

Annex

Global competitiveness clusters (specialization
Aerospace Valley (Space-aviation Toulouse-Bordeaux)
Finance Innovation (Finance Paris)
LYONBIOPOLE (vaccine Lyon)
Medicen Paris Région (medical high technologies Paris)
MINALOGIC (intelligent miniaturized products Grenoble)
SCS (Solutions communicantes sécurisées) (communication Sophia-Antipolis)
SYSTEM@TIC Paris Région (software-dominant-systems Paris)
Globally-oriented competitiveness clusters (specialization- localization in France)
Alsace Biovalley (life sciences Alsace)
AXELERA (chimistry Lyon)
Cap Digital Paris Région (creating, editing, communicating, processing and providing services Paris)
Images & Réseaux (informations, telecommunications and audio visual technologies Bretagne et Pays de loire)
i-Trans (transports Nord-Pas de Calais Picardie)
Industries & Agro-Ressources (Picardie Champagne Ardenne

Annex. Continued

Globally-oriented competitiveness clusters (specialization- localization in France)
MOV'EO (private cars and publics transport Normandie)
Pôle Mer Bretagne (sea sciences Bretagne)
Pôle Mer PACA (sea sciences Provence Alpes Cote d'Azur)
Végépolys (medicinal herbs, tree growing Pays de loire)
Competitiveness clusters
Agrimip Innovation
Arve Industries Haute-Savoie Mont-Blanc
ASTech
Atlantic Biotherapies
Automobile haut de gamme
CAPENERGIES
Céramique
Céréales Vallée
Cosmetic Valley
DERBI (Développement des énergies renouvelables bâtiment - industrie)
Elastopôle
ELOPSYS
EMC2 (Ensembles métalliques et composites complexes)
Fibres Grand'Est
Filière équine
Filière produits aquatiques
Génie Civil Ouest
Gestion des risques, vulnérabilité des territoires
Imaginove
Industries du Commerce
Industries et Pin maritime du futur
InnoViandes
Logistique Seine-Normandie
Lyon Urban Truck&Bus 2015
MAUD (Matériaux à usage domestique)
Microtechniques
MIPI (matériaux innovants et produits intelligents)
MTA (Mobilité et transports avancés)
Nutrition Santé Longévité
ORPHEME
PASS (Parfums, arômes, senteurs, saveurs)
Pegase
Photonique

Annex. Continued

Competitiveness clusters
PLASTIPOLIS
Pôle Cancer-Bio-Santé
Pôle Enfant
Pôle européen d'innovation fruits et légumes
Pôle Nucléaire Bourgogne
Prod'Innov
Q@LI-MEDiterranée
Qualitropic
Route des Lasers
S^2E^2 (Sciences et systèmes de l'énergie électrique)
SPORALTEC
TECHTERA
TENERRDIS
TES (Transactions électroniques sécurisées)
TRIMATEC (TRIcastin-MArcoule-TEChnologies)
UP-TEX
Valorial
Véhicule du futur
VIAMECA
Ville et mobilité durables
VITAGORA

For more informations see www.competitivite.gouv.fr

References

Bhagwati, J. *Lectures on International Trade,* New Delhi, OUP, 2003.

Cepremap, *Les pôles de compétitivité. Que peut-on en attendre ?*, Presses de l'École normale supérieure, 2008

Duranton, G. and Puga, D. *Microfoundations of urban agglomeration economies* in V. Henderson et J.-F. Thisse (éd.), Handbook of Regional and Urban Economics, North-Holland, Amsterdam, vol. 4, pp. 1154 - 1477. 2004.

Grubel, H. G. and Lloyd, P. J. *Intra Industry trade: The Theory and Measurement of internationally trade in Differentiated Products,* Wiley, New York 1975.

Guiso, L. and Schivardi, F. Spillovers in industrial districts, *Economic Journal*, **117**, 2007, pp. 68-93.

Jaffe, A., Trajtenberg, M. and Henderson, R. Geographic localization of knowledge spillovers as evidenced by patent citations, *Quarterly Journal of Economics*, **108** (3), 1993, pp. 577-598.

Laurent, E., et Cacheux, J. Le, «La re-construction européenne : les nouvelles frontières de l'Union », *Lettre de l'OFCE,* N° **265**, juillet 2005.

Marshall, A. *Principles of Economics,* Macmillan 8th ed, London, 1920.

Porter, M. E. *Clusters and the New Economics of Competition*, Harvard Business review, nov-déc 1998, pp. 77 - 90.

Porter, M. E. Location, competition and economic development: local clusters in a global economy, *Economic Development Quaterly*, **14** (1), 2000, pp. 15-34.

Rodrik, D. "Trade, social insurance, and the limits to globalization", *NBER Working Paper*, n°**5905**, 1997

Samuelson, P. A. Why Ricardo and Mill Rebut and Confirm Arguments of Mainstream Economist Supporting Globalization, *Journal of Economic Perspectives*, Summer, 2004, pp. 135-146.

In: Trade Liberalization and Protectionism
Editors: B. Hahn et al, pp. 153-174
ISBN: 978-1-60876-837-0

Chapter 6

TRADE, DEVELOPMENT, AND POVERTY ALLEVIATION: CONSIDERATIONS FOR INDIA AND CHINA

Pritam Banerjee[1], Ian Goldin[2] and Kenneth A. Reinert[1]
[1]School of Public Policy, George Mason University
[2]James Martin 21st Century School, Oxford University

Abstract

International trade, both exports and imports, can contribute to development and poverty alleviation by expanding markets, promoting competition, and raising productivity, each of which has the *potential* for increasing the real incomes of poor people. The potential of international trade to alleviate poverty comes from its ability to expand markets and thereby create new production and consumption opportunities for people. Such market expansion can help to generate employment and incomes for poor people. That said, long-term development and poverty alleviation requires *both* technological upgrading *and* the education and skills acquisition necessary to support it. We consider these issues in some detail and then turn to the emerging and important cases of India and China. It is our contention that these two countries pose particular challenges and offer particular opportunities in the evolving trade-development nexuses.

Introduction

International trade, both exports and imports, can contribute to development and poverty alleviation by expanding markets, promoting competition, and raising productivity, each of which has the *potential* for increasing the real incomes of poor people. We emphasize the word "potential" because the link between trade and poverty alleviation is not necessarily automatic.[1] The potential of international trade to alleviate poverty comes from its ability to expand markets and thereby create new production and consumption opportunities for people. Such market expansion can help to generate employment and incomes for poor people. That said, as emphasized by Abramovitz's (1989) discussion of *social capabilities*, long-term development and poverty alleviation requires *both* technological upgrading *and* the education and skills acquisition necessary to support it. We consider these issues in some detail and then turn to the emerging and important cases of India and China. It is our contention that these two countries pose particular challenges and offer particular opportunities in the evolving trade-development nexuses.

The focus on India and China is important because, at the end of the day, success in a global economy is defined by the ability to compete. The wider the range of sectors an economy is able to compete in, the more opportunities for its people to profit from the global economy. The level of competitiveness is shaped by the access to resources and an economy's efficiency in managing them. Traditionally, poorer countries have had access to cheap, lower-skilled labor and rich countries to higher skills and capital and the global structure of trade has evolved around this duality. However, as the Chinese and Indian economies mature, both these countries will have access to significant capital and skilled human resources *as well as* large amounts of low-skilled, relatively cheap labor. Thus, the rise of India and China, and the absolute size of both their labor-intensive and skill-intensive sectors, will have important consequences for global competitiveness and market opportunities for both low-income as well as industrialized economies. This rise will also have important lessons for the process of globalization and the strategies for poverty alleviation in the world economy.

[1] The fact that the trade-poverty alleviation linkage is not automatic has also been stressed by UNCTAD (2004) in the case of the least-developed countries. There is a long research literature on this issue, recently reviewed in some of its aspects by Rodríquez and Rodrik (2001).

Exports and Wages

Exporting can most effectively contribute to poverty alleviation when it supports labor-intensive production, human capital accumulation (both education and health), and technological learning. These characteristics were often present in the successful East Asian export expansions of recent decades. However, even successful labor-intensive, export-oriented development in and of itself might not address poverty and social distribution in its entirety.[2]

Critics of globalization point out that the wages of workers in poor-country export industries are far lower than the wages of workers in developed countries. Consequently, globalization has often been identified as poverty worsening. However, the more relevant comparison is between what people may have earned before and after trade opportunities were made manifest. From a poverty perspective, this could be between the wages of export-sector workers with agricultural day laborers, both in the same developing country. Here it can often be seen that it is the alternative of agricultural day labor that is the much worse. It is precisely this type of income comparison that draws workers into export industries.[3]

Consider the case of Bangladesh where poverty reduction during the 1990s was quite dramatic. While changes in the non-tradable sector were a significant part of the cause of this poverty reduction process, clothing exports also played a role. Nearly 2 million Bangladeshis work in the clothing sector's nearly 3,000 factories. Oxfam's (2000) description of this sector illustrates the importance of relevant wage comparisons:

> Most of the (clothing) workforce consists of young women, many of whom have migrated from desperately poor rural areas. The wages earned by these women are exceptionally low by international standards, and barely above the national poverty line. Yet their daily wage rates are around *twice* as high as those paid for agricultural labourers, and higher than could be earned on construction sites. Employment conditions in the export zones are scandalously poor, with women denied even the most basic rights. Yet for most women working in the garments sector, their employment offers a higher quality of life than might otherwise be possible (p. 56, emphasis added).

---

[2] We are in broad agreement with the assessment of Oxfam (2002) that "In itself, trade is not inherently opposed to the interests of poor people. International trade can be a force for good, or for bad.... The outcomes are not pre-determined. They are shaped by the way in which international trade relations are managed, and by national policies" (p. 28).

[3] To make this observation is not to downplay the exploitation that can often occur in export sectors. Labor standards do matter. But it is decidedly *not* the case that exploitation is absent from agricultural day labor.

While it is true that the wages in the Bangladeshi garment sector are barely US$2.00 per day, this labor-intensive employment has served as an opportunity for poor people to leave worse conditions in rural and urban poverty. To be blunt, it can be a difference between poverty and *extreme* poverty. Indeed, using survey data from 1990 and 1997, Zohir (2001), Kabeer (2004), and Kabeer and Mahmud (2004) provide evidence that work in the garment sector has had a number of beneficial impacts on women workers in Bangladesh. These include first-time access to cash income, support of families in rural areas through remittances, support of siblings' education, and increased household status. Zohir's conclusion is that "employment in the garment industry has definitely empowered women, increased their mobility and expanded their individual choice" (p. 67).[4]

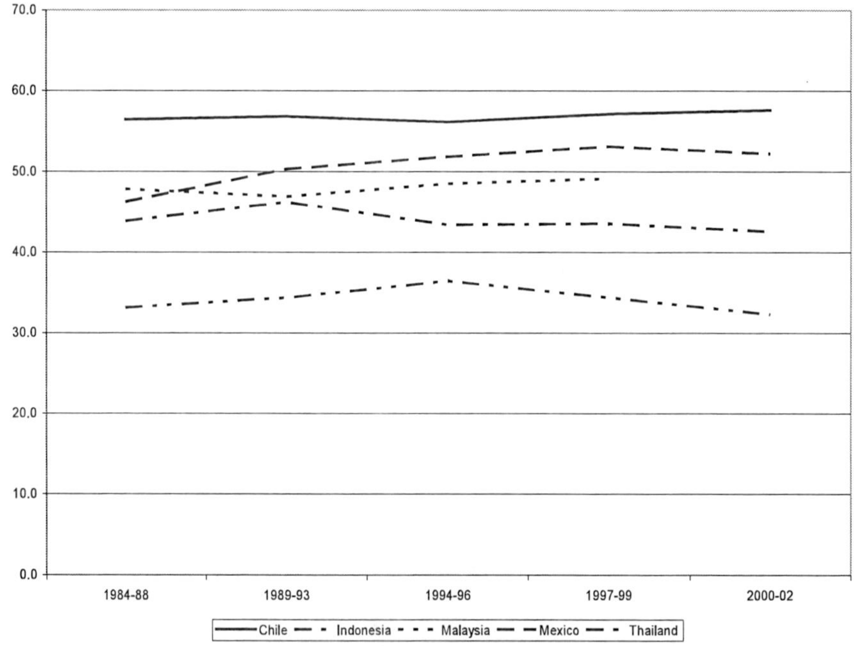

Source: World Bank Development Indicators and authors' calculations. Note that where more than one observation in a period was available, we took a simple average, and one observation was interpolated in the case of Indonesia.

Figure 1. Gini Index for Export Oriented Countries.

[4] Zohir (2001) did raise concerns about the effect of garment-sector work on women's health and the increased risk of harassment.

Similar evidence in five additional countries of the way exports can support women's incomes is provided by Nordas (2003) who concludes that export industries in Mauritius, Mexico, Peru, the Phillipines, and Sri Lanka are more likely to employ women than men and also tend to increase women's wages compared to men.

We can address these issues more directly with the help of Figures 1 and 2. Figure 1 provides the Gini Index for a set of five countries that followed labor-intensive export-oriented policies through much of the 1980's and 1990's, and Figure 2 provides the poverty head count as a percent of population for the same set of countries plus China. Figure 1 shows that export-oriented development policies did very little to address economic inequality in these countries. With the exception of Thailand, where there was a marginal change towards more equitable income distribution, all the other countries in the sample had either moved towards more income inequity or stayed more or less the same. This sort of evidence gives some credence to the critics of globalization that globalization has done little or nothing to address inequality.

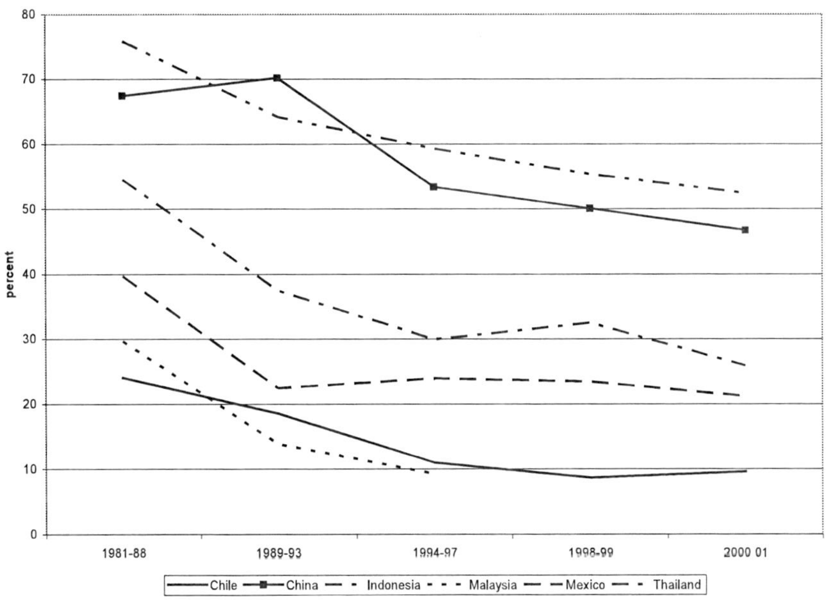

Source: World Bank Development Indicators and authors' calculations. Note that where more than one observation in a period was available, we took a simple average.

Figure 2. Percent of Population at 2 US$ per Day.

A supplement to the story of Figure 1 is that, while labor-intensive export growth might not address *inequality*, it certainly helps a section of the population move out of *absolute poverty* by giving them better employment options. Figure 2 seems to support that argument. All six countries of this figure show sharp drops in the percentage of their population living below absolute poverty. However, the drop in poverty head count takes place in the first phase of the export oriented growth trajectory (i.e. the mid 1980's to early 1990's). Subsequently, there seems to be a stagnation in the rate at which people out of poverty, exceptions being China and Indonesia. This might indicate that reducing persistent poverty, especially addressing the poorest members of society, cannot be accomplished by trade alone. A more comprehensive approach is needed that addresses multiple economic and social challenges simultaneously and emphasizes the expansion of poor people's capabilities, especially in the areas of health, education and technological upgrading.

Technological Upgrading

For export activities to support poverty alleviation in a sustained manner, it helps if those activities lend themselves to technological upgrading and associated learning processes. There is some evidence that international trade can promote productivity in exporting countries, and it is possible that productivity increases can, in turn, support the incomes of poor people. Neither of these components is automatic, however. It is not the case that exports *of all types* or *in all countries* generate positive productivity effects, but there is evidence that this is the case in certain instances.[5] Export postures can place the exporting firms in direct contact with discerning international customers, facilitating upgrading processes. There is no consensus within international economics on the extent of these upgrading effects, but they nonetheless remain an important possibility that has been active in sectors such as the Indian software industry.[6]

---

[5] As described by Rodrigo (2001), "By opening up a channel to the world market, trade… serves to promote specialization and sustain production tempos of goods in which learning effects are embodied; if constrained by domestic market size alone along with associated domestic business cycle uncertainty of demand, firms would be less willing to make the investments needed to capture gains from learning" (p. 90).

[6] See Kapur and Ramamurti (2001), for example. These authors show that the large and fast-growing software market within the United States with its sophisticated software buyers has contributed significantly to the competitiveness of the Indian software sector. The remaining issue, however, is the extent to which the expansion of incomes generated by the Indian software industry supports the incomes of poor Indians. Here the answer might be "only a little."

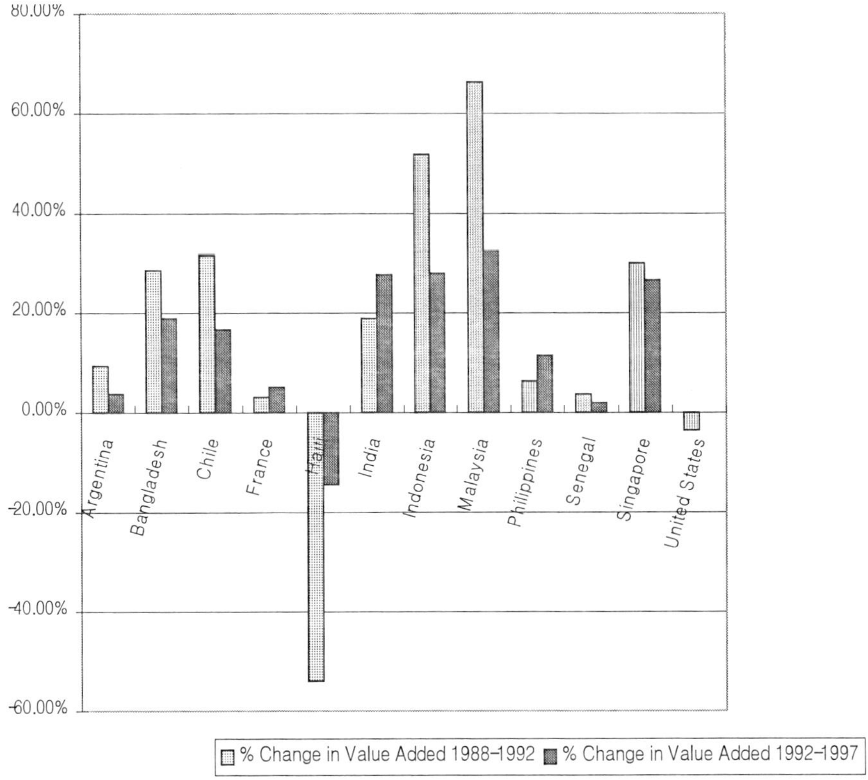

Source: Authors' calculations based on World Bank Development Indicators.

Figure 3. Percentage Change in Manufacturing Value Added.

Figure 3 provides the percentage change in manufacturing value added in the period 1988-1992 and in the period 1992-1997 as an indicator of productivity changes in a set of developing economies and compares this change with that of two developed economies also in the sample. Figure 3 seems to support the argument that trade supports productivity increases. The growth in manufacturing value added is higher for countries that have been known to follow export oriented policies in the 1980's and 1990's (i.e. Indonesia, Malaysia, Singapore, Chile and Bangladesh). On the other hand, countries that have been relatively closed seemed to show lower gains in manufacturing value added (i.e. India, Argentina, and Philippines). Further, India saw a greater increase in manufacturing value added in the later period (1992-1997) when it underwent economic reforms and opened up to the global economy. The developing countries also show relatively greater positive change in terms of their manufacturing value added compared to France and the US, indicating that there might be a process of development and technological upgrading via trade that allows developing nations to narrow their productive differences with the developed world. But institutional development and political stability are prerequisites for such positive changes. As Haiti's sharp declines in this period indicate, despite some initiatives taken by the US to jumpstart that Haitian economy through trade incentives, the political and institutional deficit in Haiti has prevented it from taking advantage of such measures.

Skills and Education

A related aspect of skill upgrading and productivity change is the distribution of skills. As manufacturing exports become more sophisticated and the means of production in terms of both domestic and imported capital (i.e. machines and processes) become more complex, the export sector starts demanding more skilled workers than the old technology that had been in use. Consequently, as trade is liberalized, unskilled workers tend to lose relative to skilled workers in terms of opportunities. Since poor people are almost always unskilled, these factor-intensity changes have traditionally worked against them.[7] As discussed by de Ferranti et al. (2002) in the context of Latin America, this is one of a number of reasons why skills upgrading is crucial for trade to have a positive impact on poverty.

Figure 4 presents the enrollment at the tertiary level (a skill upgrading capacity) as a percentage of total population for a set of developing countries along with the United States and France. Figure 4 shows that the capacity for skill upgrading is based on the resources available for development. Developed countries do better than middle-income countries and middle-income countries do better than low income countries. Thus, if trade leads to increases in per-capita incomes, it might also create the resources at both the macro level (government spending boosted by increased revenues) and micro level (higher private allocation to education) for skill upgrading.

---

[7] See Cragg and Epelbaum (1996), Chapter 5 of de Ferranti et al., Gindling and Robbins (2001), and Robbins and Gindling (1999). For the case of South Africa, see Edwards (2004). More generally, Winters, McCulloch, and McKay (2004) note that "trade liberalization may be accompanied by skill-biased technical change, which can mean the skilled labor may benefit relative to unskilled labor" (p. 75).

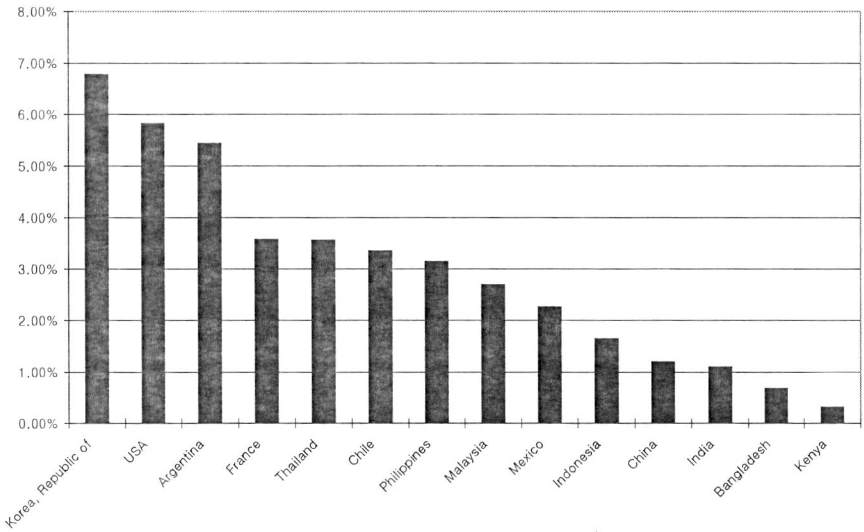

Source: Authors' calculations based on World Bank Development Indicators and UNESCO Statistics

Figure 4. Tertiary Enrollment as Percent of Total Population (2002).

Figure 5 shows the level of tertiary enrollment in 1980 relative to 2002 for the same set of countries as in Figure 4. This comparison allows us to see which countries showed the most improvement in this period. The date presented in Figure 5 show that countries that followed an export-oriented development trajectory through the 1980's and 1990's (i.e. Chile, Indonesia, Malaysia, Korea, Thailand, China and Bangladesh) have the most impressive increases in their capacity for skill upgrading. Countries that have been more insular through the 1980's (e.g. India and the Philippines, with Argentina being an exception) have less impressive increases in skill upgrading capacity.[8] Thus, Figure 5 seems to support the idea that increased resources created by trade do indeed create incentives for greater investment in tertiary educative capacity. However, it is intuitive that with increased income from trade, the micro-level increases will tend to perpetuate the skill bias in a certain section of the population since the benefits from the skill-biased, export sector will accrue mostly to skilled workers, and they in turn will reinvest in the their own education or that of their families. However, the macro-level increase in educational allocation might lead to the government

[8] Argentina did move towards greater liberalization through much of the early 1990's under the leadership of President Carlos Menem. Unfortunately, this took place under an inappropriate capital account arrangement (currency board) that proved to be disastrous.

targeting the poor, unskilled population and facilitate their access to better education. Thus, redistributive policies of the government will have a major role in determining whether opportunities created through trade can have a real impact on poverty allocation through skill upgrading.

Lall and Teubal (1998) emphasize that the learning process for skill upgrading in manufacturing requires the external support of education and training that is technology specific. This indicates that complementary educations policies on the part of the public sector are important for trade-supported productivity gains. Trade alone is not sufficient. An example of this is the initiative of the Costa Rican government to supply schools with computer technologies in support of a hoped-for emergence of an export-oriented computer products sector. This effort proved to be successful.

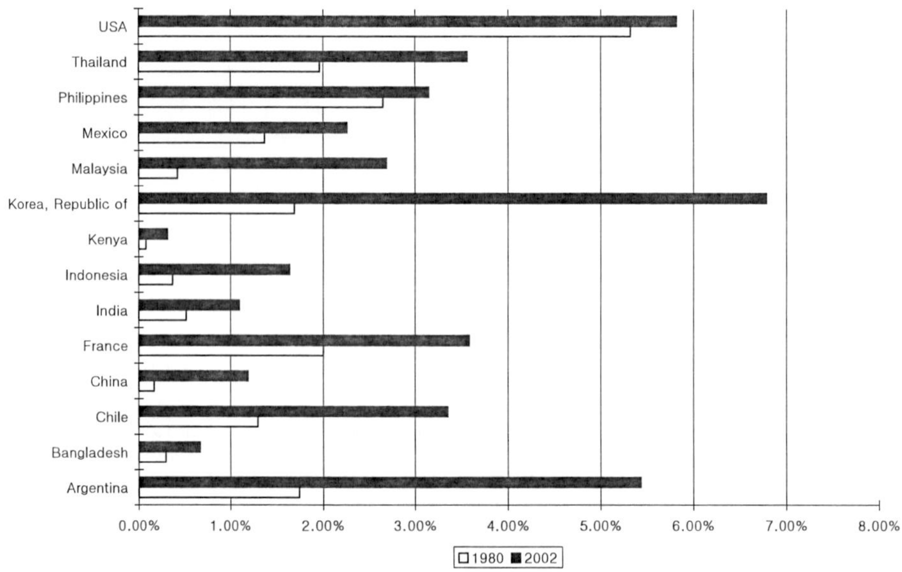

Source: Authors' Calculations based on World Bank Development Indicators and UNESCO Statistics

Figure 5. Comparing Tertiary Enrolment in 1980 and 2002.

Along with Lall (1998), one can distinguish between the *basic learning* that is required to export low-technology manufactured exports and the *deep learning* that is required to export high-technology manufactured exports. The required complementary education and training policies differ in these two instances. As stated by Lall (1998), "In early stages of industrialization, when skill needs are fairly low and general, the correct policy is functional support for schooling and basic vocational training. In later stages, with more complex activities and functions, skill needs grow more demanding, diverse, and specific to particular technologies" (p. 68). Beginning the process of basic learning, supported by functional educational advances, and then transitioning into deep learning, supported by more specific educational advances, are *both* important. Admittedly, achieving both of these objectives simultaneously is not easy, especially when educational resources are scarce, but the long-run support of real incomes depends on countries' abilities to do this.

The deep learning process that supports high-technology manufactured exports is important because there is some evidence that low-technology manufacturing exports can fail to deliver long-term real wage increases. It is becoming clear that not all manufacturing activity is supportive of productivity increases from technological learning over the long term. In the case of assembly or *maquiladora* export sector of Mexico, similar examples of which can be found all over the developing world, there are limits to productivity increases, despite the generation of substantial number of jobs. The assembly of high-technology product from imported high-technology inputs remains a low-skilled job, that of assembly. Thus, unless there effective production of high-technology products, including the value-added components of the goods and services that go into the final product, developing countries will not effectively move up the productivity ladder, and will remain low-cost assembly centers. In fact, there is a great deal of evidence that long-term productivity in exporting activities in support of long-term increases in real wages relies on manufacturing export activities being integrated into the local economy via sourcing of local inputs and local value added. Just the opposite appears to have occurred in the Mexican *maquila* sector.[9]

India and China

The relevant question, then, is what are the factors that allow a developing country to move up the productivity ladder so as to become competitive in the higher ends of the production chain? But a more subtle question is whether it is possible to manage the transition so as to continue to be competitive in the lower-skilled manufacturing exports while successfully integrating into the more high-tech global economy for a long-term economic transition. This would involve successfully doing the difficult job of creating a competitive cheap labor force and

[9] See, for example, Buitelaar and Padilla Pérez (2000).

creating a substantial number of highly skilled people *simultaneously*. We would like to argue that, given strength of numbers or scale, this is indeed possible and that China and India might become the two economies who achieve this multi-faceted transition most successfully.

In terms of conventional international economics, countries of the world can be broadly categorized into capital-abundant (both human and physical) developed economies and labor-abundant developing economies. The world's industrial geography also largely reflects this categorization with the developed economies dominating the more technologically-sophisticated and capital-intensive sectors and the developing economies specializing in the more labor-intensive sectors or in natural resource extraction (e.g., Lall 1998). To some degree, at least, this industrial geography derives from conventional trade theory. Given the relatively higher cost of labor in developed economies, labor-intensive production is offshored to places where labor costs are lower. While capital-intensive processes can profitably be substituted for labor in some instances, this is not always the case. The offshoring of labor-intensive production from developed economies in Europe and North America to lower labor cost destinations in East Asia and Latin America provide evidence that it is far easier to offshore labor-intensive processes rather than trying to redesign them as capital- and skill-intensive processes.[10]

The sensitivity of labor-intensive production process to labor costs is further underlined by the so called "flying geese" pattern of industrial location where labor-intensive production progressively moves from a relatively low-wage location to a location with even lower wages (e.g., Kwan, 2002). Such a flying geese pattern has clearly emerged in East and South-East Asia over the last four decades with low-wage export industries moving progressively from Hong Kong to Taiwan to Thailand and Malaysia and now to China and Vietnam.

Given the relative scarcity of human and physical capital in developing economies, it is difficult for them to undertake capital- and technology-intensive production. In some cases, capital scarcity can be overcome by Foreign Direct Investment (FDI) or well-organized harnessing of domestic capital resources. However, the capacity to harness domestic capital or attract FDI in technology-intensive production processes can be dependent on the size of the domestic market. Consequently, many developing countries are not in a position to create the conditions that would allow profitable investment into capital- and technology-intensive sectors.

---

[10] For one relevant discussion of the offshoring process, see Jones and Marjit (2001).

It is not that developing countries are condemned to be low-wage, labor-intensive producers for eternity. Selective strategic (in the broad sense) trade policy based on export promotion and leveraging domestic demand has been used for successful transitions from low-wage, labor-intensive production to industrialized economies as in the cases of Taiwan and Korea. The resultant focus on export-oriented industrialization allowed these countries to overcome the small size of their domestic markets by accessing markets globally. Government played a very important role in the execution of such strategic trade policies by easing access to capital (including technology) and helping in the creation of a skilled workforce.[11] More importantly, as these developing countries become more industrialized, wages increased and the more labor-intensive aspects of production re-located away from these economies to other lower-wage destinations in the "flying geese" pattern.

China and India appear to be potential exceptions to this typical evolution. A unique combination of market size, the absolute size of heterogeneous labor reserves, and international demographic trends all point to the fact that China and India can, under certain conditions, become globally competitive in *both* labor-intensive *and* capital- and technology-intensive sectors. In other words, both these countries can compete right across the manufacturing and services spectrum. This potential reflects the absolute size of their domestic markets as well as the characteristics of their labor markets. Large markets create competitive advantage for products that have substantial economies of scale. Yusuf et al. (2006) argue that, while scale economies can be achieved by initially relying on exports, access to large domestic markets offer significant advantages.[12] This has significant repercussions for global industrial geography, development and poverty alleviation.

Capital- and Technology-Intensive Sectors

Both India and China have very large domestic markets for industrial and consumer goods, including high-end goods. While both India and China are poor countries on average, sustained economic growth has created a large, urbanized

[11] See, for example, Westphal (1990).

[12] These authors argue that large domestic markets create a competitive advantage for any product that has substantial economies of scale, such as white goods or automobile assembly. Scale economies can be achieved without a large domestic market by relying from the start on exports, of course, but access to the domestic market and lower entry arriers can be significant advantages.

middle-class that provides effective demand for a large variety of consumer goods. Rapid economic growth and concomitant demand for industrial infrastructure and energy has also created a large market for producer goods. Yusuf et al. (2006) calculate the market for industrial goods in 2006 to be approximately US$950 billion in China and approximately US$350 billion in India. Using the figures provided by Yusuf et al. (2006) and based on average growth annual growth trends, the market for industrial goods in China and India in the year 2020 can estimated to be around US$3,073 billion and US$984 billion, respectively.[13] Thus, both India and China will increasingly possess huge industrial markets, providing economies of scale in production and incentives for FDI inflows. The large absolute size of India and China and their rising number of middle-class citizens also provide the basis for a large domestic capital market that can be mobilized to facilitate capital and technology intensive production.

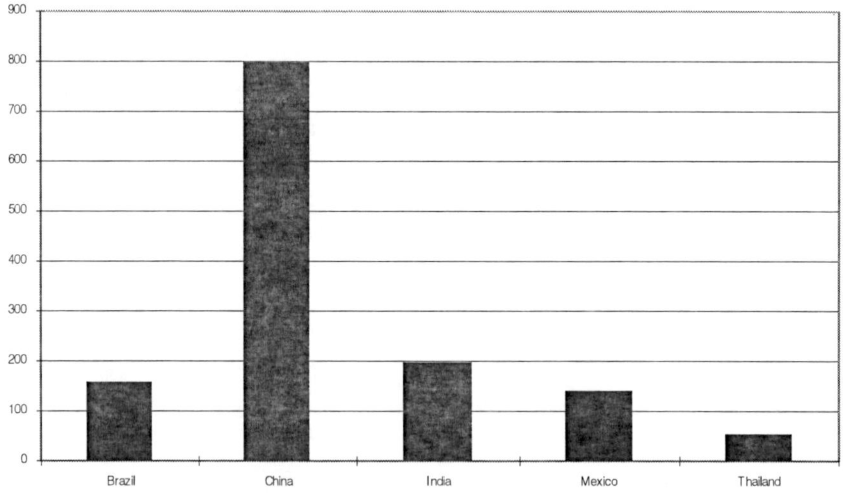

Source: World Bank Development Indicators

Figure 6. Gross Savings in USD billion for 2004.

[13] According to Yusuf et al. (2006), the industrial goods sector make up little over 50 percent of the economies of India and China. We make the assumption that growing urbanization and industrialization will increase this to about 60 percent of the economy. We also assume an annual economic growth of 8 percent for China and 7.5 percent for India in the period 2007-2020.

Figure 6 provides the gross domestic saving for a set of large developing countries. This figure shows that China has substantial domestic savings (about US$800 billion) that can be tapped for capital investments in technology-intensive sectors. Chinese gross savings is already about half of the United States (US$1.6 trillion in 2004). India, while well below China in terms of gross savings at about US$200 billion, is relatively ahead of other large developing economies such as Mexico and Brazil, and its savings and investment capacity is likely to grow substantially with increasing urbanization and expansion of the middle-class.

Table 1. Tertiary Students in Millions and as a Percent of the Population below 15

	Number of Students Enrolled in Tertiary Education (millions)	Students Enrolled in Tertiary Education as a Percent of the Population below Age 15 (percent)
China	19.4	5.5
India	11.8	4.3
USA	16.9	27.0
Europe	19.3	22.5

Source: UNESCO, World Development Indicators and authors' calculations

While a large domestic economy in absolute terms generates economies of scale and capital that can be used for the development of competitive capital and technology intensive industries, India and China's greatest competitive strength lies in their capacity to be relatively lower-cost locations for such capital and technology intensive industries. This is where China and India's advantage in having large absolute numbers of highly skilled workers comes into play. Table 1 presents both the absolute number students attending tertiary (undergraduate college or technical degree and higher levels) education in China, India, United States and the EU-15. This table shows us that the capacity for developing human capital in terms of college and technical education in China and India is comparable to that of the United States and the EU-15. While the percentage of the current population of young people who can be absorbed into tertiary education is much lower in India and China (approximately a fifth of that in EU and the US), both China and India have been increasing their tertiary educational capacity very rapidly. China is expected to increase the annual number of graduates in sciences and engineering from around 600,000 currently to about 5 million in 2020.[14] As reported in Yusuf, Nabeshima and Perkins (2006), India's training capacity for engineers increased by over five times between the years

1988 and 2003.[15] Moreover, India and China far outstrip all other developing countries in the accumulation of human capital through university training, and going by the trends, Indian and Chinese educational linkages with universities in industrialized countries will continue to increase rapidly in the coming years.[16]

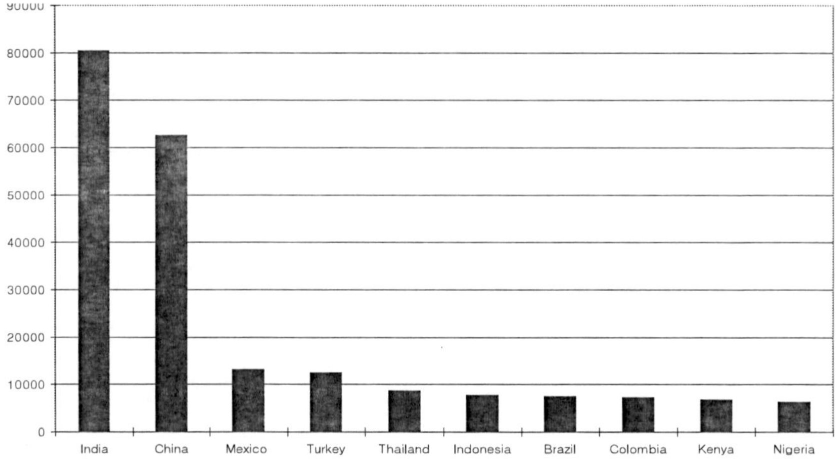

Source: Opens Doors Database 2006 on International Student Mobility, International Institute of Education (IIE)

Figure 7. International Students Entering US Universities from Top Ten Origin Countries.

Figure 7 presents the number of students entering US universities in 2006 from the top 10 developing countries. Such international educational linkages serve as important conduits of technology, innovation and production know-how to the source countries. They also lead to entrepreneurial and business linkages that facilitate the development of technology- and capital-intensive sectors in the home countries of the visiting students. The sheer numbers of Chinese and Indian

[14] See Yusuf, Nabeshima and Perkins (2006).

[15] See also Arora and Gambardella (2004).

[16] The Indian pharmaceutical industry offers an example of global competitiveness arising out of the combination of significant numbers of domestic skilled labor that can rapidly absorb complicated technological processes, large domestic market, and ability to harness entrepreneurial capital from a relatively large domestic capital base. As reported by Yusuf, Nabeshima and Perkins (2006), India graduates 15,000 chemists every year, and Indian firms like Ranbaxy, Cipla, Dr.Reddy and Wockhardt have the economies of scale and financial resources to embark on research activities involving drug discovery. These authors also report that Indian firms already control about a sixth of the global generic drugs market (US$8 billion of a US$48 billion market). India has become far more competitive as a location to develop new bulk drugs than the US or EU.

students visiting the US will thus have important positive ramifications for the development of technology- and capital-intensive sectors in these countries.

The relative cost competitiveness of Chinese and Indian skilled labor inputs has also been reported by the McKinsey report on the global labor market.[17] According to this report, the average hourly wage of a Chinese or Indian engineer is about 25 percent of that of an US engineer and about 22 percent that of a Japanese engineer. Given such vast cost savings on human resources that are often a significant portion of total costs of production in technology-intensive sectors, the incentive to relocate production to China and India will be extremely strong, especially in combination with large domestic markets. However, the McKinsey report does sound a note of caution that highly-educated Indian and Chinese workers might not be of as high a quality as elsewhere. While the students graduating from some of the best schools in these two countries are comparable to the best in the world, a vast majority of them have been considered unfit for employment in some of the more sophisticated sectors. The McKinsey findings put the number of quality engineering graduates at 10 percent of the graduating population in China and about 25 percent of the graduating population in India.[18] However, even after taking into account this cautionary note, China and India represent very deep pools of skilled labor that gives these countries a substantial competitive edge on capital and technology intensive production. The fact that they are rapidly expanding this pool of skilled labor will keep their relative cost advantage for some years to come.

The longer-term cost advantage in the highly skilled sector of labor for China and India is also based on global demographic trends. Figure 8 presents the total population below the edge of 15 in China, India, US and EU in 2005. If India and China can double their capacity for tertiary education (refer to Table 1), then in terms of the numbers presented in Figure 8, India and China will have, over a the period of the next 20 years around 31 and 30 million new workers with tertiary degrees. On the other hand, even if the US and EU increased their tertiary education capacity by 50 percent (a difficult task given the already large scale of their educational sectors), they will add around 25 and 27 million tertiary educated workers to their economies.

[17] See Farell, Laboissière and Rosenfeld (2006).
[18] See Farell, Laboissière and Rosenfeld (2006).

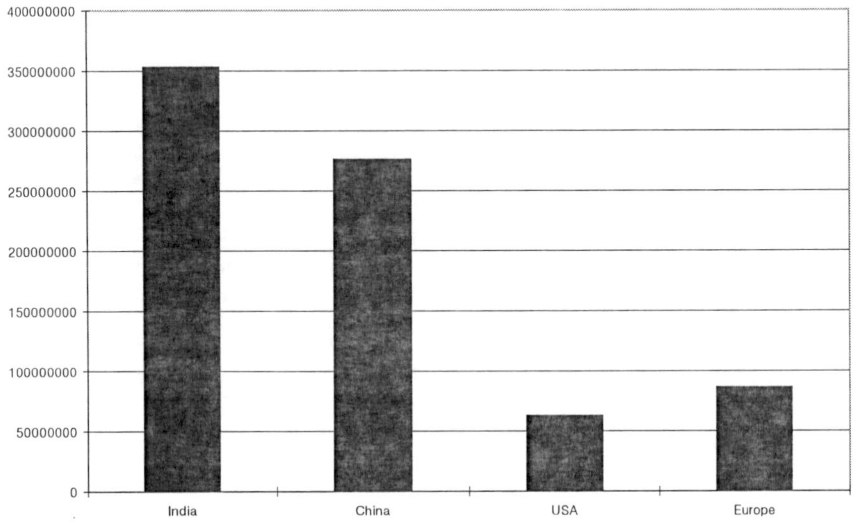

Source: United Nations Population Division, Department of Economic and Social Affairs

Figure 8. Population Below Age of 15.

Being competitive in the higher end of the production spectrum does not necessarily mean China and India will become global leaders in the *development* of cutting-edge technology products in the near term. The large absolute numbers of skilled workers will allow India and China the capacity to rapidly absorb complex production processes and undertake such production at a lower cost than the place where the technology was developed in the first place. Whalley and Xin (2006) report that foreign firms employ only 24 million out of China's 725 million workers, but the average productivity of such foreign firm employed worker is about nine times higher than the overall Chinese average and these foreign firms account for about 30 percent of Chinese industrial output. Such foreign firms also account for around 80 percent of China's total export of advanced industrial products. It is important to understand that this paper is arguing that China and India will rapidly become a competitive *production location* for high-end goods and services, not necessarily the *innovators* of such products.

Labor-Intensive Sectors

We have so far discussed Chinese and Indian competitiveness in the higher end of the value added spectrum, i.e. the capital- and technology-intensive sectors. However, as stated above, India and China will most likely be in a unique situation to be simultaneously competitive in the lower end of the value added spectrum, i.e. the labor intensive sectors. The reasons for this are identical to the argument presented for capital intensive sectors, namely, the size of the domestic market, domestic capital and competitively priced labor resources.

In terms of labor resources, if we assumed that 10 percent of India's population below 15 will be emerge as highly skilled over the next 10-15 years, there will still be a pool of over 300 million prospective workers with low and intermediate skills. This will be more than the total working age population in the US and EU combined according to current projections. Such a large pool of supply in combination with the economies of scale provided by the large domestic economies of India and China will allow the sustainability of competitive low-end assembly sector in these countries.

The ability of the Indian and Chinese economies to be competitive along the entire spectrum of the value chain has important policy repercussions globally. For the smaller emerging economies, India and China will remain a competitive challenge in labor-intensive and relatively low value added sectors such as textiles, agro-processing, and assembly of industrial products. However, as the economies of India and China continue to grow the consumption of low-cost FMCG (fast moving consumer goods) will increase substantially. This will represent a market opportunity for smaller emerging nations.

The industrialized OECD countries will face competition from China and India's advanced industrial and service sectors at the same time will be able to leverage low-cost technological inputs from them to make their own production processes more efficient and less costly. Such efficiency gains will allow OECD countries to compete with greater success in the global market. Most importantly, as production processes become more sophisticated and less standardized, driven by the low costs of processing information, niche markets will evolve. Different countries will be able to take advantage of these niches and the prospect of global production entirely dominated by India and China is highly unlikely.

Conclusion

The link from trade to development and poverty alleviation is not automatic. However, trade can be a powerful force for development by generating incomes, promoting competition and supporting productivity improvements. To move to fruition, these possibilities require the appropriate policy environments both in developing countries (e.g., supportive human capital development) and in developed countries (e.g., market access). Even within beneficial policy environments, the going can be difficult, with the need for national governments to simultaneously provide functional educational advances for basic learning and specific educational advances for deep learning (Lall, 1998). Without achieving this difficult task, the returns to export expansion can be diminishing in nature. Further difficulties arise from the fact that effective engagement with capital flows are a further requirement for positive trade-and-development trajectories. Failure to harness FDI flows can attenuate the potential positive effects of trade, and incautious opening to volatile portfolio flows and commercial bank lending can exacerbate financial stability and suppress trade.[19]

India and China together are home to just over half of both the world's poor and the world's extremely poor.[20]Consequently, any positive trade-and-development trajectories emerging in these two countries will have direct and indirect impact on global poverty alleviation.[21] Our discussion in this paper also points to the fact that India and China will be in a position to compete over very large spectrum of the value chain. How quickly and how well the Chinese and Indian economies are able to leverage their economic, institutional, and demographic advantage into real returns from globalization over the next few decades will be of continued relevance.

References

Abramovitz, M. (1989) *Thinking About Growth*, Cambridge University Press.

Arora, A. and Gambardella, A. (2004) *The Globalization of the Software Industry: Perspectives and Opportunities for Developed and Developing Countries*, National Bureau of Economic Research (NBER) Working Paper Number 10538.

[19] See Goldin and Reinert (2005) for a discussion of these issues.

[20] See the 2001 figures from Chen and Ravallion (2004) for example.

[21] This is the inequality vs. absolute poverty issue once again.

Buitelaar, R. M. and Padilla Pérez, R. (2000) "Maquila, Economic Reform and Corporate Strategies," *World Development*, **28**:9, 1627-1642.

Chen, S. and Ravallion, M. (2004) "How Have the World's Poorest Fared Since the Early 1980s?" *World Bank Research Observer*, **19**:2, 141-169.

Cragg, M. I. and Epelbaum, M. (1996) "Why Has Wage Dispersion Grown in Mexico? Is It the Incidence of Reforms or the Growing Demand for Skills?" *Journal of Development Economics*, **51**:1, 99-116.

de Ferranti, D., Perry, G. E., Lederman, D. and Maloney, W. F. (2002) *From Natural Resources to the Knowledge Economy: Trade and Job Quality*, World Bank, Washington, DC.

Edwards, L. (2004) "A Firm Level Analysis of Trade, Technology and Employment in South Africa," *Journal of International Development*, **16**:1, 45-61.

Farell, D., Laboissière, M. A. and Rosenfeld, J. (2006): Sizing the Emerging Global Labor Market: Rational Behavior from Both Companies and Countries Can Help It Work More Efficiently," *Academy of Management Perspectives*, **20**:4, 23-34.

Gindling, T.H. and Robbins, D. (2001) "Patterns and Sources of Changing Wage Inequality in Chile and Costa Rica During Structural Adjustment," *World Development*, **29**:4, 725-745.

Goldin, I. and Reinert, K. A. (2005) "Capital Flows and Development: A Survey," *Journal of International Trade and Economic Development*, **14**:4, 453-481.

Jones, R. W. and Marjit, S. (2001) "The Role of International Fragmentation in the Development Process," *American Economic Review*, **91**:2, 363-369.

Kabeer, N. (2004) "Globalization, Labor Standards, and Women's Rights: Dilemmas of Collective (In)Action in An Interdependent World," *Feminist Economics*, **10**:1, 3-35.

Kabeer, N. and Mahmud, S. (2004) "Globalization, Gender, and Poverty: Bangladeshi Women Workers in Export and Local Markets," *Journal of International Development*, **16**:1, 93-109.

Kapur, D. and Ramamurti, R. (2001) "India's Emerging Competitive Advantage in Services," *Academy of Management Executive*, **15**:2, 20-31.

Kwan, H. C. (2002), The Rise of China and Asia's Flying Geese Pattern of Economic Development: An Empirical Analysis Based on US Import Statistics, *Nomura Research Institute (NRI) Paper* no. **52**, Japan.

Lall, S. (1998) "Exports of Manufactures by Developing Countries: Emerging Patterns of Trade and Location," *Oxford Review of Economic Policy*, **14**:2, 54-73.

Lall, S. and Teubal, M. (1998) "'Market-Stimulating' Technology Policies in Developing Countries: A Framework with Examples from East Asia," *World Development*, **26**:8, 1369-1385.

Nordas, H. K. (2003) "The Impact of Trade Liberalization on Women's Job Opportunities and Earnings in Developing Countries," *World Trade Review*, **2**:2, 221-231.

Oxfam International (2002) *Rigged Rules and Double Standards: Trade, Globalization, and the Fight Against Poverty*.

Robbins, D. and Gindling, T.H. (1999) "Trade Liberalization and the Relative Wages for More-Skilled Workers in Costa Rica," *Review of Development Economics*, **3**:*2*, 140-154.

Rodrigo, G.C. (2001) *Technology, Economic Growth and Crises in East Asia*, Edward Elgar, Aldershot.

Rodríquez, F. and Rodrik, D. (2001) *"Trade Policy and Economic Growth: A Skeptic's Guide to the Cross-National Evidence,"* in B. Bernanke and K.S. Rogoff (eds.), Macroeconomics Annual 2000, MIT Press.

United Nations Conference on Trade and Development (2004) The Least Developed Country Report 2004, Geneva.

Westphal, L. E. (1990) "Industrial Policy in an Export-Propelled Economy: Lessons from South Korea's Experience," *Journal of Economic Perspectives*, **4**:3, 41-59.

Winters, L. A., McCulloch, N. and McKay, A. (2004) "Trade Liberalization and Poverty: The Evidence So Far," *Journal of Economic Literature*, **42**:1, 72-115.

Whalley, J. and Xin, X. (2006), China's FDI and Non-FDI Economies, and the Sustainability of Future High Chinese Growth, *NBER Working Paper Series*, WP 12249

Yusuf, S., Nabeshima, K. and Perkins, D. H. (2006) "China and India Reshape Industrial Geography," in S. Yusuf and L.A. Winters (eds.) *Dancing with the Giants: China, India and the Global Economy,* World Bank, Washington, DC, 35-66.

Zohir, S. C. (2001) "Social Impact of the Growth of Garment Industry in Bangladesh," *Bangladesh Development Studies*, **27**:4, 41-80.

In: Trade Liberalization and Protectionism
Editors: B. Hahn et al, pp. 175-192 ISBN: 978-1-60876-837-0

Chapter 7

TO PROTECT OR TO SERVE? ON THE ECONOMIC SIDE OF THE ANSWER

***José Caetano*[a] *and António Caleiro*[b]**
Department of Economics & Center for
Advanced Studies in Management and Economics of the
University of Évora (CEFAGE-UE),University of Évora, Portugal

Abstract

A protectionist policy on the part of the government is a recurrent behavior especially evident under severe crisis. Behind this attitude is the assumption that short-run benefits for nationals overcome the costs associated with protectionism. As a matter of fact, from a long-run perspective, the costs must include the expected reactions from the other trade partners. This, in turn, challenges even the responsibility hypothesis that supports the short-run behavior of the government as national citizens may indeed be characterized by a sufficiently large time-horizon allowing for an electoral punishment of the incumbent. The current global crisis is already contracting global trade at a rate of knots, spreading negative effects among countries, which is magnifying the impact of the fall-off in domestic demand. Nationals' crisis-fighting plans have spawned new obscure ways of protectionism, by discriminating against foreign firms, workers and investors. In this paper we scrutinize some controversial national initiatives that are gradually fragmenting the international economic field. We will emphasize the urgent need that multilateral institutions have to push trade

---

[a] E-mail address: jcaetano@uevora.pt.
[b] E-mail address: caleiro@uevora.pt.

higher up in the list of the political priorities, putting the recent Doha agenda on the right track.

JEL codes: C72, D61, D72.

Keywords: Protectionism, Multilateral institutions, Time horizons.

1. Introduction

A protectionist policy on the part of the government is a recurrent behavior especially evident under severe crisis. Behind this attitude is the assumption that short-run benefits for nationals overcome the costs associated with protectionism.

As a matter of fact, from a long-run perspective, the costs of protectionism must include the expected reactions from the other trade partners. This, in turn, challenges even the responsibility hypothesis that supports the short-run behavior of the government because national citizens may indeed be characterized by a sufficiently large time-horizon allowing for an electoral punishment of the incumbent that uses a myopic protectionist policy.

From a theoretical point of view, the situation described above can be modeled by assuming that a well-known situation, corresponding to a prisoners' dilemma, occurs. This formalization is considered in the first part of the paper. This is followed by a tentative verification of empirical support taking into account some episodes that occurred at an international trade level.

The current global crisis is already contracting global trade at a rate of knots, spreading negative effects among countries, which is magnifying the impact of the fall-off in domestic demand. Nationals' crisis-fighting plans have spawned new obscure ways of protectionism, by discriminating against foreign firms, workers and investors. In this paper we scrutinize some controversial national initiatives that are gradually fragmenting the international economic field.

In doing so, we will emphasize the urgent need that multilateral institutions have to push trade higher up in the list of political priorities, putting the recent Doha agenda on the right track.

2. A Theoretical Perspective on Protectionism

Given the costs and benefits of a protectionist policy, which most probably will be retaliated by the other trade partners/countries, it is possible to formalize the situation from a game point of view. To simplify, let us consider a country A, whose government may implement a protectionist policy (say policy p_A) or a non-protectionist policy (say policy $n\text{-}p_A$). These two kinds of policies interact with the same two kinds of policies by the government of country B, i.e. p_B and $n\text{-}p_B$, as a trade partner.

The combination of the possible policies of the two countries leads to the following pay-off matrices:

Country A			**Country B**		
	$n\text{-}p_B$	p_B		$n\text{-}p_B$	p_B
$n\text{-}p_A$	α	0	$n\text{-}p_A$	α	β
p_A	β	γ	p_A	0	γ

where, from a theoretical and an intuitive point of view, it is expected that $\beta > \alpha > \gamma > 0$.

Under those circumstances, it is straightforward to notice that the Nash equilibrium is composed by the pair of protectionist policies (p_A,p_B), leading to a welfare of γ in both countries. Plainly, both countries could be better-off by cooperating on the implementation of a non-protectionist policy, that leading to a higher welfare level for both countries, α.

As is well-known the cooperative solution of the game is not, indeed, an equilibrium as it suffers from credibility problems. Therefore, without some sort of mechanism imposing that both countries decide not to implement protectionist policies, a smaller level of welfare will be registered due to non-cooperative behavior.

As a matter of fact, one mechanism that may act as a binding constraint for the implementation of non-protectionist policies is the recognition, for instance by the electorate, that the repetition of the non-cooperative behavior may indeed be incorrect from a long(er) time-horizon.

To illustrate how the consideration of a long(er) time-horizon may induce the immediate implementation of non-protectionist policies it is enough to consider that the incumbent decides, or it is imposed by the electorate, to compare the discounted welfare, at a rate ρ, associated with the implementation of non-protectionist policies (case 1), and that associated with the implementation of a protectionist policy followed by a retaliation by country B (case 2).

In the case 1, the discounted welfare will be given by:

$$\sum_{t=0}^{\infty} \rho^t \alpha = \frac{\alpha}{1-\rho}$$

whereas in case 2, the discounted welfare will be given by:

$$\beta + \sum_{\tau=1}^{\infty} \rho^{\tau} \gamma = \beta + \rho \frac{\gamma}{1-\rho}$$

Plainly, the non-protectionist behavior should be observed whenever

$$\alpha \geq (1-\rho)\beta + \rho\gamma,$$

which is possible to be observed in case of a sufficiently large electoral punishment (Minford, 1995; Caleiro, 2004), i.e., through an increase in α and/or a decrease in γ, of protectionist behavior.

In what follows we present episodes that corroborate the ideas behind the relationship between the parameter values in the pay-off matrices, i.e., $\beta > \alpha > \gamma > 0$. In order to better understand and comprehend those episodes, it is important to note the similarities between the current crisis and the one that occurred in the 1930s, which is done in the following session.

3. Similarities on Trade Trends between the Current Crisis and the Great Depression

In the recent severe global economic downturn concerns are being raised that countries may try to improve their own trade positions in order to help domestic industries at the expense of others by imposing measures that artificially increase their exports or restrict imports. Such efforts are considered as a form of 'protectionism' and are often referred to as *beggar-thy-neighbour* policies. So, the inevitable global slowdown will intensify calls for more protection against imports and there is a real threat that the golden age of international trade will end with new waves of protectionism, in opposition to the predictions of the economic literature[1].

[1] Frankel and Romer (1999) show that trade is one of the variables which stimulates growth over longer periods of time. The economics literature also shows that well-functioning institutions depend on open markets and, clearly, the positive influence of economic freedom and private initiative in economic development is confirmed in empirical research (De Haan and Sturm, 2000).

The current financial crisis may foster protectionist behaviour, as occurred after the 1929 crisis (Eichengreen and O´Rourke, 2009). In fact, a similarity can easily be drawn between the present situation and the one that existed then: in the 1930s, unemployment was also rising, fears of deflation were prevailing, and a lack of public resources not allowed governments from remedying the economic crisis.

Moreover, today as in the 1930s, the context of decreasing prices can mechanically reinforce protectionist attitudes, as specific measures become more and more restrictive when world prices follow a downward trajectory. In this type of economic framework, protectionism is a tempting policy instrument for policymakers, because it myopically supports domestic activity, providing new public receipts, which may be seen as beneficial from an electoral point of view.

The economies of the triad (United States, Japan, and Europe) are in a deep recession and the emerging economies in Asia and Latin America are experiencing slower, if not negative, growth as well. According to the International Monetary Fund (IMF 2009b), world economic activity is projected to contract by ½ to 1 percent in 2009, the first of such fall in 60 years. As economic activity has slowed around the globe and trade finance has become harder to obtain, world trade flows have also been declined. The turn down begun in the summer of 2008 and has affected all the major trading countries.

The collapse in global demand brought on by the biggest economic downturn in decades will drive exports down by roughly 9% in volume terms in 2009, the biggest such contraction since the Second World War[2]. According to WTO projections, the contraction in developed countries will be particularly harsh with exports falling by 10% this year. In developing countries, which are far more dependent on trade for growth, exports will shrink by some 2%-3% in 2009. Economic contraction in most of the industrial world and steep export declines already posted in the early months of this year by most major economies — mainly those in Asia — makes for an strangely bleak 2009 trade assessment[3].

As the Figure 1 illustrates, by comparing current global crisis to the Great Depression, it can be seen that world trade is falling much faster now than in

[2] In projecting trade growth for 2009, WTO assumes a normal pattern for a recession, where trade falls, remains weak for a time and then resumes its upward trajectory and begins to return to its previous trend. See, WTO (2009b), "World Trade 2008, Prospects for 2009", PRESS/554, March 23, 2009.

[3] In the same line, the World Bank is also predicting that world trade flows will decline by 2 percent in real terms in 2009 after growing by 4 percent in 2008. This may prove to be optimistic because early 2009 data show signs of sharper declines in export volumes, particularly among the open Asian export economies such as Singapore, Taiwan, and China (WB, 2009).

1929-30, which is highly upsetting given the prominence attached in the historical literature to trade destruction as a factor compounding the Great Depression.

Source: Barry Eichengreen & Kevin H. O'Rourke © voxEU.org. Accessed at http://www.voxeu.org/index.php?q=node/3421 , on June 22, 2009.

Figure 1. Comparing the current and the 1930s crisis—the World Trade.

Evocative of these concerns, the leaders of the most-developed G-20 countries proposed at a November 2008 meeting to refrain from raising new barriers on trade in goods and services for at least 12 months and in the March 2009 Summit they prolonged this moratorium for one year more. Essential in this statement was a view that government efforts to protect local companies from the global economic downturn through the burden of trade barriers would only curb economic growth and prolong the global downturn.

There is an additional concern that a rise in trade barriers could turn the global downturn into a global depression. In the view of some literature, this is what happened in the 1930s as a result of the *U.S. Smoot-Hawley Tariff Act* of 1930[4], an event which triggered a cycle of retaliation trade protectionist measures, originating the world trade incurred a severe 66 percent drop between 1929 and 1934.

[4] The Smoot-Hawley Tariff Act of 1930 raised U.S. tariffs on over 20,000 products to an average level of 60 percent. After this, other countries retaliated by raising their barriers to U.S. exports. World trade flows incurred a severe 66 percent drop between 1929 and 1934.

Authors argue that this huge drop in trade contributes to augment the economic depression, by prolonging and deepening a global recession. Greater consensus appears to exist on the notion that it is better to keep markets open and boost world demand than to divert demand in domestic markets to home producers by raising trade barriers during a recession.

From the comparison between those two global crises it is easy to comprehend the reasons leading to the current evident indications of protectionism. These will be presented in the following section.

4. The Impressive Signals of Protectionist Trends on Trade

The spectre of widespread protectionism at the present time is the subject of frequent press and scientific articles. Until now it was possible to release many mass media alarms on the grounds that today's global economy has abundant firewalls against protectionism that did not exist in the 1930s. However, the accelerating global economic decline has increased pressures on policymakers to adopt a number of measures to help troubled industries that are considered by some observers to be "protectionist."

Protectionism is a resilient concept with manifold meanings. For many economists, no form of protection is legitimate because such interventions distort prices and misallocate resources over time. For some trade lawyers, only measures that are not consistent with WTO rules and obligations are protectionist and considered unacceptable. For some historians, efforts by countries to improve their own trade position and help domestic industries at the expense of others by imposing measures that artificially increase exports or limit imports express protectionism. Finally, for some politicians, protective measures that support constituents in times of global economic pain emerge as an act of political accountability, as the real aim is not to protect but to serve. In what concerns this last aspect, as pointed out in section 2, as the real aim of incumbents should be, at a minimum from a long-run point of view, to serve the social interests, this should be an incentive not to adopt protectionist policies.

In this context, pressures for protection are dampened by a world economy that is much more interdependent and integrated than in the 1930s. Leading firms have become so international in their production activities and in supply chains that they have developed a vested interest in resisting protectionism. Many industries that have faced import competition in the past have found that international diversification or joint-ventures with foreign partners are a more profitable way to cope with global competition than blocking goods at the border. In addition, lots of domestic industries have less incentive to ask for import restrictions because foreign rivals now produce in the domestic market, eliminating the benefits of trade barriers for domestic firms.

Taking into account this strong interdependence between firms around the world, the increasing trade protection is spreading and this is pushing the economy into prolonged contraction. In fact, there is already robust evidence that political pressures demanding import protection to defend employment are surfacing with increasing intensity around the world.

Based on information collected by the World Bank, a recent study performed by Gamberoni and Newfarmer (2009) shows that since the beginning of the crisis, officials have proposed 78 trade measures, excluding anti-dumping cases. Of these, 66 involved trade restrictions, and 47 trade-restricting measures eventually took effect. However, the impacs of these measures are difficult to evaluate due to the prevalence of non-tariff barriers, subsidies and contingent protection[5].

In a similar trend, the amount of antidumping cases surged in 2008, especially in the second semester. In fact, comparing to 2007, antidumping initiations grew by 15% and imposition of duties grew by 22%. Developing countries accounted for the majority of initiations, though developed countries accounted for the greatest number of duty impositions.

India was the most active country, accounting for 29% of total initiations, followed by Japan, China, South Africa, and Thailand. The US and European Union (EU) were the countries that most regularly imposed duties. For example, the EU in December 2008 imposed duties on preserved fruits from China as well as on imports of welded tubes and pipes of iron or non-alloy steel from Belarus, China and Russia.

A significant trend emerging from these actions is the reliance of developed countries on subsidies rather than border barriers, while developing countries have deployed all forms of protection. This certainly is witness to the greater financial power of public budgets in developed countries. Yet, once economic pressures for boosting economies are replaced with the inevitable need to reduce deficits, this pattern may signify similarly severe pressures on trade competition arena.

The referred measures have not considered the protectionist bias provoked in other economic activities, which had been particularly significant in the financial sector. While serving the urgent purpose of re-establishing financial stability,

[5] Curiously, 17 countries that implemented this kind of measures belong the G-20, which leaders issued a formal declaration at November 2008 meeting against the raising of new barriers on trade in goods and services.

virtually all nations have focused their subsidies on domestically owned banks rather than subsidiaries of foreign banks. Also, in the agricultural sector many national programmes have provided tough protection through price supports, so when commodity prices fall, direct payments to producers increase[6].

In a different way, workers in some countries have campaigned for restrictions on foreign labour. In the UK, for example, the dispute over the use of Portuguese and Italian contractors in oil refining at a time of swelling unemployment led workers to strike in protest and triggered several sympathy protests across Britain. Workers complained that foreign firms were overlooking skilled British workers. Malaysia banned the hiring of foreign workers in factories, stores, and restaurants to protect its citizens from mass unemployment along with the global economic downturn.

The episodes above presented are sources of an increasing concern as there are hints that do not reject the hypothesis of a toleration of the phenomenon by international organizations, as the next section shows.

5. The New Wave of Protectionism Tolerated by Multilateral Institutions

Probably, the creeping protection is not yet a most important cause of falling trade, at this point the global nature of supply chains and a lack of trade credit are the culprits. But history teaches us that protection does not move linearly, and a new murkier protection has been emerging as governments around the world massively increase their role in the economy (Baldwin and Evenett, 2009)[7]. Most examples of this kind of protectionism witnessed in recent months are not direct violations of WTO obligations but they are abuses of legitimately-created diplomacy which are used to discriminate against foreign goods, firms, workers and investors.

---

6 For example, Gamberoni and Newfarmer (2009) estimate that US overall trade distorting subsidies of about \$8.1 billion in 2008 are likely to rise to \$9.9 billion 2009. Trade-distorting subsidies push the global burden of adjustment onto commodity producers in Africa, Asia, and Latin America, where governments do not have resources to match subsidies of the wealthier countries.

7 Examples include abuses of health and safety regulations and clauses in stimulus packages that confine spending increases to domestic producers. For instance, the 'green protectionism' reproduces a clause in the recent US stimulus legislation that appropriates funds for advanced batteries and components, but only for manufacturers located in the US.

The well-known expression "buy America" generates effectively a vast storm and possibly has spread a new wave of protectionism over the word[8]. In late January, the US *House of Representatives* passed an incentive bill that would provide a 25% competitive margin for US iron and steel for all expenditures. Several governments and eminent economists objected forcefully to the provisions (Hufbauer and Schott, 2009). After the revisions included in the document, the final version expanded the coverage of the provision to all manufactured goods but added a specification that the provision be applied in a manner consistent with US obligations under international agreements.

This apparently exempts the EU member states and the 12 other countries that have signed the *WTO Agreement on Government Procurement* and the countries with Free Trade Agreements. These countries collectively supply about 25% of US iron and steel imports. It seems that this small change puts the new legislation into conformity with WTO rules and would imply no new restriction on federal purchases. It would still mean that government purchases of iron, steel and other manufactures from China, India, and Russia, among others, would be subject to the provisions.

After this, subsidies proposed for the auto industry have proliferated and total some $48 billion worldwide, mostly in high-income countries. In addition to the US direct subsidy of $17.4 billion to its national companies, other developed countries have also provided direct or indirect subsidies to its car dealers and component suppliers.

To the extent that the industry is laden with excess capacity, these subsidies hinder exit and delay adjustment and subsidies may be linked to requirements that firms preserve domestic employment, even at the cost of closing more efficient plants abroad in developing countries[9]. Likewise, to prevent this, governments have had to react to the policies of neighbours – for instance, Canada has matched the subsidies given to Detroit automakers to ensure that Canadian plants of American producers remain open.

---

[8] A more recent initiative was taken by the Chinese government that has introduced an explicit "buy Chinese" policy as part of its economic stimulus programme in a move that will amplify tensions with trade partners and increase the likelihood of protectionism around the world. In an edict released jointly the government said procurement must use only Chinese products or services unless they were not available within the country or could not be bought on reasonable commercial or legal terms. Further information is available in the *Financial Times* (online edition acceded in 19/06/2009 http://www.ft.com/cms/s/0/e1ddf11a-57b1-11de-8c47-00144feabdc0.html).

[9] President Sarkozy reportedly proposed that Renault and Peugeot-Citroen shut plants in the Czech Republic to maintain employment in France as part of its €6 billion package.

The recent bailout packages are another source that typically is characterizing these obscure ways of protectionism. For instance, UK banks receiving bailouts were encouraged to redirect lending towards the home market. French banks were encouraged to lend to airlines that might otherwise cancel Airbus orders. The examples of this new kind of protection show that the lack of transparency makes harder for politicians to resist retaliation against a trading partner's measures.

After the US started talks on a massive bailout of US automakers, Britain, Canada, France, Germany, Italy, Russia, Sweden and China are all considering or have implemented auto-industry bailout measures.[10] The automotive sector bailouts announced or discussed following the US decision evidence a deliberate pattern of retaliation/reaction, as we could confirm in the table 1[11].

Table 1. Stimulus packages in large countries (in percent of GDP)

	2008	2009	2010	Total
United States	1.1	2.0	1.8	4.8
China	0.4	2.0	2.0	4.4
Germany	0.0	1.5	2.0	3.4
Canada	0.0	1.5	1.3	2.7
Japan	0.4	1.4	0.4	2.2
United Kingdom	0.2	1.4	-0.1	1.5
France	0.0	0.7	0.7	1.3
India	0.0	0.5	……	0.5
Italy	0.0	0.2	0.1	0.3
Average	0.5	1.6	1.3	3.4

Source: IMF (2009a). "The Size of the Fiscal Expansion: An Analysis for the LargestCountries", Fiscal Affairs Department of International Monetary Fund, February.

From what was said before it is clear the urgent need that multilateral institutions have to push trade higher up in the list of the political priorities, and to reinforce the efforts for putting the recent Doha agenda on the right path. This fact will be made clearer in the next section, by taking into consideration the potential costs of a failed multilateral trade negotiation.

[10] This fact is in clear agreement with what was postulated in the pay-off matrices in section 2.

[11] President Sarkozy recently remarked "the situation in Europe means that you cannot accuse any country of being protectionist when the Americans put up $30 billion to support their automotive industry".

6. World Leadership and Institutions Must Put Doha on the Right Track

Despite the impressive evidence with reference to the spreading of the obscure protectionism over the world, several factors have clearly muted protectionist pressures and distinguish this global downturn from the pressures of the 1930s. On thc one hand, countries are far more interdependent through supply chains, imported inputs and so export interests are far more powerful than before relative to pure import-competing industries[12]. On the other hand, the successive GATT/WTO agreements and the raising of members involved in multilateral institutions, which currently involve 153 countries in WTO, should provide much greater legal stability of trading relations.

Focusing on the last issue, it could be sustained that international institutions and world leaders have to carry out additional efforts to avoid a real economic damage motivated by inaction. In fact, after seven years of intense and complex negotiations in the framework of WTO, the ministerial meeting in Geneva at July of 2008 did not reach a final agreement on the *Doha Development Agenda* (DDA).

If nothing happens to return for negotiations, the current trend of multilateral trade liberalization may not survive this failure and the global public good provided by the WTO that helps to free trade in a stable and less-distorted environment may be vanished. The context of the current crisis has been fostering protectionist behaviours and the threat of trade wars will become more and more prominent. So, as referred, the number of litigations at the WTO will continue to increase and countries may try to reverse past unilateral trade liberalization moves and this picture could be dramatic for the world economy.

A recent study performed by Bouët and Laborde (2008) evaluates the cost of a non-DDA agreement by studying cooperative as well as non-cooperative outcomes of these trade negotiations. The authors consider different scenarios, taking into account the future of the Doha negotiations, which implies an option for more or less protection in world trade (see Table 2).

Based on the results of this noteworthy study, the success of the Doha Round will reduce world protection by 22 percent, from 4.6 percent to 3.6 percent, but if it does not occur tariffs could double the level of protection in average. The elimination of recent unilateral tariff reduction during the past 13 years has a more

[12] The simple average of trade-to-GDP today is 96% compared to 55% in 1970 – and parts and components trade, an indicator of supply chains, has more than doubled as a proportion of total trade.

limited impact but still represents an increase of 40 percent in world protectionism compared to the baseline.

Table 2. Protection faced by category of countries in different scenarios of DDA

Scenarios	High-income	Middle-income	Low-income
Status quo (baseline)	4.6%	4.6%	4.0%
Success of DDA	3.6%	3.6%	3.2%
Tariffs raised to bound rates	9.0%	8.9%	11.7%
Tariffs raised to maximum of past 13 years	6.5%	6.3%	7.3%

Source: Adapted from Bouët and Laborde (2008). Reproduced with permission from the International Food Policy Research Institute www.ifpri.org <http:/www.ifpri.org>

Summing up, the Doha round will cut the applied protection by one-third for High-Income Countries (HICs) and one-tenth for the Middle-Income Countries (MIC's), a significant achievement when compared to previous rounds. Indeed, under worst scenario, protection could increase by 50 percent in HIC's, 130 percent in MIC's, and 270 percent in Least Developed Countries (LDC's) compared to the current level. In relative terms, the Doha Round manages to deliver homogeneous market access gains with an average tariff faced by the three groups of countries reduced by about 20 percent. The other scenarios, however, have significantly different results. In particular the LDC's are more harshly affected due to the losses of nonreciprocal preferences.

Under the Doha scenario considered here, focusing on only a tariff liberalization and domestic support discipline[13], world trade is augmented by a mere 1.46 percent, confirming the findings of other studies. In case of the *up to bound* scenario, world trade would contract by 7.7 percent and in the case of the less damaging scenario, world trade would be reduced by 3.2 percent[14]. These figures allow for a clear re-assessment of what is really at stake. A disagreement between WTO countries over the DDA would signal international non-cooperation, but, if the contrary prevails, results could be understood as a strong attitude and a firm commitment against protectionist policies.

---

[13] Tariff liberalization is just a part of the global agenda, which includes other source of potential gains that are liberalization in services, trade facilitation, and intellectual property rights.

[14] While such an increase in duties would especially impact agricultural exports (-6.9 percent), particularly harming developing countries' agricultural exports (-11.5 percent), the exports of industrial goods could also face a substantial reduction: 2 percent in developed countries and 4.8 percent in developing countries.

So, the success of DDA will not only play its international public good role by securing the trade setting but could actively contribute for decreasing the costs associated to probable trade wars in the future. Taking these fundamentals into consideration, the cost of inaction on the Doha Agenda is quickly rising, reinforcing the importance of pushing forward with a rapid conclusion of the Doha round[15].

The new world player G-20 should play an important role in this process by adopting additional measures and serious advices in order to strength the fragile consensus against this perilous wave of protectionism. The key commitments would be as such as to make countries give up from imposing new protectionist measures, to get the Doha round back on track, and to fund additional financing mechanisms for trade credit. However, these commitments require follow up and determined additional action.

The recent G-20 London Summit took place in late March at a time when global trade is falling at the fastest rate since the period of the Great Depression[16]. Some analyst sustain that the Summit strengthened the commitment made in the previous Washington Summit (November, 2008) in different important ways[17]. Firstly, going beyond simply measures that impact directly on trade, leaders committed themselves to minimising any negative impact on trade and investment of domestic policy actions, including fiscal policy and action in support of the financial sector. This represented a strong commitment to avoid a retreat into financial protectionism, particularly in measures that constrain worldwide capital flows to developing countries.

Secondly, a promising point was the G-20 call for the WTO and other international organizations to enhance their surveillance of protectionist measures and to report back publicly on a quarterly basis. This explicit call for a public and transparent WTO-led monitoring process to report regularly on all measures might potentially avoid distorting trade. This will lead to regular, clear and

[15] The decision by the WTO membership on 9 February 2009, in the Trade Policy Review Body will, in the meantime, contribute to regular multilateral surveillance of the world trading system (WTO, 2009).

[16] The WTO is forecasting world trade to decline by as much as 9% in 2009, driven by falling global demand and a shortage of trade finance. By one set of estimates, the volume of world trade fell month-on-month by 5% in November 2008, 7% in December 2008, and a further 7% in January 2009 – a 17% decline year-on-year.

[17] More information on this issue can be obtained at the "Global crisis debate" on http://www.voxeu.org/index.php?q=node/2824. In the section "Open Markets" (moderated by Richard Baldwin) the objective is to help answering the following question: *What should be done to maintain open markets and promote an environmentally sound recovery?*

comprehensive reporting of all policies that could have an impact on trade, putting pressure on G-20 members to refrain from protectionism and consider effects on other countries when setting their economic policies.

Finally, in what concerns to the Doha agenda, in their final communication, the G-20 called for the conclusion of an ambitious and balanced round. Nevertheless, what is important is not the conclusion of just any Doha Round, but rather a Round that fulfils the mandate that launched the DDA one, which explicitly prioritizes the needs of developing countries and addresses the imbalances already present in the rules of the global trading regime. G-20 leaders pledged their personal commitment to the round and agreed to prioritise the negotiations on the basis of the significant progress achieved so far.

In sum, this commitment to complete the round recognise these negotiation as a legally-binding long-term insurance policy against protectionism that would send a strong indication that the international community can work together to support open markets.

To reinforce this line, a novel WTO Ministerial Conference would provide an opportunity for political dialogue on how the global trading system can play a stronger role in addressing global issues, including poverty reduction, climate change, food security, and the sustainability of natural resources. It would also promote an enlarged discussion of governance reforms that would boost up the responsiveness of the WTO to developing countries and to exchange views on the future of the trading system.

The Conference could also take up other key topics, as the proliferation of bilateral and regional agreements spawned through asymmetric negotiating processes[18]. Indeed, for developing countries, a multilateral approach to trade rules, despite all its imperfections, offers them the best prospect for managing collectively the bargaining power that define global trade relations.

7. Conclusion

Trade growth data show declines that are larger than in past slow-downs. A number of factors may explain this. One of these is that the fall-off in demand is more widespread than in the past, as all regions of the world economy are slowing at once. A second reason for the magnitude of recent declines relates to the increasing presence of global supply chains in total trade. As a matter of fact,

[18] There are a lot of reasons to believe that the proliferation of preferential trade agreements have slowed down the progress on the multilateral freeing of trade, as with the Doha Round of multilateral trade negotiations. See Bhagwati (2008).

trade contraction or expansion is no longer simply a question of changes in trade flows between a producing country and a consuming country, as goods cross many frontiers during the production process, and components in the final product are counted every time they cross a frontier. A third element in current conditions that is likely to contribute to the reduction of trade is a shortage of trade finance. This has clearly been a problem and it is receiving meticulous attention from international institutions and governments[19]. A fourth factor that could contribute to trade contraction is protection. Any rises in protection will threaten the prospects for recovery and prolong the downturn. The risk of the spreading of protectionism is rightly a source of concern going forward.

In this context, the revival of the Doha Round will not be the magic pill to end global recession. However, monetary and budgetary policies only cannot bring back confidence to investors. The success of fiscal stimuli, while needed, might also be limited. A quick success of the Doha Round could thus be an essential element to foster investor confidence, which is crucial for the recovery in the real sector of the economy; but particularly confidence that spirals of regulations, spreading from the financial to the real sector might not occur.

At the same time, government action would also infuse confidence in the ability of political actors to work together in reducing the impact of a global slowdown and in indicating the ability of the world community to understand this crisis as an opportunity to look beyond short-ranged interests to lock in long-lasting benefits to the world economy. From this point of view, incumbents should be electorally penalized when adopting protectionist policies, despite being evident, in particular in the short-run, that this may only correspond to the (best) reaction to protectionism behaviour by trade partners.

The WTO will work with others to provide regular, clear, and publicly available reports to raise the level of peer pressure and public scrutiny on policies affecting trade. There is an obligation on all G-20 countries to rapidly and transparently declare their policies to WTO monitoring committees. For concluding the Doha round, trade ministers must now take action to deliver on leaders' commitments. Finally, individual countries and multilateral development banks must put in place additional trade finance resources and adequate measures, consistent with their international obligations, which last until market conditions recover. In concert with wider action to boost global demand and get financial markets working again, this will help keep trade flowing through the recession and support its strong recovery as the economy returns to growth.

---

[19] The WTO has been playing a role as broker by bringing together the key players to work on ensuring the availability and affordability of trade finance.

Given the constraints and conflicts in other areas such as fiscal stimulus and financial regulation, the outcome of the London Summit on trade is pretty good. This is especially true since it is hard to argue that trade policy failures have had anything to do with the crisis—at least so far. The impressive failure of banks put regulation high on the agenda. The nose-diving economy put budget stimulus on the agenda. While worldwide trade is in collapse, we have no choice when it comes to protectionism or the Doha Round.

Thus the stakes in WTO are very high and the July 2008 package appears to be the closest and the most hopeful step toward a global development agenda for a world turmoil. This requires an overall understanding that a world where political frontiers distinguishing nationals from foreign may be in conflict with a globalized world, i.e., one without economic frontiers to trade.

References

Baldwin, R. and Evenett, S. eds, (2009). *The Collapse of Global Trade, Murky Protectionism, and the Crisis: Recommendations for the G20,* VoxEU.org. Accessed at http://www.voxeu.org/reports/Murky_ Protectionism. pdf on June 22, 2009.

Bhagwati, J. (2008). *Termites in the Trading System: How Preferential Agreements Undermine Free Trade,* Oxford University Press, Oxford.

Bouët, A. and Laborde, D. (2008). *The Potential Cost of a Failed Doha Round.* International Food Policy Research Institute, Issue Brief 56. Accessed at http://www.ifpri.org/pubs/ib/ib56.pdf on 22 June 2009.

Caleiro, A. (2004). "Economic Policies and Elections. A principal-agent point of view", *Notas Económicas*, **20**, 89-101.

Eichengreen, B. and O'Rourke, M. (2009). *A tale of two Depressions, voxEU.org.* Accessed at http://www.voxeu.org/index.php? q=node/3421, on June 22, 2009.

Frankel, J. and Romer, D. (1999). "Does Trade Cause Growth?", *American Economic Review*, **89**, 3: 379-399.

Gamberoni, E. and Newfarmer, R. (2009). "Trade Protection: Incipient but Worrisome Trends," *World Bank Trade Notes,* **37**, March.

Haan, J. and J. Sturm (2000). "On the relationship between economic freedom and economic growth", *European Journal of Political Economy*, **16**: 215-241.

Hufbauer, G. and Schott, J. (2009). *Buy American: Bad for Jobs, Worse for Reputation.* Policy Brief Washington: Peterson Institution for International

Economics, February. Accessed at http://www.petersoninstitute.org/publications/pb/pb09-2.pdf on June 22, 2009.

IMF (2009a). *The Size of the Fiscal Expansion: An Analysis for the Largest Countries,* Fiscal Affairs Department - International Monetary Fund, February. Accessed on http://www.imf.org/external/ np/pp/eng/2009/020109.pdf at June 22, 2009.

IMF (2009b). "IMF Survey Online", International Monetary Fund, March 19, Acessed on http://www.imf.org/external/pubs/ft/survey/so/2009/NEW031909A.htm at June 22, 2009.

Minford, P. (1995). "Time-Inconsistency, Democracy, and Optimal Contingent Rules", *Oxford Economic Papers*, **47**, 195-210.

WB (2009). *"Global Development Finance 2009: Outlook summary",* World Bank Prospects for the Global Economy, June. Acessed on http://web.worldbank.org/external/default/main?theSitePK=659149&pagePK=2470434&contentMDK=20370063&menuPK=659159&piPK=2470429 at June 22, 2009.

WTO (2009a). *"Report to the TPRB from the Director-General on the Financial and Economic Crisis and Trade-Related Developments",* World Trade Organization, February 9. Accessed on http://www.tradeobservatory.org/library.cfm?refid=105042 at June 22, 2009.

WTO (2009b). *World Trade 2008, Prospects for 2009, World Trade Organization,* Press/ 554, March 23, 2009. Accessed on http://www.wto.org/english/news_e/pres09_e/pr554_e.pdf at June 22, 2009.

In: Trade Liberalization and Protectionism
Editors: B. Hahn et al, pp. 193-205
ISBN: 978-1-60876-837-0

Chapter 8

EU REGULATION CONCERNING GENETICALLY MODIFIED PRODUCTS: AN ISSUE OF FOOD SECURITY OR A MEASURE OF DISGUISED PROTECTIONISM?

Ana Maria Morgado dos Santos[1,a]
and José Manuel Martins Caetano[2,b]
Department of Economics,
University of Évora, Portugal

Abstract

The biggest producers and exporters of agricultural products have been adopting genetic engineering in order to improve the factors productivity and the firms profits. In the last decade, the United States of America (U.S.) and the European Union (EU) have established a high divergent regulation on production, distribution and consumption of genetically modified organisms (GMOs). Apparently, the EU's complex legislative framework related to GMOs was intended to satisfy the European consumers which are concerned about food safety and wish to make a more informed choice about the food they eat. The aim

[a] E-mail address: asantos1234@sapo.pt.
[b] E-mail address: jcaetano@uevora.pt.

of this paper is to understand the potential motivations behind the different policies on GM products adopted by the U.S. and EU.

Key-words: Consumers preferences; Food security; Genetically Modified Organisms; Technical barriers to trade.

1. Introduction

Gene technology allows an organism to be altered by introducing genetic information from another organism, across species boundaries (ANZFSC, 2003). This technology, also called biotechnology, has been used in sectors such as agriculture in order to increase the size of the crop that can be harvested from the same amount of land. For instance, particular traits have been added to the plants` genetic make-up to reduce the need for pesticides, to prevent insect and disease damage or to increase crops' tolerance to drought (Paarlberg, 2002; Zarilli, 2005).

However, no one has foreseen the widespread opposition or the strong public concerns elicited by the introduction of GM foods that took place especially in the EU markets. While firms with major interests in the sector, such as Monsanto, argue that GMOs protect the environment and reduce starvation, opponents, such as groups of consumers and environmentalists, namely Greenpeace, contest and assure that GMOs damage the environment, are responsible for allergic reactions in humans and increase the monopoly of the multinationals (Ackerman and Richardson, 2002).

According to the *International Service for the Acquisition of Agribiotech Applications* (ISAAA) the global area of biotech crops increased approximately 47 fold from 1996 to 2004 (James, 2004). In 2004, 29% of the global cultivated area was biotech (Zarilli, 2005). So far, the main genetically modified crops are corn, cotton, soybean and canola, and the leading biotech crop countries are the U.S., Argentina, Canada and Brazil.

The U.S. is the main producer and consumer of GM crops and the mandatory labelling of GM food is required only where the approved GM food has altered the characteristics when compared to its conventional counterpart (ANZFSC, 2003). In contrast, in the EU, only a few GM crop varieties were approved due to the moratorium imposed from 1998 until April 2004 that has limited the production, imports and sale of the vast majority of GMOs. Since then, strict rules requiring food labelling, traceability and a slow process of approval of new GM varieties has had a similar effect (Jackson and Anderson, 2005).

Such high divergent regulatory policies have had a significant negative effect on U.S. exports of food and agriculture products to the EU and led to a GM food US-EU trade dispute (Pew Initiative on Food and Biotechnology, 2003). Apparently, the European consumers' behaviour, who exhibit strong uncertainty avoidance towards the unknown, was the main reason behind the EU moratorium and the strict regulation concerning OGMs. However, despite the fact that consumer preferences have a recognized influence on international trade, an essential question remains: were, in fact, the European consumers the fuel of the US-EU dispute or were they merely used as pawns of protectionist interests? In fact, despite the economic rhetoric surrounding consumer sovereignty, trade policies have focused on the supply side and on regulations. In addition, some authors suggest that nations are seeking innovative ways to protect their domestic agriculture, namely through non tariff barriers to trade (OECD, 2003).

The objective of this paper is to understand why the U.S. and EU have adapted such different policies towards GM food. We aim to explore whether this issue is in fact a question of food security or just a protectionist measure against free trade.

2. The EU Legal Framework for Production and Sale of GMOS

In Europe, prior to 1998, crops such as GM corn and soybeans were viewed as equivalent to conventional varieties, implying that they did not need a separate GM label. This approach, which requires scientific evidence of risk for human health to establish security measures, became unacceptable in the EU following the mad cow disease (BSE) crisis in 1996. This crisis undermined the credibility of official food safety regulators, who had originally assured consumers it was safe to eat meat from BSE-diseased animals. As a consequence, consumers after 1996 began to mistrust authorities on GM products and to avoid eating this type of product. Consumer confidence was further undercut when a variety of groups, led by Greenpeace and green party leaders, started to attack GM food (Paarlberg, 2002).

Invoking the Precautionary Principle[1], which allows measures to be adopted in case of uncertainty or insufficient information, the European Commission (EC) decided in 1998 to place a moratorium on the approval of any new GM crop that

[1] The Article 5.7 of the SPS Agreement permits WTO Members to provisionally adopt SPS measures in the absence of sufficient evidence.

lasted until April of 2004. As a result, the production, the import and the domestic sales of GM crop varieties in the European area were dramatically reduced. Apparently, the pressure of the EU consumers who wanted to make informed choices about what they eat, led the EC to set up a tighter regulation concerning labeling and traceability of food and feed products produced from GMOs. This regulation requires labs for all products that contain GMOs above 1% threshold, and also call for procedures to ensure the traceability of all GM foods through the chain of production and distribution. The traceability requirement obliges the operators to keep a record for five years of all the individual GMOs that have passed through their hands, including information on where they come from, and to whom they were sold or delivered.

According to the EU, the regulation concerning the labeling was designed to enhance consumer confidence on GM foods and to facilitate consumer informed choices by providing on labels more detailed and verifiable information about GM content of foods and feeds. Moreover, the EU hoped this proposal would reestablish consumer trust in official food safety regulators. On the other hand, traceability of GMOs allows the monitoring and checking of information given on labels, the monitoring of effects on the environment and the withdrawal of GMOs which are potentially dangerous for human or animal health (Paarlberg, 2002).

Díez (2005) argued that the EU policy, by maintaining harsh standards of food safety, is unfairly discriminating against foreign suppliers. Roberts et al. (1999)[2] who have developed a classification scheme for the analysis of trade barriers in agricultural markets, included labeling in the list of the technical barriers to trade. In fact, foreign suppliers have to pay for different labels and compliance procedures in order to conform to labeling standards that differ across national markets. These additional costs can be so substantial that they prevent some of them from competing in the market and reduce trade (OECD, 2004).

At the moment, international trade in GMOs has to take place according to the rules of the World Trade Organization (WTO), in particular, to those spelled out in the *Agreement on the Application of Sanitary and Phytosanitary Measures*, the *Agreement on Technical Barriers to Trade* and the *General Agreement on Tariff and Trade* (GATT). Since biotechnology is propriety technology, the rules of the *Agreement on Trade-Related Aspects of Intellectual Property Rights* have to be taken into account on international trade in GMOs (Zarilli, 2005).

[2] Cited by "Organisation for Economic Co-operation and Development" (OECD, 2003)

3. Implications of the EU Mandatory Regulation for GMOs on US-EU Trade

The EU and the U.S. are each other`s main trading partners and account for the largest bilateral trade relationship in the world[3]. The main U.S. exports on agricultural products are cotton, soybeans and corn. In 2004, about 45% of the corn, 85% of soybeans and 76% of cotton planted in the U.S. were GM varictics (Pew Initiative on Food and Biotechnology, 2005). Furthermore, in 2003, the U.S. was responsible for 2/3 of the GM crops produced in the world (Pew Initiative on Food and Biotechnology, 2003), which shows the importance of this country as a global source of GMOs.

In this context, the EU moratorium has had a significant negative effect on U.S. exports to the EU. As a consequence of the U.S. loss of market share, the *American Bureau Federation* estimated a global loss of 300 million dollars per year. The decline of corn exports to the EU was dramatic: the EU share of the total corn export market had fallen from 4% in 1998 to less than 0.1% in 2004. On the other hand, GM soybean exports to the EU have not been affected by the moratorium because the EU had approved one variety of GM soybean prior to 1998 that American soybean producers planted exclusively. Since the EU market has a significant share (11.7% in 2004) of U.S. soybean exports, American producers have been reluctant to introduce new GM soybean varieties that have not been approved for the EU market. However, soybean exports to the EU have fallen (from 9.8 million tons in 1995 to 3.6 million tons in 2004). The EC argued that this decline is more likely due to the increased competition from lower cost producers such as Brazil, whose exports have risen from 3.0 million ton in 2005 to 9 million tons in 2002 (Pew Initiative on Food and Biotechnology, 2005).

In August 2003, the U.S., Canada and Argentina challenged the EU moratorium in the WTO, since food industry and farms of these countries have seen the moratorium as a clear infringement of WTO trade rules. In September 2006 a WTO dispute panel has decided against the EU`s application of its approval process for GMOs. The panel rejected the EU`s defence of the national-level bans as precautionary measures, arguing that enough scientific evidence was in fact available to carry out an adequate risk assessment (Bridges Trade BioRes, 2006).

---

[3] More detailed information can be found at the Web site of the Directorate of External Trade of the European Commission http://ec.europa.eu/trade/issues/index_en.htm.

4. Public Sentiment about GMOs in the U.S. and EU

Why has the EU not followed American adoption of GM food? The conventional wisdom is that Europeans have less trust in their food safety regulators than Americans (Jackson and Anderson, 2005). In fact, public opinion polls revealed that Europeans, in particular those of the North of Europe, tend to trust consumer and environmental groups while screening little trust in institutions such as government (Zechendorf, 1998). This is important since groups of consumers and environmentalists have been actively involved in campaigns against GMOs. In an opposite way, Americans tend to trust scientific and academic sources of information while tending to have very little trust in consumer and environmental groups (Lang and Hallman, 2005). Similarly, Loureiro and Hine (2004) suggested that whereas American consumers say they would like GM foods to be labelled, they remain confident in the policy of the *Food Drug Administration* (FDA) that does not require such labelling. This is also consistent with the historically high level of trust American consumers have had for regulatory agencies like the FDA.

Some authors have suggested that EU rejection of GMOs is linked to fear of the unknown and risk averting (Gaskell et al., 2003; Laros and Steenkamp, 2004). According to Vogel (2001), Europeans are more risk averse than Americans, especially with respect to issues of public health. However, The *Pew Initiative on Food and Biotechnology* (2005) argued that concerns on food safety are not the only factor influencing EU public opinion about GM crops and food. This research project pointed out that historically Europeans have a deeper cultural connection to their food than do most Americans. In Europe, in spite of the increasing of the supermarkets, they have not entirely replaced the traditional markets and the local specialized providers, such as bakers or butchers. In the other hand, most American consumers have little relationship with the food production process and acquire food from big supermarkets.

The GMOs issue is not a major source of controversy in the U.S. This is partially explained by the fact that Americans remain relatively unaware of agricultural biotechnology itself (Pew Initiative on Food and Biotechnology, 2005). Hallman et al. (2004) stressed that less than half of Americans realize that foods containing GM ingredients are sold in supermarkets and less than one in three believe that they have personally consumed GM foods. These authors argued that it is unlikely that many Americans are aware that there is a worldwide controversy surrounding the OGMs: little more than a third of Americans have heard of European demonstrations against GM foods, and less than a quarter were aware of the refusal of African nations to accept U.S. GM food aid.

Though Americans claim they are interested in various topics related to agricultural biotechnology, only about one in five Americans say they have discussed the topic more than once or twice with anyone (Hallman et al., 2004), a figure comparable to that of the United Kingdom, Greece, Portugal, Spain, and Belgium, though considerably less than Europe as a whole and substantially less than such countries as Germany and Denmark where reported discussion is at its highest (Gaskell et al., 2003). In general, Americans are more optimists about biotech products than Europeans and see the technological progress as a positive sign of economic and social development (Gaskell et al., 2003).

The differences on the agriculture scale and structure in the US and Europe may be another important influence on the EU public opinion towards GMOs. In the U.S. farms are private property and often posted against intrude. Besides, agriculture in the U.S. typically occurs on farms that are set apart from the urban centres. In contrast, in many parts of Europe, farms are much smaller and located closer to the urban centres and often adjacent to or in natural areas. Furthermore, the agricultural lands, in spite of being private property, may be crossed by hikers in some countries. These differences may help to make clear why many in Europe see what happens on farms as occurring in nature and why many in U.S. see farming as something separated from nature (Zechendorf, 1998).

Finally, the media are the main way to convey information about the scientific knowledge, like agricultural biotechnology, to the majority of the consumers. The presence or absence of an issue within the media plays an important role in public awareness and participation in that topic. The American press has not covered the GM foods topic extensively. That explains, probably, why so many American consumers seem apathetic toward this topic. The European press, however, has covered the biotechnology issues rather extensively, and this may have had an effect on public awareness and opinion, driving European consumers to be both cognizant of the technology and wary of it (McInerney et al., 2004).

5. Is There a Market for GMOs in Europe?

Since April 2004 a tough labelling law for GM food has been in force in the EU. However, and contrary to the expectations, consumers rarely find labels indicating the use of genetic engineering (GMO-Compass, 2006). Most the EU food companies have expressed their confidence in the safety of biotechnology. Nevertheless, they have pointed out that they avoid putting GM label on their products because consumers perceive label as health warnings rather than a way of conveying information about the application of genetic engineering.

The results of a Eurobarometer poll suggested that the opposition to the crops and the food GM has been decreasing gradually in the last years among the Europeans, though the majority of those inquired confirmed that they will continue to reject GMOs despite any potential benefit associated to them.

Trade association, representing the EU food companies (CIAA), stated that the new labelling rules do not have a helpful effect in terms of facilitating consumers informed choices, as it was the announced objective of the EU, since there are very few GMO labelled products on the market and, therefore, customers have no opportunity to exercise choice. The CIAA stressed that food industry and retailers are avoiding products displaying GMOs labelling in response to consumers` preferences for non-GM products. Apparently, no firm wants to take the risk of suffering competitive disadvantage due to lobbying moved by anti-GMOs activists. As a result, CIAA argued that industry will take all measures to guarantee that products on the market are derived from conventional plant material (ASA, 2006). Many producers have already changed the composition of their products replacing, for instance, soy lecithin by emulsifiers. Other producers are paying out a premium for soy with a written guarantee that GM content does not exceed the 0.9% threshold (GMO-Compass, 2006).

The CIAA suggests that if it was the intention of the EC to create an OGMs market in Europe, then the EU needs to go over the scope of the regulation or undertake a massive consumer education programme. This is because consumers` behaviour does not change rapidly but over time. Some authors secure that the old consumer's habit has to be "unfrozen" before a new one is acquired (Lewin, 1958 cited by Magnusson, 2004). The educative campaigns have an important role in this process since they may reverse the impact of media scare stories and the undermining of confidence in the safety of GM derived food products engendered by anti-GM activists.

6. What`s behind the Regulation Concerning GMOs in the EU and the U.S.?

A first step in solving the GM food US-EU trade dispute is to understand the true EU policymakers` motives. What is behind this trade dispute? The EU moratorium and strict regulation concerning GMOs was intended to satisfy consumers` desires to make informed decisions about the food they eat or was a hidden protectionist measure?

Consumer groups such as the *European Consumer Organization* (BEUC) and the *European Organization of Consumer Cooperatives* (EuroCoop) have, certainly, influenced EU policy. Furthermore, environmental groups opposed to GM foods have flourished at the same time. However, that is unlikely to be the main reason for the policy difference between the counterparts, since both groups have been active in America as well (Jackson and Anderson, 2005).

Thornsbury and Fairchild (2004) argued that as consumer preferences become more important in international trade, some groups of interests will attempt to influence those preferences. Therefore, and despite the dignified goals of the consumer groups, their pursuits may have been manipulated and influenced by political and economic interests of the EU.

So far, there is no evidence that GM food can be more toxic or carcinogenic, result in more allergies, or be less nutritive than GM-free food. Moreover, no evidence was found that the modified genes may survive digestion and alter the genome of the person or animal consuming them. A report issued by eminent scientists and published by the UK government found no adverse effects anywhere in the world. Like other reports it concluded: "the risks to human health are very low for GM crops currently on the market". Moreover, no theoretical reason or empirical evidence was found in the study to suggest that GM crops "would be any more invasive or persistent, or toxic to soil or wildlife outside the farmed environment than conventional crop varieties, or spread their genes to other plants" (King, 2003).

This suggests the need to consider the influence of producers and economic interest on the EU policy towards GMOs as well. Anderson et al. (2004) developed a political economy model that takes into account the political influence of special interest groups, namely, farmers. Their results showed that consumers or environmentalist opposition to GM crops were not the only reasons behind the EU moratorium and the strict EU regulation concerning GMOs. These authors suggested that difference in comparative advantage in the adoption of GM crops might have been sufficient to explain the different trans-Atlantic GM policies.

On the one hand, the optimal response of farmers in a country with a comparative advantage in GM technology may be to lobby for lax controls of GM production and usage. On the other hand, farmers in a country with a comparative disadvantage in GM adoption can obtain cost advantage by lobbying for more strict GM standards.

The US farmers have strong interest in a lax GMOs regulation of production, in order to exploit the new technology before it is disseminated beyond the US. They also have a strong interest in a low degree of GMOs consumer regulation either at home either in their export markets, given that they supply more than half of global exports (Jackson and Andersons, 2005). In fact, US producers will be less competitive if they have to comply with EU labelling and traceability rules since they drive up prices. International financial consultancy, KPMG, estimated that mandatory labelling in Canada would result in an increasing cost equal 35–41% of producer prices. It is important to stress that KPMG study did not include any cost estimates for the numerous products recalls that will inevitably occur annually due to accidental "GMOs" mislabelling (ASA, 2006). As Holm and Kildevang (1996) pointed out, price is a powerful determinant of consumer choices.

The U.S. agricultural biotechnology firms, also have a clear boost for promoting GM adoption. Since they were more prevalent, more politically influential, and/or more advanced in the US than in the EU, that would be an additional reason for the observed difference in GM policies (Anderson et al., 2004).

In contrast, EU farmers have strong interest in a high degree of GMOs regulation of production and distribution. Even if they could benefit from a more productive technology, the first-available GM food crops (corn and soybean) are not of major importance to them. Besides, GM technology would be less profitable in the European landescape since non-GM crops and nature areas are much closer than in U.S. That would required more buffer zoning per hectare of GM crop in Europe than in the broad-acre landscapes of the U.S. As a consequence, for EU small farmers, the potential productivity gains may be offset by the management cost of buffer zoning. Therefore, there would be a higher number of EU than U.S .farmers that will continue to produce just non-GM. That proportion would be higher as greater would be the opposition against the environmental and consumer groups to the selling GM foods in Europe.

Other important issue that probably European farmers are taking into account is the extent to which their crop products are internationally competitive. Since the U.S. and other countries have already adopted GM technology, EU producers may be more competitive in their own and in third country markets due to the fact that consumers in those markets are GM averse, and more so the stricter are policies towards GM foods. The EU livestock producers are unlikely to benefit as much from the GM technology as the more corn and soybean intensive livestock producers. Therefore, they also could support anti-GM policies (Jackson and Anderson, 2005).

Jackson and Anderson (2005) suggested another possible reason for the EU`s strict GM food policy. They hypothesized that government is giving EU biotech firms time to catch up with American competitors so that intellectual property rights are paid to domestic rather than foreign patent holders. The slow approval process of new GM varieties in EU may, probably, support this idea.

7. Conclusion

The controversy surrounding the GMOs continues to be emotional due to the lack of conclusive scientific evidence on the current or potential impact of agricultural biotechnology on human and animal health and on the environment. The EU and the U.S. have adopted domestic regulation on the approval, labelling and documentation requirements for GMOs that varies substantially. Apparently, the EU tight mandatory labelling and traceability of GMOs was intend to satisfy the European consumers who are concerned about food safety and whish to make more informed choice about the risks related with the food they eat. However, some authors suggested that this regulation just meant to protect the interests of some agents of the EU. The discussion presented above take us some way towards arguing that, apparently, in the case of OGMs the European consumers were used as pawns of protectionist. The exploratory nature of this paper stressed the importance of consumer preferences on international trade disputes and how those preferences can potentially be manipulated by organized groups of interests.

References

Anderson, K., Damania, R., and Jackson, L. A. (2004), *Trade, standards, and the political economy of Genetically Modified food*, Centre for International Economic Studies, Paper 0410.

ANZFSC (2003). *Report on the review of labelling of genetically modified foods*. Australian New Zealand Food Standards Council.

Ackerman, J. and Richardson, J. (2002). Alimentos muito alterados? *National Geographic Portugal* **14**: 3-21.

ASA (2006). *EU labeling and traceability rules for biotech products – Trade effects*. American Soybean Association, May 2006.

Bridges Trade BioRes (2006). *Biotech panel calls on EU to Conform with WTO rules*, Volume 6, Number 7.

Díez, M. C. F. (2005). Welfare measures and mandatory regulation for transogenic food in the European Union: a theoretical framework for the analysis. *Proceedings of the 11th Congress of the EAAE* "Future of Rural

Europe in the Global Agri-food System", Copenhagen, Denmark, August 24-27.

Gaskell, G., Allum, N. C., and Stares, S. R. (2003). *Europeans and Biotechnology in 2002: Eurobarometer 58.0.* Brussels: European Commission.

GMO-Compass (2006). *Labelled goods hard to find.*

Hallman, W. K., Hebden, W. C., Cuite, C. L., Aquino, H. L., and Lang, J. T. (2004). *Americans and GM Food: Knowledge, Opinion & Interest in 2004.* (Food Policy Institute Report No. RR-1104-007). New Brunswick, NJ: Rutgers University, Food Policy Institute.

Holm, L. and Kildevang, H. (1996). Consumers` views on food quality. A qualitative interview study. *Appetite* **27**: 1-14.

IFIC (2006). Food biotechnology. *A study of US consumer attitudinal trends. 2006 Report.* International Food Information Council.

Jackson, L. A. and Anderson, K. (2005). What`s behind GM food trade dispute? *World Trade Review* **4**: 203-228.

James, C. (2004). *Global status of commercialised biotech/GM food: 2004.* International Service for the Acquisition of Agri-biotech Applications, Ithaca NY.

King, D. K. (2003). *GM Science Review: First Report.* Prepared by the GM Science Review Panel under the chairmanship of Sir David King for the UK Government, July.

Lang, J. T., and Hallman, W. K. (2005). Who Does the Public Trust? The Case of Genetically Modified Food in the United States. *Risk Analysis* **25**: 1241-1252.

Laros, F. J. M. and Steenkamp, J. E. M. (2004). Importance of fear in the case of genetically modified food. *Psychology & Marketing*, **21**: 889-908.

Loureiro, M. L. and Hine, S. (2004). Preferences and willingness to pay for GM labeling policies. *Food Policy*, **29**: 467-483.

Magnusson, M. (2004). *Consumer Perception of Organic and Genetically Modified Food.* PhD thesis. Uppsala University.

McInerney, C., Bird, N. and Nucci, M. (2004). The Flow of Scientific Knowledge From Lab to the Lay Public: the Case of Genetically Modified Food. *Science Communication,* **26**: 75-106.

OECD (2004). *Analysis of non-tariff measures.* The case of labelling: overview and analysis of WTO data, TD/TC/WP(2002)40/FINAL, Organisation for Economic Co-operation and Development, Paris.

Paarlberg, R. L. (2002). *The contested governance of GM foods: implications for US-EU trade and the developing world,* Paper Nº 02-04, July 2002.

Pew Initiative on Food and Biotechnology (2005). U.S. *vs* E.U.: An examination of the trade issues surrounding genetically modified food.

Pew Initiative on Food and Biotechnology (2003). U.S. *vs* E.U.: An examination of the trade issues surrounding genetically modified food.

Thornsbury, S. and Fairchild, G. (2004). King or Pawn? Consumer Preferences in International Trade. *Choices,* 1st quarter 2004.

Unnevehr, L. and Roberts, D. (2003). Food safety and quality: regulations, trade, and the WTO. *Proceedings of the International Conference on Agricultural policy reform and the WTO: where are we heading?*. June 23-26, Capri, Italy.

Vogel, D. (2001). *The new politics of risk regulation in Europe.* London School of Economics and Political Science. London, United Kingdom.

Zarrilli, S. (2005). International trade in GMOs and GM products: national and multilateral legal frameworks, *Policy Issues in International Trade and Commodities Study Series* nº **29**, UNCTAD, New York and Geneva.

Zechendorf, B. (1998). Agricultural biotechnology: Why do Europeans have difficulty accepting it? *AgBioForum*, **1**: 8-13.

In: Trade Liberalization and Protectionism ISBN 978-1-60876-837-0
Editors: B. Hahn et al, pp. 207-231

Chapter 9

BILATERAL FREE TRADE AGREEMENT IN VERTICAL TRADE STRUCTURE*

Hiroshi Kurata[a,†] ***Yasushi Kawabata***[b] ***and Akihiko Yanase***[c]
[a]Faculty of Economics, Tohoku Gakuin University, Japan
[b]Faculty of Education, Mie University, Japan
[c]Graduate School of International Cultural Studies, Tohoku University, Japan

Abstract

We investigate the welfare effect of the bilateral free trade agreement (FTA) in a vertical trade structure. We consider a three-country model with one country exporting intermediate goods (upstream country) and two countries exporting final goods (downstream countries). We focus on the situation where both the upstream and downstream countries impose positive import tariffs before forming the FTA. We then consider an FTA between the upstream country and one of the downstream countries. The other downstream country is regarded as a nonmember country. After forming the FTA, all of the tariffs between the member countries are

*We would like to thank Kenzo Abe, Ichiroh Daitoh, Taiji Furusawa, Yoichi Hizen, Jun-ichi Itaya, Yukio Karasawa, Kazuharu Kiyono, Noritaka Kudoh, Kazuo Machino, Ryoichi Nomura, Masao Oda, Takao Ohkawa, Makoto Okamura, Masayuki Okawa, Chisato Shibayama, Nobuhito Suga, Hajime Sugeta, Yasunobu Tomoda, Kei-ichi Umada, Shigemi Yabuuchi, and Chisato Yoshida for their constructive comments and suggestions. The usual disclaimer applies. This work has been financially supported by the Japan Economic Research Foundation and Grants-in-Aid for Scientific Research (C) (No. 21530217).

†E-mail address: hkurata@tscc.tohoku-gakuin.ac.jp

eliminated, whereas the tariffs between the FTA member and nonmember are maintained. We have two scenarios in relation to the FTA; the first one is the case where external tariff reform by the FTA member country is not allowed, and the second one is the case where external tariff reform is allowed. Then, in the first scenario, the FTA unambiguously decreases the nonmember's welfare, while it may or may not increase the FTA members' welfare. The latter result depends on the number of firms producing the intermediate and the final goods and on the levels of the initial tariffs. Irrespective of an increase of the FTA members' welfare, Pareto-improving FTA is not possible. In contrast, in the second scenario, if an external tariff reform, *i.e.*, a reduction of tariff by the FTA member, is available, there exist some possibilities that the FTA increases both of the FTA members' welfare without changing the nonmember's welfare. Therefore, Pareto-improving welfare is possible.

Key Words: Free trade agreements; Vertical trade; External tariff reform; Cournot competition

JEL classifications: F12; F13; F53

1. Introduction

In the last two decades, free trade agreements (FTAs) have rapidly increased in the world economy. According to the Japanese Ministry of Economy, Trade and Industry (2006), there were 24 FTAs worldwide in 1986, and there were 193 by 2006. In particular, countries in Asia, the Middle East and Africa, which previously lacked FTAs, are now driving forward the formation of FTAs.

As the number of FTAs increases, research on FTAs has become a prominent issue in the international trade theory. The previous literature (*e.g.*, Kiyono, 1993; Kose and Riezman, 2000; Yi, 2000; Raff, 2001; Bond et al., 2004) focuses on horizontal trade, *i.e.*, international trade in which countries mutually export final goods.

However, vertical trade, *i.e.*, international trade in which one country exports intermediate goods to other countries that process the imported inputs into final goods for their exports, is of growing importance in recent trade transactions. Such vertical trade relationships are of particular note in the Asian region. For example, Japan exports some parts such as semiconductors for computers to other Asian countries, including China, and imports computers mainly from China (JETRO, 2006). It is necessary to reevaluate FTAs, taking account of the vertical trade structure in the Asian region.

Thus, the purpose of this chapter is to examine the welfare effect of FTAs in the context of vertical trade. To analyze this, we construct a simple three-country model with one country exporting intermediate goods and importing final goods (*upstream country*) and two countries importing intermediate goods and exporting final goods (*downstream countries*). Before forming the FTA, each country imposes positive import tariffs. We then consider an FTA between the upstream country and one of the downstream countries. The other down-stream country is regarded as a non-member country. After forming the FTA, all tariffs between the FTA member countries are eliminated, while an external tariff of the upstream country and the tariff of the non-member downstream country are maintained. In this setting, we investigate how the formation of the FTA affects each country's welfare.

We have two scenarios in relation to the FTA; the first one is the case where external tariff reform by the FTA member country is not allowed, and the second one is the case where external tariff reform is allowed.[1] In the latter case, in particular, we consider a reduction of the member's external tariff such that the trade volume from the nonmember country and, as a result, the nonmember's welfare are unchanged.[2] In other words, we consider the Kemp-Wan-Ohyama-type tariff reduction (Ohyama, 1972; Kemp and Wan, 1976).

Under these scenarios, we have the following outcomes. In the first scenario, where external tariff reform by the FTA member is not allowed, the FTA unambiguously makes the nonmember worse off, whereas it may or may not make the FTA member countries better off, depending on the number of firms producing the intermediate and the final goods and the initial tariff levels. Irrespective of an increase of the FTA members' welfare, the FTA is not Pareto-improving,

[1]On the external tariff reform, Naito and Abe (2008) examine welfare and revenue effects of tariff and tax reform in a country importing final and intermediate goods under imperfect competition. The analysis of this chapter is related to theirs, but is different in that the upstream and downstream countries mutually trade the final and intermediate goods and in that our focus is on the effect of the bilateral FTA with the external tariff reform.

[2]The assumption of a reduction of the external tariff by the FTA member country is reasonable from two viewpoints. First, from the institutional viewpoint, the GATT article XXIV prohibits the imposition of an external tariff that is more restrictive relative to the situation before the formation of the FTA. Following this article, we propose a reduction of the external tariff such that the trade volume is unchanged. Second, from the theoretical viewpoint, the tariff complementarity effect (Bagwell and Staiger, 1999) is well known in the studies on FTAs. That is, the reduction of the external tariff makes the FTA member countries better off because it promotes competition between exporting countries. Therefore, it is quite reasonable to assume that the FTA member countries implement a reduction of the external tariff.

because it gives welfare loss to the nonmbember country. In contrast, in the second scenario, if the FTA member reduces the external tariff so as to keep the nonmenmer's welfare before and after the FTA, there exist some possibilities that the FTA makes both of the members better off under certain conditions regarding the number of firms producing the intermediate and the final goods and the initial tariff levels. That is, the FTA can be Pareto-improving. These results are explained by the properties of vertical trade. Therefore, it is worthwhile to investigate the welfare effect of FTAs.

For the setup of our analysis, we apply the models in the research on trade policy under vertical trade (*e.g.*, Bernhofen, 1997; Ishikawa and Spencer, 1999; Chang and Sugeta, 2004; Yanase and Kawabata, 2008). As we noted above, the main focus of this chapter is on the welfare effect of FTAs. Therefore, this chapter links these two research streams and provides a new insight into the research on FTAs.

The rest of the chapter is organized as follows. Section 2 presents the basic model and finds the equilibrium. Section 3 refers to the first scenario of the FTA. We focus on the effect of an FTA on welfare for each country without external tariff reform. Section 4 considers the second scenario, which allows the FTA member country to reform the external tariff. Finally, section 5 briefly concludes this chapter.

2. The Model and Equilibrium

The world economy consists of three countries, A, B and C, between which a final good and an intermediate good are traded. The intermediate good is produced only in country A, which has m identical firms. In contrast, there exist n identical firms producing the final good in countries B and C, respectively, whereas there are no firms producing the final good in country A. Moreover, we assume that consumption of the final good takes place only in country A. Therefore, the trade pattern is that the upstream country A exports the intermediate good to the downstream countries B and C,[3] and imports the final good from these downstream countries.

Markets in the final and intermediate good industries are both imperfectly competitive. We assume that all firms behave in the Cournot way in these mar-

[3]Even if the markets in the intermediate good are integrated, the following results are qualitatively unchanged.

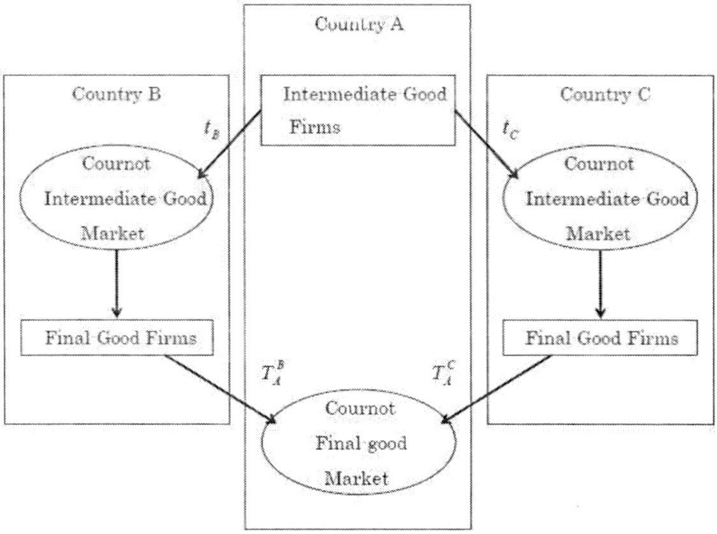

Figure 1.

kets.

The government in country A imposes a specific tariff, T_A^i, on imports of the final good from country i ($i = B, C$), whereas the government in country i imposes a specific tariff, t_i, on imports of the intermediate good from country A. Our setting is briefly illustrated in Figure 1.

In the subsequent analysis, we consider an FTA between the upstream country A and the downstream country B, and regard the downstream country C as a nonmember country. The FTA eliminates tariffs between its member countries A and B. Therefore, the values of T_A^B and t_B move toward zero after the FTA. In contrast, tariffs between the member country A and the nonmember country are maintained. In this setting, we investigate how the formation of the FTA affects each country's welfare.

The model involves two stages of decisions. In the first stage, firms producing the intermediate goods in country A (*intermediate-good firms A*) compete in the Cournot way and sell the intermediate goods to firms producing the final goods in countries B and C (*final-good firms B* and C). In the second stage, given the prices of the intermediate good, the final-good firms perform under

Cournot competition in the final-good market in country A.[4] We derive the subgame-perfect equilibrium of this model in the following subsections.

2.1. Equilibrium in the Final-good Market

We assume that producing one unit of the final good requires one unit of the intermediate good. Let us introduce an index ij to express the jth firm in country i ($i = B,C$; $j = 1,\dots,n$). Let y_{ij} and Y be the output of the final-good firm ij and the total output of the final good. Then, the profit of the final-good firm ij, denoted by π_{ij}, is given by

$$\pi_{ij} = \left(P(Y) - r_i - T_A^i\right) y_{ij}, \tag{1}$$

where $P(Y)$ is the inverse demand for the final good, and r_i is the price of the intermediate good in the market in country i ($i = B,C$). Firm ij chooses output y_{ij} so as to maximize its profit (1), taking the outputs of rivals and the prices of the intermediate good as given. From equation (1), the first-order condition for profit maximization for the final-good firm ij is obtained by

$$P(Y) - r_i - T_A^i + P'(Y) y_{ij} = 0, \tag{2}$$

$i = B,C$; $j = 1,\dots,k$. Since these firms are identical, $y_{ij} = y_{ik}$ holds in equilibrium for all $i = B,C$, $j,k = 1,\dots,n$, and $j \neq k$. Let us denote $y_{ij} \equiv y_i$, then we have $Y = \sum_{i=B,C} \sum_{j=1}^{n} y_{ij} = n y_B + n y_C$. Condition (2) derives the Cournot-Nash equilibrium outputs in the final good market, $y_i = \tilde{y}_i$ ($i = B,C$), where the tilde is used to express the equilibrium value. The Cournot-Nash equilibrium outputs are functions of price of the intermediate good, r_i, and tariff for the final good, T_A^i ($i = B,C$).

2.2. Equilibrium in the Intermediate-good Market

Before analyzing the Cournot competition by the intermediate-good firms A, we refer to the inverse demands for the intermediate good. Because the final-good firms are identical, the total demand for the intermediate input in country i is

[4] This setting implies that the final-good firms recognize their market power in the final-good market but act as price-takers in the intermediate-good market. This setting is often adopted in the literature on vertical trade (*e.g.*, Bernhofen, 1997; Hwang, *et al.*, 2007; Yanase and Kawabata, 2008). Ishikawa and Spencer (1999) provide a detailed discussion of the justification for this setting.

$n\tilde{y}_i$ $(i = B, C)$. Letting X^i be the total export supply of the intermediate good to country i, the market-clearing condition in country i is

$$X^i = n\tilde{y}_i, \quad i = B, C. \tag{3}$$

Equation (3) yields the inverse demand of the intermediate good, $r_i = \tilde{r}_i$, which is a function of supply for the intermediate good, X_i, and and tariff for the final good, T_A^i $(i = B, C)$.

We assume a constant marginal cost for producing the intermediate good, $k > 0$. Same as the final-good firms, we introduce index h to express hth intermediate firms in country A $(h = 1, \ldots, m)$. Then, profit for the intermediate-good firm h, denoted by Π_h, is expressed by

$$\Pi_h = \sum_{i=B,C} (\tilde{r}_i - k - t_i) x_h^B, \tag{4}$$

where x_h^i is the intermediate-good firm h's supply to country i $(i = B, C)$. The intermedaite-good firm h determines x_h^B and x_h^C so as to maximize (4), taking the output of rival intermediate-good firms as given. From equation (4), the first-order conditions for profit maximization for the intermediate-good firm h are

$$\begin{aligned} \tilde{r}_B - k - t_B + \frac{\partial \tilde{r}_B}{\partial X^B} x_h^B + \frac{\partial \tilde{r}_C}{\partial X^B} x_h^C = 0, \\ \tilde{r}_C - k - t_C + \frac{\partial \tilde{r}_B}{\partial X^C} x_h^B + \frac{\partial \tilde{r}_C}{\partial X^C} x_h^C = 0. \end{aligned} \tag{5}$$

Because firms are identical, we have $x_h^i = x_k^i$ for all $i = B, C$, $h, k = 1, \ldots, m$, and $h \neq k$. Let us denote $x_h^i \equiv x^i$, and then, we have $X^i = mx^i$. Conditions (5) determine the Cournot-Nash equilibrium outputs in the intermediate-good market, $x^i = \tilde{x}^i$ $(i = B, C)$, as a function of the tariff rates T_A^B, T_A^C, t_B, and t_C, and the number of firms, m and n.

Substituting the equilibrim outputs in the first stage into the equilibrium outputs and prices in the second stage, we have the subgame-perfect equilibrium solutions as functions of the tariff rates T_A^B, T_A^C, t_B, and t_C, and the number of firms, m and n.

Finally, we take a look at economic welfare. The welfare of country A consists of the sum of the profits of the intermediate-good firms, consumer surplus and country A's tariff revenue. That is,

$$W_A(T_A^B, T_A^C, t_B, t_C) = m\pi_A + CS + T_A^B n y_B + T_A^C n y_C, \tag{6}$$

where $CS = \int_0^Y p(s)ds - p(Y)Y$ is the consumer surplus. In contrast, the welfare function of country i consists of the sum of the profits of the final-good firms in country i and country i's tariff revenue ($i = B, C$). That is,

$$W_i(T_A^B, T_A^C, t_B, t_C) = n\pi_i + t_i m x_A^i, \quad i = B, C. \tag{7}$$

In the subsequent analysis, we assume a linear demand: $p(Y) = \alpha - Y$, where $\alpha > 0$ is large enough to ensure positive outputs. Then, the uniqueness and stability of the Cournot-Nash equilibrium are guaranteed and the second-order conditions for profit maximization for any firms are satisfied in both the final-good and the intermediate-good markets.

3. Welfare Effect of an FTA Without External Tariff Reform

In this section, we focus on the welfare effect of an FTA in the case where the FTA member countries and the nonmember country keep their tariff levels constant before and after forming the FTA. We first discuss how the FTA affects the nonmember country's welfare, and then investigate whether the FTA increase welfare levels for member countries, A and B.

We assume that, before the formation of the FTA, country A levies a nondiscriminatory tariff on imports from countries B and C because of the principle of most-favored-nation treatment, *i.e.*, $T_A^B = T_A^C = T_0 > 0$, and that countries B and C impose the same level of tariff on imports from country A, *i.e.*, $t_B = t_C = t_0 > 0$. After the FTA formation, countries A and B entirely eliminate the tariffs applying to trade between them, *i.e.*, $T_A^B = t_B = 0$. Country A retains the tariff level on imports from country C, *i.e.*, $T_A^C = T_0$. Moreover, country C does not change its tariff level on imports from country A, *i.e.*, $t_C = t_0$.

Throughout the analysis in this section, we assume that the following condition is satisfied:

$$t_0 < \frac{\alpha - k}{n+1} - T_0. \tag{8}$$

This condition guarantees that all intermediate-good and final-good firms produce positive outputs before and after the FTA formation. That is, $x_A^i > 0$ and $y_i > 0$ are satisfied ($i = B, C$). This condition (8) often appears in the following as *positive-output condition*.

In order to examine the welfare effect of the FTA, we focus on the change between the post-FTA welfare level with $T_A^B = t_B = 0$, $T_A^C = T_0$, and $t_C = t_0$ and the pre-FTA welfare level with $T_A^B = T_A^C = T_0$ and $t_B = t_C = t_0$. In our setting, we obtain such welfare change in country i, ΔW_i, as follows:[5]

$$\Delta W_A \equiv W_A(0,T_0,0,t_0) - W_A(T_0,T_0,t_0,t_0) = \frac{mn}{2(2n+1)^2(m+1)^2} f_A(T_0,t_0), \quad (9)$$

$$\Delta W_B \equiv W_B(0,T_0,0,t_0) - W_B(T_0,T_0,t_0,t_0) = \frac{mn}{(2n+1)^2(m+1)^2} f_B(T_0,t_0), \quad (10)$$

$$\Delta W_C \equiv W_C(0,T_0,0,t_0) - W_C(T_0,T_0,t_0,t_0) = -\frac{mn^2(T_0+t_0)}{(2n+1)^2(m+1)^2} f_C(T_0,t_0), \quad (11)$$

where

$$\begin{aligned} f_A(T_0,t_0) \equiv\ & 2(\alpha-k)\{(2n-m+1)T_0 + 2(mn+2n+1)t_0\} \\ & -(T_0+t_0)\left\{m(4n^2+n-2)T_0 + (3mn-4n^2+2n+2)t_0\right\}, \\ f_B(T_0,t_0) \equiv\ & (\alpha-k)\{2m(n+1)T_0 - (2n-m+1)t_0\} \\ & +(T_0+t_0)\left\{m(n+1)(n-1)T_0 + (mn^2+2mn+2n+1)t_0\right\}, \\ f_C(T_0,t_0) \equiv\ & \{2m(\alpha-k) - m(n+2)T_0 + (mn-m+2n+1)t_0\}. \end{aligned}$$

First, focusing on the change in welfare in country C (equation (11)) , we obtain the following result.[6]

Proposition 1. *If any external tariff reforms are not allowed, the FTA unambigously decreases the nonmember country C's welfare.*

Thus, we find that the FTA between countries A and B is unambiguously harmful for the nonmember country C in the absence of external tariff reforms. The intuition is explained as follows. The FTA eliminates T_A^B, which decreases the imports of the final good from country C, y_C. This reduces profit of the final-good firms C. Further, it decreases the amount of imports of the intermediate good from country A, and then decreases the country C's tariff revenue. Therefore, the FTA is harmful for the non-member country C.

Next we turn to the welfare changes in the FTA member countries, A and B. Figures 2, 3 and 4 illustrate the changes in welfare in countries A and B

[5] The detailed derivations are upon request for the authors.

[6] All proofs of the upcoming Propositions appear in Appendices.

from the pre-FTA to the post-FTA situation.[7] The horizontal axis shows T_0, the initial tariff level imposed by country A, and the vertical axis describes t_0, the initial tariff level levied by countries B and C. Along the curve $\Delta W_A = 0$, country A's welfare is unaffected by the FTA between countries A and B, *i.e.*, $W_A(0,T_0,0,t_0) = W_A(T_0,T_0,t_0,t_0)$. Above (*resp.* below) the curve $\Delta W_A = 0$, the FTA improves (*resp.* reduces) country A's welfare. For similar reasons, along thc curve $\Delta W_B = 0$, country B's welfare is unaffected by the FTA, *i.e.*, $W_B(0,T_0,0,t_0) = W_B(T_0,T_0,t_0,t_0)$, whereas the FTA decreases (*resp.* increases) country B's welfare on the left (*resp.* right) of the curve $\Delta W_B = 0$.

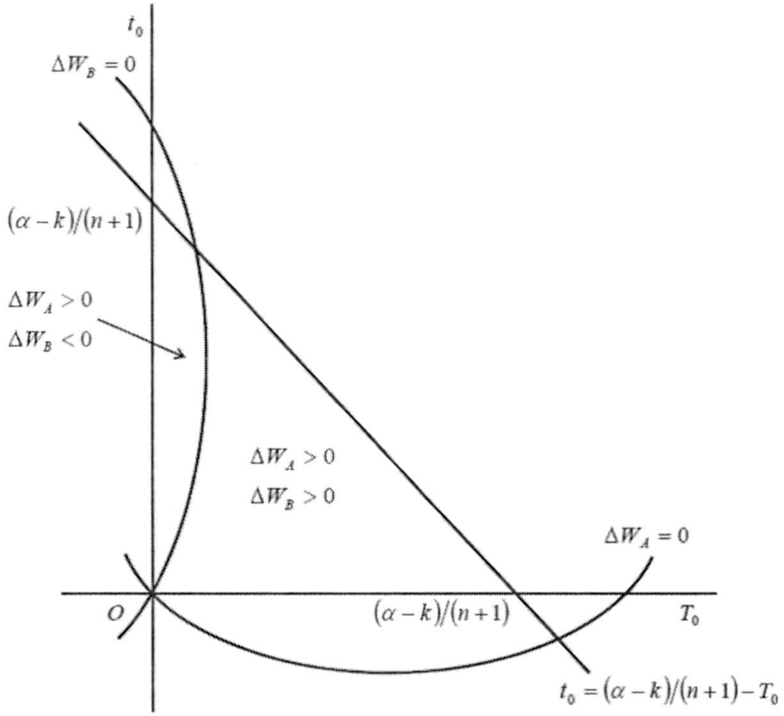

Figure 2.

Figure 2 describes the case of $m = 1$, *i.e.*, monopoly in the intermediate-good market. An FTA between countries A and B is always beneficial for coun-

[7]Here, we develop graphical explanations. The mathematical explanation appears in Appendix B.

try A. In contrast, it may or may not be beneficial for country B, depending on country A's initial tariff level, T_0. If T_0 is low enough, the FTA is harmful to country B; otherwise, it is beneficial for country B.

Figure 3 shows the case where $2 \leq m < 2n+1$, *i.e.*, there is a smaller number of intermediate-good firms relative to the number of final-good firms. In this case, the FTA may or may not be beneficial for both countries, depending on the initial tariff levels, T_0 and t_0. At least one of the countries will gain from the FTA in this case. There are some cases where the FTA is mutually beneficial for both countries, but no cases where neither of them becomes better off.

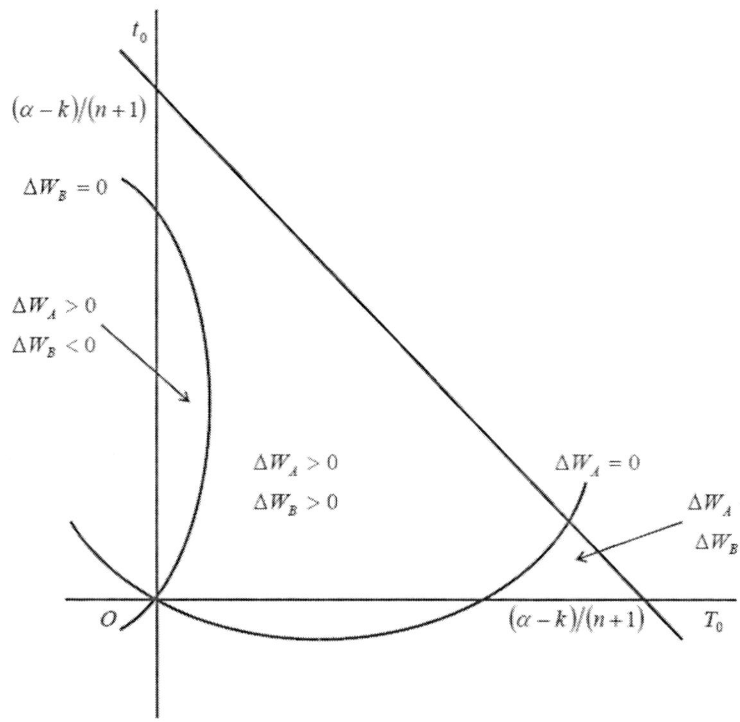

Figure 3.

Figure 4 illustrates the case where $2n+1 \leq m$. *i.e.*, there is a larger number of intermediate-good firms relative to the number of final-good firms. In this case, country B always gains from the FTA. In contrast, it may or may not be beneficial for country A, depending on country B's initial tariff level, t_0. If t_0

is low enough, the FTA is harmful to country A; otherwise, it is beneficial for country A.

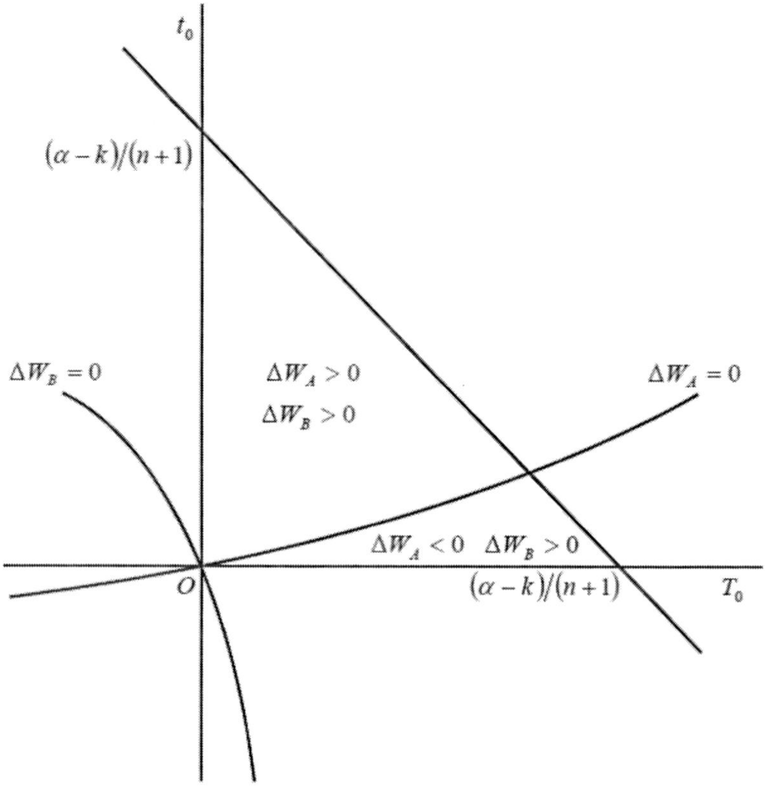

Figure 4.

We summarize these results as Proposition 2.

Proposition 2. *Suppose that tariff coordination between the FTA members and the nonmember is not allowed. Then,*
(i) For $m = 1$, the FTA increases country A's welfare and may or may not increase country B's welfare. It lowers country B's welfare when T_0 is sufficiently low.
(ii) For $2 \leq m < 2n + 1$, the FTA may or may not increase both of the member countries' welfare. It lowers country A's welfare when T_0 is sufficiently high and t_0 is sufficiently low, and it lowers country B's welfare when T_0 is sufficiently

low.
(iii) For $2n+1 \leq m$, the FTA increases country B's welfare and may or may not increase country A's welfare. It lowers country A's welfare when t_0 is sufficiently low.

The intuition behind Proposition 2 can be explained as follows. First, we focus on the effect of the FTA on country B. A decrease in T_A^B directly reduces the marginal costs of the final-good firms in country B. In addition, a decrease in t_B lowers the price of the intermediate good in country B and reduces the marginal costs of the final-good firms in country B. Such reductions in the marginal costs increase the output of final-good firms in country B, thereby shifting some of the profits from the final-good firms in country C to those in country B. These changes are summarized as *horizontal profit-shifting* of the FTA.

On the other hand, a decrease in T_A^B raises the demand for the intermediate good in country B, and thereby increases the price of the intermediate good, r_B. As payments to the intermediate-good firms increase, some of the profits are shifted from the final-good firms in country B to the intermediate-good firms in country A. In addition, a decrease in t_B worsens country B's terms of trade on imports of the intermediate good, $r_B - t_B$.[8] These changes are summarized as *vertical profit-shifting* of the FTA.

As the number of intermediate-good firms in country A, m, becomes smaller, the negative vertical profit-shifting becomes larger. In addition, as country A's initial tariff, T_0, is lower, the positive horizontal profit-shifting is weaker. Therefore, when the number of intermediate-good firms is small and country A's initial tariff is sufficiently low, the FTA makes country B worse off.

Second, we consider the effect of the FTA on country A. As we saw above, decreases in T_B^A and t_B increase the output of the final-good firms in country B. This raises the demand for the intermediate good, and thereby increases the outputs and profits of the intermediate-good firms in country A. This is the vertical profit-shifting of the FTA. Furthermore, a decrease in t_B reduces the price of the final good, p, which induces an increase in consumer surplus.

On the other hand, a decrease in T_A^B worsens country A's terms of trade on the final-good imports from country B, $p - T_A^B$.[9] In addition, decreases in

[8]Country B's import tariff, t_B, extracts the profits of the intermediate-good firms in country A. A decrease in t_B implies that such profit extraction is weakened.

[9]For similar reasons as stated in footnote 8, country A's import tariff, T_A^B, extracts the profits

T_A^B and t_B reduce the imports from country C, which reduces country A's tariff revenue.

As the number of intermediate-good firms increases, the positive vertical profit-shifting becomes weaker. As the number of final-good firms decreases, the negative terms of trade effect becomes larger. Further, as country B's initial tariff level, t_0, becomes lower, the positive effect from the elimination of t_0 becomes smaller. Therefore, when the number of intermediate-good firms relative to the number of final-good firms is sufficiently large and country B's initial tariff level is sufficiently low, the FTA makes country A worse off.

4. Welfare Effect of an FTA with External Tariff Reform

In the previous section, we found that the formation of an FTA between countries A and B makes the nonmember country C unambiguously worse off, if the external tariff reform by the FTA member is not allowed. That is, Pareto-improving FTA is not possible in that case. In this section, we show the possibility of a Pareto-improving FTA in the present model by proposing an external tariff reform; *i.e.*, a proportional reduction of the FTA member country's external tariff level.

GATT Article XXIV 5 prescribes the following requirement for FTA[10].

> Article XXIV 5 : $\cdots$ the provisions of this Agreement shall not prevent, as between the territories of contracting parties, the formation of a customs union or of a free-trade area or the adoption of an interim agreement necessary for the formation of a customs union or of a free-trade area; Provided that: $\cdots$
>
> (b) with respect to a free-trade area, or an interim agreement leading to the formation of a free-trade area, the duties and other regulations of commerce maintained in each of the constituent territories and applicable at the formation of such free-trade area or the adoption of such interim agreement to the trade of contracting parties not included in such area or not parties to such agreement shall not be higher or more restrictive than the corresponding duties and other

of the final-good firms in country B. A decrease in T_A^B implies that such profit extraction is weakened.

[10]For the detail, see the WTO webpage (http://www.wto.org).

regulations of commerce existing in the same constituent territories prior to the formation of the free-trade area, or interim agreement as the case may be; ···

We interpret the above requirement 5 (b), as meaning that the trade volume between the FTA member and the nonmember is not reduced after the formation of the FTA. More specifically, we propose a reduction rate λ such that country C's export remains unchanged before and after the FTA. After all, the nonmember's welfare is unchanged by the FTA.[11]

Suppose that when signing the FTA with country B, country A reduces its tariff on imports from country C by $(1-\lambda)\times 100\%$, where $\lambda \in (0,1)$ is the rate of reduction. That is, country A is assumed to set the post-FTA external tariff rate to $T_A^C = \lambda T_0$. The welfare changes in countries A, B and C are now given by

$$\Delta W_A \equiv W_A(0,\lambda T_0,0,t_0) - W_A(T_0,T_0,t_0,t_0), \quad (12)$$

$$\Delta W_B \equiv W_B(0,\lambda T_0,0,t_0) - W_B(T_0,T_0,t_0,t_0), \quad (13)$$

$$\Delta W_C \equiv W_C(0,\lambda T_0,0,t_0) - W_C(T_0,T_0,t_0,t_0). \quad (14)$$

Let $\bar{\lambda}$ be the rate of tariff reduction such that $y_C(T_0,T_0,t_0,t_0) = y_C(0,\lambda T_0,0,t_0)$. Solving $y_C(T_0,T_0,t_0,t_0) = y_C(0,\lambda T_0,0,t_0)$ for λ, we have

$$\bar{\lambda} = \frac{T_0 - nt_0}{(n+1)T_0}. \quad (15)$$

Equation (14) is calculated as follows:

$$\Delta W_C = \frac{mn\{(\lambda-1)T_0 + n(t_0+\lambda T_0)\}}{(m+1)^2(2n+1)^2} \times [-2m(\alpha-k) + m\{1+(n+1)\lambda\}T_0 + \{m-1-(m+2)n\}t_0]. \quad (16)$$

Substituting equation (15) into (16) and rearranging it, we have $\Delta W_C = 0$. That is, if the rate of external tariff reduction by country A is given by equation (15), the FTA between countries A and B accompanied by the reform of external tariffs not only does not reduce the volume of trade between the FTA member country A and the nonmember country C, but also does not make the nonmember worse off.

[11] On this external tariff reform, we apply the tariff compensating customs union (Kemp, 1964; Ohyama, 1974).

Under $\bar{\lambda}$, the positive-output condition changes from equation (8) to

$$t_0 < \alpha - k - T_0. \tag{17}$$

Because we consider the reduction of the external tariff by country A, the sign of $\bar{\lambda}$ given by equation (15) must be nonnegative. This means that, in the following analysis, we focus on the set of initial tariffs (T_0, t_0) such that $T_0 - nt_0 \geq 0$ is satisfied. This condition implies that country A's initial tariff level T_0 must be large enough to support the reduction of the external tariff. In the light of the positive-output condition (17), the set of (T_0, t_0) must exist below the line $t_0 = \frac{1}{n}T_0$ in Figures 5 and 6. In addition, rewriting equation (15), we obtain

$$1 - \bar{\lambda} = \frac{n(T_0 + t_0)}{(n+1)T_0} > 0. \tag{18}$$

Equation (18) implies that we find a unique $\bar{\lambda}$ such that $0 \leq \bar{\lambda} < 1$.

Using the same method as in the previous section, let us discuss whether the FTA increases welfare levels of countries A and B if a proportional reduction in the external tariff $\bar{\lambda}$ is implemented.

We begin with country B. Substituting equation (15) into equation (13), the welfare change of country B is calculated as follows:

$$\Delta W_B = \frac{mn}{(m+1)^2(n+1)^2(2n+1)} g_B(T_0, t_0), \tag{19}$$

where

$$\begin{aligned} g_B(T_0, t_0) \equiv{} & (n+1)\{2mT_0 - (mn - m + n + 1)t_0\}(\alpha - k) \\ & + (T_0 + t_0)[\{n(n+2)(m+1) + 1\}t_0 - mT_0]. \end{aligned}$$

As in the previous section, we investigate the sign of ΔW_B by depicting a $W_B = 0$ curve in the (T_0, t_0) space. As shown in Appendix C, the $\Delta W_B = 0$ curve is backward bending, and $\Delta W_B > 0$ (*resp.* $\Delta W_B < 0$) holds on the right (*resp.* left)-hand side of the curve.

It is clear from Figures 5 and 6 that $\Delta W_B > 0$ holds for any combination of (T_0, t_0) satisfying $0 \leq \bar{\lambda} < 1$. That is, the FTA always increases country B's welfare insofar as the reduction of the external tariff, *i.e.*, $0 \leq \bar{\lambda} < 1$, is possible.

By substituting equation (15) into equation (12), Country A's welfare change is analogously calculated as follows:

$$\Delta W_A = \frac{mn}{2(m+1)^2(n+1)^2(2n+1)} g_A(T_0, t_0), \tag{20}$$

where

$$\begin{aligned} g_A(T_0, t_0) \equiv\ & 2(n+1)\{(2n-m+1)T_0 + (mn+3n+2)t_0\}(\alpha - k) \\ & + (T_0 + t_0)\{m(2n^2+3n+2)t_0 - (mn+2n^2+4n+2)T_0\}. \end{aligned}$$

As for the case of country B, we can obtain a $\Delta W_A = 0$ curve in the (T_0, t_0) space. As shown in Appendix C, the $\Delta W_A = 0$ curve is inverted U-shaped and $\Delta W_A > 0$ (*resp.* $\Delta W_A < 0$) holds above (*resp.* below) the curve.

From Figures 5 and 6, in the set of initial tariffs satisfying $0 \leq \bar{\lambda} < 1$, we see that country A unambiguously gains from signing the FTA, *i.e.*, $\Delta W_A > 0$, if $m \leq 2n+1$. If $m > 2n+1$, the FTA may make country A worse off, *i.e.*, $\Delta W_A < 0$, if the initial tariff levels T_0 and t_0 are sufficiently small; otherwise, the FTA makes country A better off.

Therefore, the analysis so far is summarized as Proposition 3.

Proposition 3. *Consider the FTA with a proportional reduction in country A's tariff level on imports from country C by* $(1-\bar{\lambda})$. *If* $m \leq 2n+1$, *the FTA increases both of the member countries' welfare. If* $m > 2n+1$, *the FTA incrases country B's welfare and may or may not increase country A's welfare. It lowers country A's welfare when the initial tariff levels* T_0 *and* t_0 *are sufficiently small.*

The intuition behind Proposition 3 can be explained as follows. In terms of country B, there are no horizontal profit-shifting from country C because the reduction in the external tariff does not change the trade volume of country C. However, the elimination of T_A^B increases the export of country B and thus increases its welfare. The vertical profit-shifting decreases the profit of the final-good firms B and thus decreases country B's welfare. As we see before, the initial tariff T_0 must be large relative to t_0 to support the reduction in the external tariff (*i.e.*, $0 \leq \bar{\lambda}$). Thus, the positive effect of the tariff elimination is significantly large, and the negative vertical profit-shifting is significantly small. Therefore, the FTA unambiguously increases country B's welfare.

In terms of country A, the same mechanism works in Proposition 2. Although the reduction in the external tariff works positively for country A because

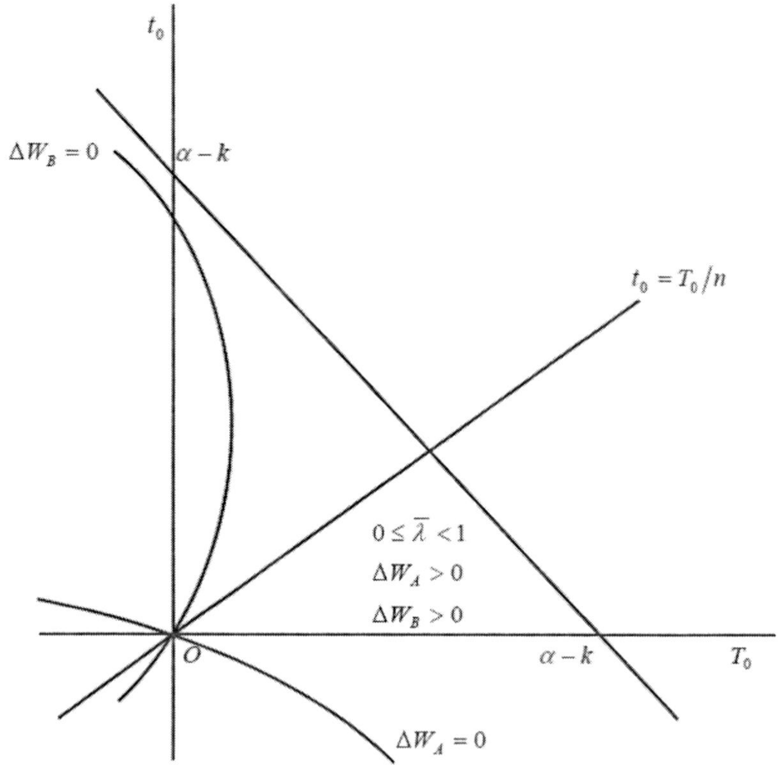

Figure 5.

of the tariff complementarity effect (Bagwell and Staiger, 1999), the FTA decreases country A's welfare if the number of the intermediate-good firms is large and the initial tariff level T_0 is relatively small[12]. Otherwise, the FTA increases country A's welfare.

Proposition 3 has two interpretations. Interpreting it positively, this proposition states that a Pareto-improving FTA is possible. At the same time, this proposition can be interpreted negatively; the Kemp-Wan-Ohyama theorem may

[12]Because $T_0 \geq nt_0$ must be satisfied to support the reduction in the external tariff (*i.e.*, $0 \leq \bar{\lambda}$), if the initial tariff T_0 is small, the other initial tariff t_0 is smaller (see Figures 5 and 6). Therefore, in the case where the FTA decreases country A's welfare, the positive vertical profit-shifting is small.

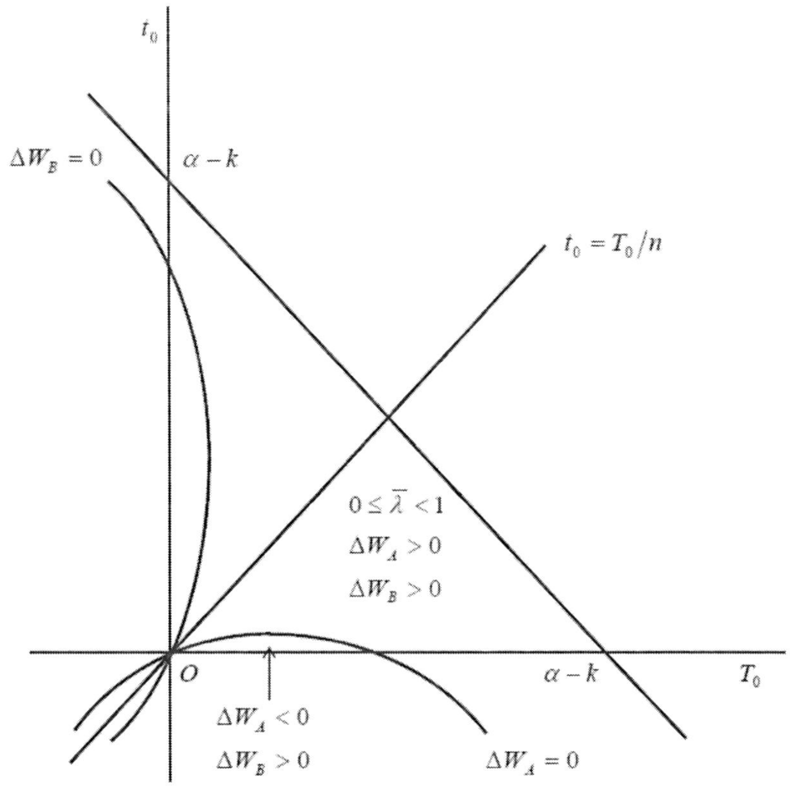

Figure 6.

or may not hold in the vertical trade structure depending on the initial tariff levels and the number of firms producing the intermediate and the final goods.

5. Conclusion

In this chapter, we have investigated the welfare effect of an FTA in the context of vertical trade. We considered two scenarios: the first one is the case where any external tariff reform is not allowed, and the second one is the case where an external tariff reform is allowed. In particular, the second scenario focuses on the reduction in external tariff by an FTA member, which maintains the nonmember country's welfare at the same level before and after the FTA.

In the first scenario, we find that the FTA unambiguously makes the non-member country worse off. This result implies Pareto-improving FTA is not possible when the external tariff reform is not allowed. We also show that the FTA may or may not increase the member countries' welfare, depending on the number of the intermediate-good and final-good firms m and n, and the initial tariff levels T_0 and t_0. In contrast, in the second scenario, we show that the FTA increases the member countries' welfare levels with a proportional reduction of the external tariff which keeps the non-member country's welfare unchanged before and after the FTA. That is, a Pareto-improving FTA is possible when the external tariff reform is allowed.

Some extensions are available in our model. For example, we treat all tariffs exogenously in this chapter. Endogenizing tariff is an interesting extension. Including heterogeneities of countries and/or firms in, *e.g.*, the number of firms, production cost, and so on, would enrich our analysis. Further, including firm entry or a determination of trade pattern would provide additional interesting results. We would like to extend our model by including these topics in our future research.

Appendix A: Proof of Proposition 1

From the positive-output condition (8), $\alpha - k > (n+1)(T_0 + t_0)$. Using this relation in $f_C(T_0, t_0)$ of equation (11), we find that

$$\begin{aligned} &2m(\alpha - k) - m(n+2)T_0 + (mn - m + 2n + 1)t_0 \\ &> 2m(n+1)(T_0 + t_0) - m(n+2)T_0 + (mn - m + 2n + 1)t_0 \\ &= mnT_0 + (3mn + m + 2n + 1)t_0 > 0. \end{aligned}$$

Therefore, $\Delta W_C < 0$ holds. ∎

Appendix B: Proof of Proposition 2

We begin with country B. To obtain the $\Delta W_B = 0$ curve, we make equation (10) equal to zero.

The $\Delta W_B = 0$ curve intersects the t_0 axis twice. This is verified by solving $f_B(0, t_0) = 0$ for t_0. The intersections are derived as follows:

$$(T_0, t_0) = (0, 0) \quad \text{and} \quad (T_0, t_0) = \left(0, \frac{(2n - m + 1)(\alpha - k)}{mn^2 + 2mn + 2n + 1}\right).$$

Now, we compare the latter intersection with the intersection of the positive-output condition (equation (8)). Then,

$$\frac{\alpha-k}{n+1} < \frac{(2n-m+1)(\alpha-k)}{mn^2+2mn+2n+1} \quad \text{if} \quad m=1 \text{ and } n \geq 3, \tag{A.1}$$

$$\frac{\alpha-k}{n+1} > \frac{(2n-m+1)(\alpha-k)}{mn^2+2mn+2n+1} \quad \text{otherwise.} \tag{A.2}$$

Moreover, we have

$$\left.\frac{dt_0}{dT_0}\right|_{\Delta W_B=0;(T_0,t_0)=(0,0)} = -\frac{\partial f_B/\partial T_0}{\partial f_B/\partial t_0} = \frac{2m(n+1)}{2n-m+1}. \tag{A.3}$$

From (A.1), (A.2) and (A.3), we find that

$$\left.\frac{dt_0}{dT_0}\right|_{\Delta W_B=0;(T_0,t_0)=(0,0)} > 0 \quad \text{if} \quad m < 2n+1 \quad \text{(see Figures 2 and 3),}$$

$$\left.\frac{dt_0}{dT_0}\right|_{\Delta W_B=0;(T_0,t_0)=(0,0)} < 0 \quad \text{if} \quad 2n+1 < m \quad \text{(see Figure 4).}$$

Note that $\left.\frac{dt_0}{dT_0}\right|_{\Delta W_B=0;(T_0,t_0)=(0,0)} = \infty$ if $m = 2n+1$. In any case, the $\Delta W_B = 0$ curve is backward bending. Furthermore, on the right-hand (*resp.* left-hand) of the curve, $\Delta W_B > 0$ (*resp.* $\Delta W_B < 0$) holds because

$$\frac{\partial(\Delta W_B)}{\partial T_0} = \frac{mn}{(m+1)^2(2n+1)^2}\frac{\partial f_B}{\partial T_0} > 0.$$

Next, we consider country A. In order to obtain the $\Delta W_A = 0$ curve, we make equation (9) equal to zero.

The $\Delta W_A = 0$ curve intersects the T_0 axis twice. This is verified by solving $f_A(T_0, 0) = 0$ for T_0. The intersections are derived as follows:

$$(T_0,t_0) = (0,0) \quad \text{and} \quad (T_0,t_0) = \left(\frac{2(2n-m+1)(\alpha-k)}{m(4n^2+n-2)}, 0\right).$$

Now, we compare the latter intersection with the intersection of the positive-output condition (equation (8)). Then,

$$\frac{\alpha-k}{n+1} < \frac{(2n-m+1)(\alpha-k)}{m(4n^2+n-2)} \quad \text{if} \quad m=1, \tag{A.4}$$

$$\frac{\alpha-k}{n+1} > \frac{(2n-m+1)(\alpha-k)}{m(4n^2+n-2)} \quad \text{if} \quad m \geq 2. \tag{A.5}$$

Moreover, we have

$$\left.\frac{dt_0}{dT_0}\right|_{\Delta W_A=0;(T_0,t_0)=(0,0)} = -\frac{\partial f_A/\partial T_0}{\partial f_A/\partial t_0} = -\frac{2n-m+1}{2(mn+2n+1)}. \tag{A.6}$$

From (A.4), (A.5), and (A.6), we find that

$$\left.\frac{dt_0}{dT_0}\right|_{\Delta W_A=0;(T_0,t_0)=(0,0)} < 0 \quad \text{if} \quad m < 2n+1 \quad \text{(see Figures 2 and 3)},$$
$$\left.\frac{dt_0}{dT_0}\right|_{\Delta W_A=0;(T_0,t_0)=(0,0)} \geq 0 \quad \text{if} \quad 2n+1 \leq m \quad \text{(see Figure 4)}.$$

In any case, the $\Delta W_A = 0$ curve is U-shaped. Furthermore, above (*resp.* below) the curve, $\Delta W_A > 0$ (*resp.* $\Delta W_A < 0$) holds because

$$\frac{\partial(\Delta W_A)}{\partial t_0} = \frac{mn}{2(m+1)^2(n+1)^2(2n+1)}\frac{\partial f_A}{\partial t_0} > 0.$$

As a result of analyzing the shapes of the $\Delta W_A = 0$ and $\Delta W_B = 0$ curves, we have the following results:
(i) For $m = 1$, in the case of a sufficiently low T_0, the FTA decreases country B's welfare;
(ii) For $2 \leq m < 2n+1$, in the case of a sufficiently high T_0 and a sufficiently low t_0, the FTA decreases country A's welfare. In the case of a sufficiently low T_0, the FTA decreases country B's welfare; and.
(iii) For $2n+1 \leq m$, in the case of a sufficiently low t_0, the FTA decreases country A's welfare.
In the case of the other sets of initial tariffs (T_0, t_0), the FTA increases both of the member countries' welfare. ■

Appendix C: Proof of Proposition 3

We begin with country B. To obtain the $\Delta W_B = 0$ curve, we make equation (13) equal to zero.

The $\Delta W_B = 0$ curve intersects the t_0 axis twice. This is verified by solving $g_B(0, t_0) = 0$ for t_0. The intersections are derived as follows:

$$(T_0, t_0) = (0, 0) \quad \text{and} \quad (T_0, t_0) = \left(0, \frac{(mn-m+n+1)(n+1)(\alpha-k)}{n(m+1)(n+2)+1}\right).$$

We compare the latter intersection with the intersections of the positive-output condition (equation (17)) and find that the intersection of the positive-output condition $\alpha - k$ is greater than the latter intersection.

Moreover, we have

$$\left.\frac{dt_0}{dT_0}\right|_{\Delta W_B=0;(T_0,t_0)=(0,0)} = -\frac{\partial g_B/\partial T_0}{\partial g_B/\partial t_0} = \frac{2m}{mn-m+n+1}. \tag{A.7}$$

From (A.7), the $\Delta W_B = 0$ curve is upward sloping at the origin, and is backward bending. Furthermore, on the right-hand (*resp.* left-hand) of the curve, $\Delta W_B > 0$ (*resp.* $\Delta W_B < 0$) holds because

$$\frac{\partial(\Delta W_B)}{\partial T_0} = \frac{mn}{(m+1)^2(n+1)^2(2n+1)}\frac{\partial g_B}{\partial T_0} > 0.$$

It is clear from Figures 5 and 6 that $\Delta W_B > 0$ for any pair (T_0, t_0) such that $0 \leq \lambda < 1$ holds. That is, the FTA always increases country B's welfare if the initial tariffs satisfy $0 \leq \lambda < 1$.

Next, we consider country A. To obtain the $\Delta W_A = 0$ curve, we make equation (12) equal to zero.

The $\Delta W_A = 0$ curve intersects the T_0 axis twice. This is verified by solving $g_A(T_0, 0) = 0$ for T_0. The intersections are derived as follows:

$$(T_0, t_0) = (0,0) \quad \text{and} \quad (T_0, t_0) = \left(\frac{2(m-2n+1)(n+1)(\alpha-k)}{m(2n^2+3n+2)}, 0\right).$$

Now, we compare the latter intersection with the intersection of the positive-output condition (equation (17)). Then,

$$\alpha - k > \frac{2(m-2n+1)(n+1)(\alpha-k)}{m(2n^2+3n+2)}. \tag{A.8}$$

Moreover, we have

$$\left.\frac{dt_0}{dT_0}\right|_{\Delta W_A=0;(T_0,t_0)=(0,0)} = -\frac{\partial g_A/\partial T_0}{\partial g_A/\partial t_0} = -\frac{2n-m+1}{mn+3n+2}. \tag{A.9}$$

From (A.8) and (A.9), we find that

$$\left.\frac{dt_0}{dT_0}\right|_{\Delta W_A=0;(T_0,t_0)=(0,0)} \leq 0 \quad \text{if} \quad m \leq 2n+1 \quad \text{(see Figure 5)},$$

$$\left.\frac{dt_0}{dT_0}\right|_{\Delta W_A=0;(T_0,t_0)=(0,0)} > 0 \quad \text{if} \quad 2n+1 < m \quad \text{(see Figure 6)}.$$

In any case, the $\Delta W_A = 0$ curve is inverted U-shaped as illustrated by Figures 5 and 6. Furthermore, above (*resp.* below) of the curve, $\Delta W_A > 0$ (*resp.* $\Delta W_A < 0$) holds because

$$\frac{\partial(\Delta W_A)}{\partial t_0} = \frac{mn}{2(m+1)^2(n+1)^2(2n+1)} \frac{\partial g_A}{\partial t_0} > 0.$$

As a result of analyzing the shapes of the $\Delta W_A = 0$ curve, we have the following results:
(i) For $m \leq 2n+1$, the FTA increases country A's welfare; and
(ii) For $2n+1 < m$, the FTA decreases country A's welfare. ■

References

[1] Bernhorfen, D. M. (1997). Strategic trade policy in a vertical related industry. *Review of International Economics,* **5**, pp.429-433.

[2] Bagwell, K., and Staiger, R. W. (1999). *Regionalism and multilateral tariff co-operation.* in J. Pigott and A. Woodland (Eds.), International Trade Policy and the Pacific Rim (pp. 157-185). London: Macmillan.

[3] Bond, E. W., Riezman, R. G. and Syropoulos, C. (2004). A strategic and welfare theoretic analysis of free trade areas. *Journal of International Economics,* **64**, pp.1-27.

[4] Chang, W. W. and Sugeta, H. (2004). Conjectural variation, market power, and optimal trade policy in a vertical related industry. *Review of International Economics,* **12**, pp.12-26.

[5] Hwang, H., Lin, Y.S., and Yang, Y. P. (2007). Optimal trade policies and production technology in vertically related markets. *Review of International Economics*, **15**, pp.823-835.

[6] Ishikawa, J. and Spencer, B.J. (1999). Rent-shifting export subsidies with an imported intermediate product. *Journal of International Economics,* **48**, pp.199-232.

[7] Japanese Ministry of Economy, Trade and Industry. (2006). *White paper on international economy and trade (in Japanese).* Tokyo: Gyosei.

[8] JETRO. (2006). *JETRO white paper on foreign direct investment (in Japanese).* Tokyo. Japan External Trade Organization.

[9] Kemp, M. C. (1964). *The Pure theory of international trade.* Englewood Cliffs: Prentice-Hall.

[10] Kemp, M. C. and Wan, H. (1976). An elementary proposition concerning the formation of customs unions. *Journal of International Economics,* **6**, pp.95-97.

[11] Kiyono, K. (1993). Who will be called partner? An importing country's incentive to form a free trade area. *Economic Studies Quarterly,* **44**, pp.289-310.

[12] Kose, M. A. and Riezman, R. G. (2000). Understanding the welfare implications of preferential trade agreements. *Review of International Economics,* **8**, pp.619-633.

[13] Naito, T. and Abe, K. (2008). Welfare- and revenue-enhancing tariff and tax reform under imperfect competition. *Journal of Public Economic Theory,* **10**, pp.1085-1094.

[14] Ohyama, M. (1972). Trade and welfare in general equilibrium. Keio Economic Studies, **9**, pp.37-73.

[15] Raff, H. (2001). Preferential trade liberalization under Cournot competition. *Review of International Economics,* **9**, pp.455-461.

[16] Yanase, A. and Kawabata, Y. (2008). Strategic import policies in a three country model with vertically related industries. *Economics Bulletin*, **6**, pp.1-7.

[17] Yi, S.S. (2000), Free-trade areas and welfare: an equilibrium analysis. *Review of International Economics,* **8**, pp.336-347.

INDEX

A

B

C

D

E

F

G

H

I

J

K

L

M

N

O

P

R

S

U

V

W

Z